ASIMOV TELLS, AS NO ONE ELSE CAN:

- How to make a trillion seem small
- Why imaginary numbers are real
- The real size of the universe—in photons
- How much water the world really has
- Why googles and T-formations are larger than you can imagine
- Why the zero isn't "good for nothing" at all

"With his usual aplomb, the science popularizer steers readers through some historic brainteasers and on to numerical oddities. . . . Asimov's remarkable ability to simplify the complex, and his good-humored informality, once again transform potentially difficult material into a pleasurable reading experience."

—BOOKLIST

Books by Isaac Asimov

Asimov on Numbers
The Beginning and the End
The Collapsing Universe

Published by POCKET BOOKS

ISAAC ASIMOV

ASIMOV ON NUMBERS

PUBLISHED BY POCKET BOOKS NEW YORK

POCKET BOOKS, a Simon & Schuster division of
GULF & WESTERN CORPORATION
1230 Avenue of the Americas, New York, N.Y. 10020

Published by arrangement with Doubleday & Company, Inc.
Library of Congress Catalog Card Number: 76-23747

ISBN: 0-671-41186-1

First Pocket Books printing October, 1978

10 9 8 7 6 5 4 3

POCKET and colophon are trademarks of Simon & Schuster.

Printed in the U.S.A.

All essays in this volume originally appeared in *The Magazine of Fantasy and Science Fiction*. Individual essays were in the following issues.

CONTENTS

x   *Contents*

INTRODUCTION

BACK in 1959, I began writing a monthly science column for *The Magazine of Fantasy and Science Fiction*. I was given carte blanche as to subject matter, approach, style, and everything else, and I made full use of that. I have used the column to range through every science in an informal and very personal way so that of all the writing I do (and I do a great deal) nothing gives me so much pleasure as these monthly essays.

And as though that were not pleasure enough in itself, why, every time I complete seventeen essays, Doubleday & Company, Inc., puts them into a book and publishes them. Twelve books of my F & SF essays have been published by now, containing a total of 204 essays. A thirteenth, of course, is on its way.

Few books, however, can be expected to sell indefinitely; at least, not well enough to be worth the investment of keeping them forever in print. The estimable gentlemen at Doubleday have therefore (with some reluctance, for they are fond of me and know how my lower lip tends to tremble on these occasions) allowed the first five of my books of essays to go out of print.

Out of *hardback* print, I hasten to say. All five of the books are flourishing in paperback, so that they are still available to the public. Nevertheless, there is a cachet about the hardback that I am reluctant to lose. It is the hardbacks that supply the libraries; and for those who really want a permanent addition to their large personal collections of Asimov books * there is nothing like a hardback.

My first impulse, then, was to ask the kind people at Doubleday to put the books back into print and gamble on a kind of second wind. This is done periodically in the case of my science fiction books, with success even when paperback editions are simultaneously available. But I could see that with my essays the case was different. My science fiction is ever fresh, but science essays do tend to get out of date, for the advance of science is inexorable.

And then I got to thinking. . . .

I deliberately range widely over the various sciences both to satisfy my own restless interests and to give each member of my heterogeneous audience a chance to satisfy his or her own particular taste now and then. The result is that each collection of essays has some on astronomy, some on chemistry, some on physics, some on biology, some on mathematics, and so on.

But what about the reader who is interested in science but is *particularly* interested in one particular branch? He has to read through all the articles in the book to find three or four that may be just up his alley.

Why not, then, go through the five out-of-print books, cull the articles on a particular branch of science, and put them together in a more specialized volume.

Doubleday agreed and I made up a collection of astronomical articles which appeared as *Asimov on Astronomy*. This introduction appeared at the start, explaining to the readers just what I had done and why I had done it, so that everything was open and on the table. It was an experimental project, of course, and might have done very poorly. It did not; it did very well. The people at Doubleday rejoiced and I got to work at once (grinning) and put together *Asimov on Chemistry* and *Asimov on Physics*, each with the same introduction, as in the first one of this series, so that the reader will continue to be warned of what is going on.

---

* Well, start one!

These, too, did well, and now I am preparing a fourth and last * of these volumes, *Asimov on Numbers,* which contains one article from *View from a Height,* seven articles from *Adding a Dimension,* four articles from *Of Time and Space and Other Things,* and five articles from *Earth to Heaven.* The articles are arranged, not chronologically, but conceptually.

Aside from grouping the articles into a more homogeneous mass in an orderly arrangement, what more have I done? Well, the articles are anywhere from nine to sixteen years old and their age shows here and there. I feel rather pleased that the advance of science has not knocked out a single one of the articles here included, or even seriously dented any, but minor changes must be made, and I have made them.

In doing this, I have tried not to revise the articles themselves since that would deprive you of the fun of seeing me eat my words now and then, or, anyway, chew them a little. So I have made changes by adding footnotes here and there where something I said needed modification or where I was forced to make a change to avoid presenting misinformation in the course of the article. Where it was necessary to make a number of small changes in the statistics and doing it in footnotes would be unbearably clumsy, I *did* revise the article, but in that case I warn the reader I am doing so.

In addition to that, my good friends at Doubleday have decided to prepare these books on the individual branches of science in a consistent and more elaborate format than they have use for my ordinary essay collections and have added illustrations to which I have written captions that give information above and beyond what is in the essays themselves.

Finally, since the subject matter is so much more homogeneous than in my ordinary grab-bag essay collections, I have prepared an index (though I must admit that this will be less useful in this case than in the first three books of the series).

---

* *There are, of course, seventeen essays in the five out-of-print books that have appeared in none of the four collections, but they are a miscellaneous lot. Perhaps when more of my essay books go out of print, I can combine some of them with additional articles from the later books to add to the subject-centered collections.*

So, although the individual essays are old, I hope you find the book new and enjoyable just the same. And at least I have explained, in all honesty, exactly what I have done and why. The rest is up to you.

ISAAC ASIMOV
New York, November 1975

ASIMOV
ON NUMBERS

Part I

NUMBERS AND
COUNTING

1 NOTHING COUNTS

ROMAN NUMERALS seem, even after five centuries of obsolescence, to exert a peculiar fascination over the inquiring mind.

It is my theory that the reason for this is that Roman numerals appeal to the ego. When one passes a cornerstone which says: "Erected MCMXVIII," it gives one a sensation of power to say, "Ah, yes, nineteen eighteen" to one's self. Whatever the reason, they are worth further discussion.

The notion of number and of counting, as well as the names of the smaller and more-often-used numbers, dates back to prehistoric times and I don't believe that there is a tribe of human beings on Earth today, however primitive, that does not have some notion of number.

With the invention of writing (a step which marks the boundary line between "prehistoric" and "historic"), the next step had to be taken—numbers had to be written. One can, of course, easily devise written symbols for the words that represent particular numbers, as easily as for any other word. In English we can write the number of fingers on one hand as "five" and the number of digits on all four limbs as "twenty."

Early in the game, however, the kings' tax-collectors,

3

chroniclers, and scribes saw that numbers had the peculiarity of being ordered. There was one set way of counting numbers and any number could be defined by counting up to it. Therefore why not make marks which need be counted up to the proper number.

Thus, if we let "one" be represented as ′ and "two" as ″, and "three" as ‴, we can then work out the number indicated by a given symbol without trouble. You can see, for instance, that the symbol ′′′′′′′′′′′′′′′′′′′′′′′ stands for "twenty-three." What's more, such a symbol is universal. Whatever language you count in, the symbol stands for the number "twenty-three" in whatever sound your particular language uses to represent it.

It gets hard to read too many marks in an unbroken row, so it is only natural to break it up into smaller groups. If we are used to counting on the fingers of one hand, it seems natural to break up the marks into groups of five. "Twenty-three" then becomes ′′′′′ ′′′′′ ′′′′′ ′′′′′ ′′′. If we are more sophisticated and use both hands in counting, we would write it ′′′′′′′′′′ ′′′′′′′′′′ ′′′. If we go barefoot and use our toes, too, we might break numbers into twenties.

All three methods of breaking up number symbols into more easily handled groups have left their mark on the various number systems of mankind, but the favorite was division into ten. Twenty symbols in one group are, on the whole, too many for easy grasping, while five symbols in one group produce too many groups as numbers grow larger. Division into ten is the happy compromise.

It seems a natural thought to go on to indicate groups of ten by a separate mark. There is no reason to insist on writing out a group of ten as ′′′′′′′′′′ every time, when a separate mark, let us say -, can be used for the purpose. In that case "twenty-three" could be written as --‴.

Once you've started this way, the next steps are clear. By the time you have ten groups of ten (a hundred), you can introduce another symbol, for instance +. Ten hundreds, or a thousand, can become = and so on. In that case, the number "four thousand six hundred seventy-five" can be written ==== ++++++ ------- ′′′′′.

To make such a set of symbols more easily graspable, we can take advantage of the ability of the eye to form a pattern. (You know how you can tell the numbers displayed by a pack of cards or a pair of dice by the pattern itself.) We could therefore write "four thousand six hundred seventy-five" as

$$== +++ --- \prime\prime\prime\prime$$
$$== +++ --- \prime\prime.$$

And, as a matter of fact, the ancient Babylonians used just this system of writing numbers, but they used cuneiform wedges to express it.

The Greeks, in the earlier stages of their development, used a system similar to that of the Babylonians, but in later times an alternate method grew popular. They made use of another order system—that of the letters of the alphabet.

It is natural to correlate the alphabet and the number system. We are taught both about the same time in childhood, and the two ordered systems of objects naturally tend to match up. The series "ay, bee, see, dee . . ." comes as glibly as "one, two, three, four . . ." and there is no difficulty in substituting one for the other.

If we use undifferentiated symbols such as $\prime\prime\prime\prime\prime\prime\prime$ for "seven," all the components of the symbol are identical and all must be included without exception if the symbol is to mean "seven" and nothing else. On the other hand, if "ABCDEFG" stands for "seven" (count the letters and see) then, since each symbol is different, only the last need to be written. You can't confuse the fact that G is the seventh letter of the alphabet and therefore stands for "seven." In this way, a one-component symbol does the work of a seven-component symbol. Furthermore, $\prime\prime\prime\prime\prime\prime$ (six) looks very much like $\prime\prime\prime\prime\prime\prime\prime$ (seven); whereas F (six) looks nothing at all like G (seven).

The Greeks used their own alphabet, of course, but let's use our alphabet here for the complete demonstration: A=one, B=two, C=three, D=four, E=five, F=six, G=seven, H=eight, I=nine, and J=ten.

We could let the letter K go on to equal "eleven," but at that rate our alphabet will only help us up through "twenty-six." The Greeks had a better system. The Babylonian notion of groups of ten had left its mark. If J=ten, than J equals not only ten objects but also one group of tens? Why not, then, continue the next letters as numbering groups of tens?

In other words J=ten, K=twenty, L=thirty, M=forty, N=fifty, O=sixty, P=seventy, Q=eighty, R=ninety. Then we can go on to number groups of hundreds: S=one hundred, T=two hundred, U=three hundred, V=four hundred, W=five hundred, X=six hundred, Y=seven hundred, Z=eight hundred. It would be convenient to go on to nine hundred, but we have run out of letters. However, in old-fashioned alphabets the ampersand (&) was sometimes placed at the end of the alphabet, so we can say that &=nine hundred.

The first nine letters, in other words, represent the units from one to nine, the second nine letters represent the tens groups from one to nine, the third nine letters represent the hundreds groups from one to nine. (The Greek alphabet, in classic times, had only twenty-four letters where twenty-seven are needed, so the Greek made use of three archaic letters to fill out the list.)

This system possesses its advantages and disadvantages over the Babylonian system. One advantage is that any number under a thousand can be given in three symbols. For instance, by the system I have just set up with our alphabet, six hundred seventy-five is XPE, while eight hundred sixteen is ZJF.

One disadvantage of the Greek system, however, is that the significance of twenty-seven different symbols must be carefully memorized for the use of numbers to a thousand, where as in the Babylonian system only three different symbols must be memorized.

Furthermore, the Greek system comes to a natural end when the letters of the alphabet are used up. Nine hundred ninety-nine (&RI) is the largest number that can be written without introducing special markings to indicate that a particular symbol indicates groups of thousands, tens of thousands, and so on. I will get back to this later.

A rather subtle disadvantage of the Greek system was that the same symbols were used for numbers and words so that the mind could be easily distracted. For instance, the Jews of Graeco-Roman times adopted the Greek system of representing numbers but, of course, used the Hebrew alphabet—and promptly ran into difficulty. The number "fifteen" would naturally be written as "ten-five."

In the Hebrew alphabet, however, "ten-five" represents a short version of the ineffable name of the Lord, and the Jews, uneasy at the sacrilege, allowed "fifteen" to be represented as "nine-six" instead.

Worse yet, words in the Greek-Hebrew system look like numbers. For instance, to use our own alphabet, WRA is "five hundred ninety-one." In the alphabet system it doesn't usually matter in which order we place the symbols though, as we shall see, this came to be untrue for the Roman numerals, which are also alphabetic, and WAR also means "five hundred ninety-one." (After all, we can say "five hundred one-and-ninety" if we wish.) Consequently, it is easy to believe that there is something warlike, martial, and of ominous import in the number "five hundred ninety-one."

The Jews, poring over every syllable of the Bible in their effort to copy the word of the Lord with the exactness that reverence required, saw numbers in all the words, and in New Testament times a whole system of mysticism arose over the numerical inter-relationships within the Bible. This was the nearest the Jews came to mathematics, and they called this numbering of words *gematria,* which is a distortion of the Greek *geometria.* We now call it "numerology."

Some poor souls, even today, assign numbers to the different letters and decide which names are lucky and which unlucky, and which boy should marry which girl and so on. It is one of the more laughable pseudo-sciences.

In one case, a piece of gematria had repercussions in later history. This bit of gematria is to be found in "The Revelation of St. John the Divine," the last book of the New Testament—a book which is written in a mystical fashion that defies literal understanding. The reason for the lack of clarity seems quite clear to me. The author of Revelation was denouncing the Roman government and was laying himself open to a charge of treason and to subsequent crucifixion if he made his words too clear. Consequently, he made an effort to write in such a way as to be perfectly clear to his "in-group" audience, while remaining completely meaningless to the Roman authorities.

In the thirteenth chapter he speaks of beasts of diabolical powers, and in the eighteenth verse he says, "Here is wisdom. Let him that hath understanding count the number of the beast: for it is the number of a man; and his number is Six hundred three-score and six."

Clearly, this is designed not to give the pseudo-science of gematria holy sanction, but merely to serve as a guide to the actual person meant by the obscure imagery of the chapter. Revelation, as nearly as is known, was written only a few decades after the first great persecution of Christians under Nero. If Nero's name ("Neron Caesar") is written in Hebrew characters the sum of the numbers represented by the individual letters does indeed come out to be six hundred sixty-six, "the number of the beast."

Of course, other interpretations are possible. In fact, if Revelation is taken as having significance for all time as well as for the particular time in which it was written, it may also refer to some anti-Christ of the future. For this reason, generation after generation, people have made attempts to show that, by the appropriate jugglings of the spelling of a name in an appropriate language, and by the appropriate assignment of numbers to letters, some particular personal enemy could be made to possess the number of the beast.

If the Christians could apply it to Nero, the Jews themselves might easily have applied it in the next century to Hadrian, if they had wished. Five centuries later it could be (and was) applied to Mohammed. At the time of the Reformation, Catholics calculated Martin Luther's name and found it to be the number of the beast, and Protestants returned the compliment by making the same discovery in the case of several popes.

Later still, when religious rivalries were replaced by nationalistic ones, Napoleon Bonaparte and William II were appropriately worked out. What's more, a few minutes' work with my own system of alphabet-numbers shows me that "Herr Adolff Hitler" has the number of the beast. (I need that extra "l" to make it work.)

The Roman system of number symbols had similarities to both the Greek and Babylonian systems. Like the Greeks, the Romans used letters of the alphabet. However, they did not use them in order, but used just a few letters which they repeated as often as necessary—as in the Babylonian system. Unlike the Babylonians, the Romans did not invent a new symbol for every tenfold increase of number, but (more primitively) used new symbols for five-fold increases as well.

Thus, to begin with, the symbol for "one" is I, and "two," "three," and "four," can be written II, III, and IIII.

The symbol for five, then, is *not* IIIII, but V. People have amused themselves no end trying to work out the reasons for the particular letters chosen as symbols, but there are no explanations that are universally accepted. However, it is pleasant to think that I represents the upheld finger and that V might symbolize the hand itself with all five fingers—one branch of the V would be the outheld thumb, the other, the remaining fingers. For "six," "seven," "eight," and "nine," we would then have VI, VII, VIII, and VIIII.

For "ten" we would then have X, which (some people think) represents both hands held wrist to wrist. "Twenty-three" would be XXIII, "forty-eight" would be XXXXVIII, and so on.

The symbol for "fifty" is L, for "one hundred" is C, for "five hundred" is D, and for "one thousand" is M. The C and M are easy to understand, for C is the first leter of *centum* (meaning "one hundred") and M is the first letter of *mille* (one thousand).

For that very reason, however, those symbols are suspicious. As initials they may have come to oust the original less-meaningful symbols for those numbers. For instance, an alternative symbol for "thousand" looks something like this (I). Half of a thousand or "five hundred" is the right half of the symbol, or I) and this may have been converted into D. As for the L which stands for "fifty," I don't know why it is used.

Now, then, we can write nineteen sixty-four, in Roman numerals, as follows: MDCCCCLXIIII.

One advantage of writing numbers according to this system is that it doesn't matter in which order the numbers are written. If I decided to write nineteen sixty-four as CDCLIIMXCICI, it would still represent nineteen sixty-four if I add up the number values of each letter. However, it is not likely that anyone would ever scramble the letters in this fashion. If the letters were written in strict order of decreasing value, as I did the first time, it would then be much simpler to add the values of the letters. And, in fact, this order of decreasing value is (except for special cases) always used.

Once the order of writing the letters in Roman numerals is made an established convention, one can make use of

ROMAN NUMERALS

This is a horoscope cast for Albrecht von Wallenstein, an Imperial general during the Thirty Years' War, by the great astronomer Johann Kepler. (Kepler cast horoscopes in order to make a living, just as a modern actor, even a good one, might do commercials on the side.)

Even though the numerals used are mostly Arabic, the twelve signs of the zodiac are numbered in Roman style for their greater effect. Roman numerals carried a cachet of stateliness for centuries after they were seen to be useless in computation.

Although our own familiar system is based on 10 and powers of 10, the Roman numerals are based on both 5 and 10 with special symbols for 1, 5, 10, 50, 100, 500, and 1,000. Obviously, this arises because we have five fingers on each hand and ten fingers altogether.

In a barefoot society it doesn't take much of an intellectual jump to decide to base a number system on 20. The Mayans of Central America counted by both tens and twenties and had special symbols for 20, for 400 (20^2), 8,000 (20^3), 160,000 (20^4) and so on.

Although there is no formal vigesimal (by twenties) number system in Western tradition, we still count by "scores" and say "four score and seven" (four twenties and seven) when we mean 87. Counting by twenties is so common, in fact, that we speak of keeping score and ask "What's the score?" in connection with a ball game.

Duodecimal systems are also used, in words anyway, if not in symbols, because 12 can be divided evenly by 2, 3, 4, and 6. We speak of dozens, therefore, and of grosses, where a gross is a dozen dozen, or 144. For that matter, the ancient Sumerians used a 60-based system and we still have 60 seconds to the minute and 60 minutes to the hour.

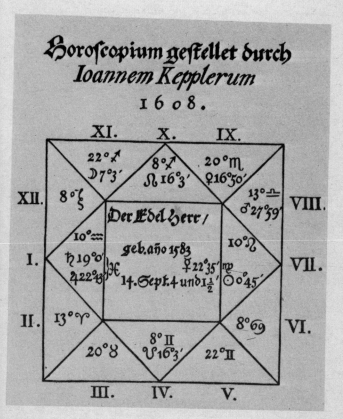

The Granger Collection

deviations from that set order if it will help simplify matters. For instance, suppose we decide that when a symbol of smaller value *follows* one of larger value, the two are added; while if the symbol of smaller value *precedes* one of larger value, the first is subtracted from the second. Thus VI is "five" plus "one" or "six," while IV is "five" minus "one" or "four." (One might even say that IIV is "three," but it is conventional to subtract no more than one symbol.) In the same way LX is "sixty" while XL is "forty"; CX is "one hundred ten," while XC is "ninety"; MC is "one thousand one hundred," while CM is "nine hundred."

The value of this "subtractive principle" is that two symbols can do the work of five. Why write VIIII if you can write IX; or DCCCC if you can write CM? The year nineteen sixty-four, instead of being written MDCCCC-LXIIII (twelve symbols), can be written MCMLXIV (seven symbols). On the other hand, once you make the order of writing letters significant, you can no longer scramble them even if you wanted to. For instance, if MCMLXIV is scrambled to MMCLXVI it becomes "two thousand one hundred sixty-six."

The subtractive principle was used on and off in ancient times but was not regularly adopted until the Middle Ages. One interesting theory for the delay involves the simplest use of the principle—that of IV ("four"). These are the first letters of IVPITER the chief of the Roman gods, and the Romans may have had a delicacy about writing even the beginning of the name. Even today, on clockfaces bearing Roman numerals, "four" is represented as IIII and never as IV. This is not because the clockface does not accept the subtractive principle, for "nine" is represented as IX and never as VIIII.

With the symbols already given, we can go up to the number "four thousand nine hundred ninety-nine" in Roman numerals. This would be MMMMDCCCCLXXXX-VIIII or, if the subtractive principle is used, MMMMCM-XCIX. You might suppose that "five thousand" (the next number) could be written MMMMM, but this is not quite right. Strictly speaking, the Roman system never requires a symbol to be repeated more than four times. A new symbol is always invented to prevent that: IIIII=V; XXXXX =L; and CCCCC=D. Well, then, what is MMMMM?

No letter was decided upon for "five thousand." In ancient times there was little need in ordinary life for numbers that high. And if scholars and tax collectors had occasion for large numbers, their systems did not percolate down to the common man.

One method of penetrating to "five thousand" and beyond is to use a bar to represent thousands. Thus, $\overline{V}$ would represent not "five" but "five thousand." And sixty-seven thousand four hundred eighty-two would be $\overline{\text{LXVII}}$CD-LXXXII.

But another method of writing large numbers harks back to the primitive symbol (I) for "thousand." By adding to the curved lines we can increase the number by ratios of ten. Thus "ten thousand" would be ((I)), and "one hundred thousand" would be (((I))). Then just as "five hundred" was I) or D, "five thousand" would be I)) and "fifty thousand" would be I))).

Just as the Romans made special marks to indicate thousands, so did the Greeks. What's more, the Greeks made special marks for ten thousands and for millions (or at least some of the Greek writers did). That the Romans didn't carry this to the logical extreme is no surprise. The Romans prided themselves on being non-intellectual. That the Greeks missed it also, however, will never cease to astonish me.

Suppose that instead of making special marks for large numbers only, one were to make special marks for every type of group from the units on. If we stick to the system I introduced at the start of the chapter—that is, the one in which ′ stands for units, - for tens, + for hundreds, and = for thousands—then we could get by with but one set of nine symbols. We could write every number with a little heading, marking off the type of groups =+-′. Then for "two thousand five hundred eighty-one" we could get by with only the letters from A to I and write it $\overset{= + \cdot \prime}{\text{BEHA}}$. What's more for "five thousand five hundred fifty-five" we could write $\overset{= + \cdot \prime}{\text{EEEE}}$. There would be no confusion with all the E's since the symbol above each E would indicate that one was a "five," another a "fifty," another a "five hundred," and another a "five thousand." By using additional symbols for ten thousands, hundred thousands, millions, and so on, any number, however large, could be written in this same fashion.

Yet it is not surprising that this would not be popular.

Even if a Greek had thought of it he would have been repelled by the necessity of writing those tiny symbols. In an age of hand-copying, additional symbols meant additional labor and scribes would resent that furiously.

Of course, one might easily decide that the symbols weren't necessary. The groups, one could agree, could always be written right to left in increasing values. The units would be at the right end, the tens next on the left, the hundreds next, and so on. In that case BEHA would be "two thousand five hundred eighty-one" and EEEE would be "five thousand five hundred fifty-five" even without the little symbols on top.

Here, though, a difficulty would creep in. What if there were no groups of ten, or perhaps no units, in a particular number? Consider the number "ten" or the number "one hundred and one." The former is made up of one group of ten and no units, while the latter is made up of one group of hundreds, no groups of tens, and one unit. Using symbols over the columns, the numbers could be written $\overset{\prime}{A}$ and $\overset{+\cdot\prime}{A}A$, but now you would not dare leave out the little symbols. If you did, how could you differentiate A meaning "ten" from A meaning "one" or AA meaning "one hundred and one" from AA meaning "eleven" or AA meaning "one hundred and ten"?

You might try to leave a gap so as to indicate "one hundred and one" by A A. But then, in an age of hand-copying, how quickly would that become AA, or, for that matter, how quickly might AA become A A? Then, too, how would you indicate a gap at the end of a symbol? No, even if the Greeks throught of this system, they must obviously have come to the conclusion that the existence of gaps in numbers made this attempted simplification impractical. They decided it was safer to let J stand for "ten" and SA for "one hundred and one" and to Hades with little symbols.

What no Greek ever thought of—not even Archimedes himself—was that it wasn't absolutely necessary to work with gaps. One could fill the gap with a symbol by letting one stand for nothing—for "no groups." Suppose we use $ as such a symbol. Then, if "one hundred and one" is made up of one group of hundreds, no groups of tens, and one unit, it can be written A$A. If we do that sort of thing, all gaps are eliminated and we don't need the little

symbols on top. "One" becomes A, "ten" becomes A$,
"one hundred" becomes A$$, "one hundred and one" be-
comes A$A, "one hundred and ten" becomes AA$, and
so on. Any number, however large, can be written with the
use of exactly nine letters plus a symbol for nothing.

Surely this is the simplest thing in the world—after you
think of it.

Yet it took men about five thousand years, counting
from the beginning of number symbols, to think of a sym-
bol for nothing. The man who succeeded (one of the most
creative and original thinkers in history) is unknown. We
know only that he was some Hindu who lived no later
than the ninth century.

The Hindus called the symbol *sunya,* meaning "empty."
This symbol for nothing was picked up by the Arabs, who
termed it *sifr,* which in their language meant "empty."
This has been distorted into our own words "cipher" and,
by way of *zefirum,* into "zero."

Very slowly, the new system of numerals (called "Ara-
bic numerals" because the Europeans learned of them from
the Arabs) reached the West and replaced the Roman
system.

Because the Arabic numerals came from lands which
did not use the Roman alphabet, the shape of the numerals
was nothing like the letters of the Roman alphabet and
this was good, too. It removed word-number confusion
and reduced gematria from the everyday occupation of
anyone who could read, to a burdensome folly that only a
few would wish to bother with.

The Arabic numerals as now used by us are, of course,
1, 2, 3, 4, 5, 6, 7, 8, 9, and the all-important 0. Such is
our reliance on these numerals (which are internationally
accepted) that we are not even aware of the extent to
which we rely on them. For instance if this chapter has
seemed vaguely queer to you, perhaps it was because I
had deliberately refrained from using Arabic numerals all
through.

We all know the great simplicity Arabic numerals have
lent to arithmetical computation. The unnecessary load
they took off the human mind, all because of the presence
of the zero, is simply incalculable. Nor has this fact gone
unnoticed in the English language. The importance of the
zero is reflected in the fact that when we work out an
arithmetical computation we are (to use a term now

ARABIC NUMERALS

Quite apart from the greater ease of computation with Arabic numerals, as compared with any other system man has invented, there is the compactness of it. Imagine all the numerical information in the table given here translated into Roman numerals (or any other kind). It would become a bulky mass that only an expert could make any sense of.

For instance, it is obvious just in the number of digits of the number that 12,000 is greater than 787. You can go down the final column of the illustration in one quick sweep of the eye and see at a glance that the greatest number of sales listed for any item in it is the 285,800 for Montgomery Ward. It happens to be the only six-digit number in the column that starts with a numeral higher than 1. You don't even have to read the other digits to know it's highest.

This cannot be done in any other number system. For instance, of the two numbers XVIII and XL, the two-symbol number is over twice as great as the five-symbol number.

Of course, there are disadvantages to the Arabic numeral system, too. There is no redundancy in it. Every digit has one and only one value, and every place has one and only one value. Drop a single digit or interchange a digit and you are lost. For instance, there is redundancy in words. Leave a letter out of "redundancy" and you have "redundncy" and hardly anyone will fail to see the correct word. Or invert two letters and you have "rednudancy" and people see the mistake and allow for it.

On the other hand, change 2835 to 235 by dropping the 8, or to 2385 by inverting two digits, and there is no sign that any mistake has been made or any chance of retrieving the correct value.

This illustration, by the way, shows the famous stock market crash of 1929. Midland Steel Products, preferred, dropped 60 points. Murray Corp. was at 20 from a year's high of 100⅞. Oh, boy.

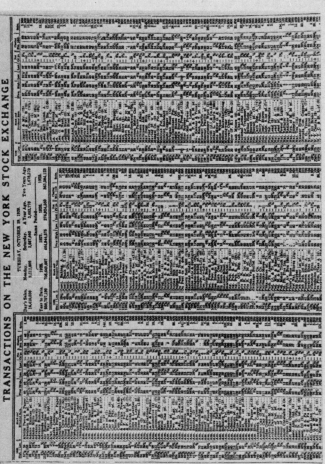

slightly old-fashioned) "ciphering." And when we work out some code, we are "deciphering" it.

So if you look once more at the title of this chapter, you will see that I am not being cynical. I mean it literally. Nothing counts! The symbol for nothing makes all the difference in the world.

2 ONE, TEN, BUCKLE MY SHOE

I HAVE always been taken aback a little at my inability to solve mathematical conundrums since (in my secret heart of hearts) I feel this to be out of character for me. To be sure, numerous dear friends have offered the explanation that, deep within me, there rests an artfully concealed vein of stupidity, but this theory has somehow never commended itself to me.

Unfortunately, I have no alternate explanation to suggest.

You can well imagine, then, that when I come across a puzzle to which I *can* find the answer, my heart fairly sings. This happened to me once when I was quite young and I have never forgotten it. Let me explain it to you in some detail because it will get me somewhere I want to go.

The problem, in essence, is this. You are offered any number of unit weights: one-gram, two-gram, three-gram, four-gram, and so on. Out of these you may choose a sufficient number so that by adding them together in the proper manner, you may be able to weigh out any integral number of grams from one to a thousand. Well, then, how can you choose the weights in such a way as to end with the fewest possible number that will turn the trick?

I reasoned this way—

I must start with a 1-gram weight, because only by using

19

it can I weigh out one gram. Now if I take a second 1-gram weight, I can weigh out two grams by using both 1-gram weights. However, I can economize by taking a 2-gram weight instead of a second 1-gram weight, for then not only can I weigh out two grams with it, but I can also weigh out three grams, by using the 2-gram plus the 1-gram.

What's next? A 3-gram weight perhaps? That would be wasteful, because three grams can already be weighed out by the 2-gram plus the 1-gram. So I went up a step and chose a 4-gram weight. That gave me not only the possibility of weighing four grams, but also five grams (4-gram plus 1-gram), six grams (4-gram plus 2-gram), and seven grams (4-gram plus 2-gram plus 1-gram).

By then I was beginning to see a pattern. If seven grams was the most I could reach, I would take an 8-gram weight as my next choice and that would carry me through each intergral weight to fifteen grams (8-grams plus 4-grams plus 2-gram plus 1-gram). The next weight would be a 16-gram one, and it was clear to me that in order to weigh out any number of grams one had to take a series of weights (beginning with the 1-gram) each one of which was double the next smaller.

That meant that I could weigh out any number of grams from one to a thousand by means of ten and only ten weights: a 1-gram, 2-gram, 4-gram, 8-gram, 16-gram, 32-gram, 64-gram, 128-gram, 256-gram, and 512-gram. In fact, these weights would carry me up to 1023 grams.

Now we can forget weights and work with numbers only. Using the numbers 1, 2, 4, 8, 16, 32, 64, 128, 256, and 512, and those only, you can express any other number up to and including 1023 by adding two or more of them. For instance the number 100 can be expressed as 64 plus 32 plus 4. The number 729 can be expressed as 512 plus 128 plus 64 plus 16 plus 8 plus 1. And, of course, 1023 can be expressed as the sum of all ten numbers.

If you add to this list of numbers 1024, then you can continue forming numbers up to 2047; and if you next add 2048, you can continue forming numbers up to 4095; and if you next—

Well, if you start with 1 and continue doubling indefinitely, you will have a series of numbers which, by appropriate addition, can be used to express any finite number at all.

So far, so good; but our interesting series of numbers— 1, 2, 4, 8, 16, 32, 64, . . .—seems a little miscellaneous. Surely there must be a neater way of expressing it. And there is.

Let's forget 1 for a minute and tackle 2. If we do that, we can begin with the momentous statement that 2 is 2. (Any argument?) Going to the next number, we can say that 4 is 2 times 2. Then 8 is 2 times 2 times 2; 16 is 2 times 2 times 2 times 2; 32 is . . . But you get the idea.

So we can set up the series (continuing to ignore 1) as 2, 2 times 2, 2 times 2 times 2, 2 times 2 times 2 times 2, and so on. There is a kind of pleasing uniformity and regularity about this but all those 2 times 2 times 2's create spots before the eyes. Therefore, instead of writing out all the 2's, it would be convenient to note how many 2's are being multiplied together by using an exponential method.

Thus, if 4 is equal to 2 times 2, we will call it 2^2 (two to the second power, or two squared). Again if 8 is 2 times 2 times 2, we can take note of the three 2's multiplied together by writing 8 as 2^3 (two to the third power, or two cubed). Following that line of attack we would have 16 as 2^4 (two to the fourth power), 32 as 2^5 (two to the fifth power), and so on. As for 2 itself, only one 2 is involved and we can call it 2^1 (two to the first power).

One more thing. We can decide to let 2^0 (two to the zero power) be equal to 1. (In fact, it is convenient to let any number to the zero power be equal to 1. Thus, 3^0 equals 1, and so does 17^0 and $1,965,211^0$. For the moment, however, we are interested only in 2^0 and we are letting that equal 1.)

Well, then, instead of having the series 1, 2, 4, 8, 16, 32, 64, . . . , we can have 2^0, 2^1, 2^2, 2^3, 2^4, 2^5, 2^6. . . . It's the same series as far as the value of the individual members are concerned, but the second way of writing it is prettier somehow and, as we shall see, more useful.

We can express any number in terms of these powers of 2. I said earlier that 100 could be expressed as 64 plus 32 plus 4. This means it can be expressed as 2^6 plus 2^5 plus 2^2. In the same way, if 729 is equal to 512 plus 128 plus 64 plus 16 plus 8 plus 1, then it can also be expressed as 2^9 plus 2^7 plus 2^6 plus 2^4 plus 2^3 plus 2^0. And of course, 1023 is 2^9 plus 2^8 plus 2^7 plus 2^6 plus 2^5 plus 2^4 plus 2^3 plus 2^2 plus 2^1 plus 2^0.

But let's be systematic about this. We are using ten different powers of 2 to express any number below 1024, so let's mention all of them as a matter of course. If we don't want to use a certain power in the addition that is required to express a particular number, then we need merely multiple it by 0. If we want to use it, we multiply it by 1. Those are the only alternatives; we either use a certain power, or we don't use it; we either multiply it by 1 or by 0.

Using a dot to signify multiplication, we can say that 1023 is: $1 \cdot 2^9$ plus $1 \cdot 2^8$ plus $1 \cdot 2^7$ plus $1 \cdot 2^6$ plus $1 \cdot 2^5$ plus $1 \cdot 2^4$ used. In expressing 729, however, we would have: $1 \cdot 2^9$ plus $1 \cdot 2^3$ plus $1 \cdot 2^2$ plus $1 \cdot 2^1$ plus $1 \cdot 2^0$. All the powers are used. In expressing 729, however, we would have: $1 \cdot 2^9$ plus $0 \cdot 2^8$ plus $1 \cdot 2^7$ plus $1 \cdot 2^6$ plus $0 \cdot 2^5$ plus $1 \cdot 2^4$ plus $1 \cdot 2^3$ plus $0 \cdot 2^2$ plus $0 \cdot 2^1$ plus $1 \cdot 2^0$. And again, in expressing 100, we can write: $0 \cdot 2^9$ plus $0 \cdot 2^8$ plus $0 \cdot 2^7$ plus $1 \cdot 2^6$ plus $1 \cdot 2^5$ plus $0 \cdot 2^4$ plus $0 \cdot 2^3$ plus $1 \cdot 2^2$ plus $0 \cdot 2^1$ plus $0 \cdot 2^0$.

But why bother, you might ask, to include those powers you don't use? You write them out and then wipe them out by multiplying them by zero. The point is, however, that if you systematically write them all out, without exception, you can take it for granted that they are there and omit them altogether, keeping only the 1's and the 0's.

Thus, we can write 1023 as 1111111111; we can write 729 as 1011011001; and we can write 100 as 0001100100.

In fact, we can be systematic about this and, remembering the order of the powers, we can use the ten powers to express all the numbers up to 1023 this way:

0000000001 equals 1
0000000010 equals 2
0000000011 equals 3
0000000100 equals 4
0000000101 equals 5
0000000110 equals 6
0000000111 equals 7, all the way up to

. . .

1111111111 equals 1023.

Of course, we don't have to confine ourselves to ten powers of 2, we can have eleven powers, or fourteen, or fifty-three, or an infinite number. However, it would get wearisome writing down an infinite number of 1's and 0's just to indicate whether each one of an infinite number of powers of 2 is used or is not used. So it is conventional to leave out all the high powers of 2 that are not used for a particular number and just begin with the highest power that *is* used and continue from there. In other words, leave out the unbroken line of zeroes at the left. In that case, the numbers can be represented as

> 1 equals 1
> 10 equals 2
> 11 equals 3
> 100 equals 4
> 101 equals 5
> 110 equals 6
> 111 equals 7, and so on.

Any number at all can be expressed by some combination of 1's and 0's in this fashion, and a few primitive tribes have actually used a number system like this. The first civilized mathematician to work it out systematically, however, was Gottfried Wilhelm Leibniz, about three centuries ago. He was amazed and gratified because he reasoned that 1, representing unity, was clearly a symbol for God, while 0 represented the nothingness which, aside from God, existed in the beginning. Therefore, if all numbers can be represented merely by the use of 1 and 0, surely this is the same as saying that God created the universe out of nothing.

Despite this awesome symbolism, this business of 1's and 0's made no impression whatsoever on practical men of affairs. It might be a fascinating mathematical curiosity, but no accountant is going to work with 1011011001 instead of 729.

But then it suddenly turned out that this two-based system of numbers (also called the "binary system," from the Latin word *binarius,* meaning "two at a time") is ideal for electronic computers.

After all, the two different digits, 1 and 0, can be matched in the computer by the two different positions

GOTTFRIED WILHELM LEIBNIZ

Leibniz was born in Leipzig, Saxony, on July 1, 1646, and was an amazing child prodigy. He taught himself Latin at eight and Greek at fourteen. He obtained a degree in law in 1665 and, in addition, was a diplomat, philosopher, political writer, and an attempted reconciler of Catholics and Protestants. On occasion he acted as adviser to Peter the Great of Russia. In 1671 he was the first person to devise a mechanical device that would multiply and divide as well as add and subtract.

Leibniz visited London in 1673 and thereafter began to work out that branch of mathematics called calculus, which he published in 1684. Isaac Newton had worked out the calculus independently at about the same time, but Newton was rather small-minded in all things where his genius didn't apply and he accused Leibniz of plagiarism. There was a long battle between defenders of the two men, but actually Leibniz's development was superior, and Great Britain, by sticking stubbornly to Newton, fell behind in mathematics and stayed behind for a century and a half.

In 1700 Leibniz induced King Frederick I of Prussia to found the Academy of Sciences in Berlin and served as it first president. However, he spent almost all his mature years in the service of the Electors of Hanover. In 1714 the then-elector succeeded to the throne of Great Britain as George I, and Leibniz was eager to go with him to London.

Kings are not notorious for anything but self-centeredness, however, and George I had no need of Leibniz. Leibniz died in Hanover on November 14, 1716, neglected and forgotten, with only his secretary attending the funeral.

The Granger Collection

of a particular switch: "on" and "off." Let "on" represent 1 and "off" represent 0. Then, if the machine contained ten switches, the number 1023 could be indicated as on-on-on-on-on-on-on-on-on-on; the number 729 could be on-off-on-on-off-on-on-off-off-on; and the number 100 could be off-off-off-on-on-off-off-on-off-off.

By adding more switches we can express any number we want simply by this on-off combination. It may seem complicated to us, but it is simplicity itself to the computer. In fact, no other conceivable system could be as simple— for the computer.

However, since we are only human beings, the question is, can *we* handle the two-based system? For instance, can we convert back and forth between two-based numbers and ordinary numbers? If we are shown 110001 in the two-based system, what does it mean in ordinary numbers?

Actually, this is not difficult. The two-based system uses powers of 2, starting at the extreme right with 2^0 and moving up a power at a time as we move leftward. So we can write 110001 with little numbers underneath to represent the exponents, thus 110001. Only the exponents
$$5\,4\,3\,2\,1\,0$$
under the 1's are used, so 110001 represents 2^5 plus 2^4 plus 2^0 or 32 plus 16 plus 1. In other words, 110001 in the two-based system is 49 in ordinary numbers.

Working the other way is even simpler. You can, if you wish, try to fit the powers of 2 into an ordinary number by hit and miss, but you don't have to. There is a routine you can use which always works and I will describe it (though, if you will forgive me, I will not bother to explain why it works).

Suppose you wish to convert an ordinary number into the two-based system. You divide it by 2 and set the remainder to one side. (If the number is even, the remainder will be zero; if odd, it will be 1.) Working only with the whole-number portion of the quotient, you divide that by 2 again, and again set the remainder to one side and work only with the whole-number portion of the new quotient. When the whole-number portion of the quotient is reduced to 0 as a result of the repeated divisions by 2, you stop. The remainders, read backward, give the original number in the two-based system.

If this sounds complicated, it can be made simple enough by use of an example. Let's try 131:

> 131 divided by 2 is 65 with a remainder of 1
> 65 divided by 2 is 32 with a remainder of 1
> 32 divided by 2 is 16 with a remainder of 0
> 16 divided by 2 is 8 with a remainder of 0
> 8 divided by 2 is 4 with a remainder of 0
> 4 divided by 2 is 2 with a remainder of 0
> 2 divided by 2 is 1 with a remainder of 0
> 1 divided by 2 is 0 with a remainder of 1

In the two-based system, then, 131 is written 10000011. With a little practice anyone who knows fourth-grade arithmetic can switch back and forth between ordinary numbers and two-based numbers.

The two-based system has the added value that it makes the ordinary operations of arithmetic childishly simple. In using ordinary numbers, we spend several years in the early grades memorizing the fact that 9 plus 5 is 14, that 8 times 3 is 24, and so on.

In two-based numbers, however, the only digits involved are 1 and 0, so there are only four possible sums of digits taken two at a time: 0 plus 0, 1 plus 0, 0 plus 1, and 1 plus 1. The first three are just what one would expect in ordinary arithmetic:

> 0 plus 0 equals 0
> 1 plus 0 equals 1
> 0 plus 1 equals 1

The fourth sum involves a slight difference. In ordinary arithmetic 1 plus 1 is 2, but there is no digit like 2 in the two-based system. There 2 is represented as 10. Therefore:

> 1 plus 1 equals 10 (put down 0 and carry 1)

Imagine, then, how simple addition is in the two-based system. If you want to add 1001101 and 11001, the sum would look like this:

> 1001101
> 11001
> ———————
> 1100110

You can follow this easily from the addition table I've just given you, and by converting to ordinary numbers (as you ought also to be able to do) you will see that the addition is equivalent to 77 plus 25 equals 102.

It may seem to you that following the 1's and 0's is difficult indeed and that the ease of memorizing the rules of addition is more than made up for by the ease of losing track of the whole thing. This is true enough—for a human. In a computer, however, on-off switches are easily designed in such combinations as to make it possible for the on's and off's to follow the rules of addition in the two-based system. Computers don't get confused and surges of electrons bouncing this way and that add numbers by two-based addition in microseconds.

Of course (to get back to humans) if you want to add more than two numbers, you can always, at worst, break them up into groups of two. If you want to add 110, 101, 100, and 111, you can first add 110 and 101 to get 1011, then add 100 and 111 to get 1011, and finally add 1011 and 1011 to get 10110. (The last addition involves adding 1 plus 1 plus 1 as a result of carrying a 1 into a column which is already 1 plus 1. Well, 1 plus 1 is 10 and 10 plus 1 is 11, so 1 plus 1 plus 1 is 11, put down 1 and carry 1.)

Multiplication in the two-based system is even simpler. Again, there are only four possible combinations: 0 times 0, 0 times 1, 1 times 0, and 1 times 1. Here, each multiplication in the two-based system is exactly as it would be in ordinary numbers. In other words:

0 times 0 is 0
0 times 1 is 0
1 times 0 is 0
1 times 1 is 1

To multiply 101 by 1101, we would have

```
     101
    1101
    ----
     101
    000
   101
  101
  -------
 1000001
```

In ordinary numbers, this is equivalent to saying 5 times 13 is 65. Again, the computer can be designed to manipulate the on's and off's of its switches to match the requirements of the two-based multiplication table—and to do it with blinding speed.

It is possible to have a number system based on powers of 3, also (a three-based or "ternary" system). The series of number 3^0, 3^1, 3^2, 3^3, 3^4, and so on (that is, 1, 3, 9, 27, 81, and so on) can be used to express any finite number provided you are allowed to use up to two of each member of the series.

Thus 17 is 9 plus 3 plus 3 plus 1 plus 1 and 72 is 27 plus 27 plus 9 plus 9.

If you wanted to write the series of integers according to the three-based system, they would be: 1, 2, 10, 11, 12, 20, 21, 22, 100, 101, 102, 110, 111, 112, 120, 121, 122, 200, and so on.

You could have a four-based number system based on powers of 4, with each power used up to three times; a five-based number system based on power of 5 with each power used up to four times; and so on.

To convert an ordinary number into any one of these other systems, you need only use a device similar to the one I have demonstrated for conversion into the two-based system, you would repeatedly divide by 3 for the three-based system, by 4 for the four-based system, and so on.

Thus, I have already converted the ordinary number 131 into 11000001 by dividing 131 repeatedly by 2 and using the remainders. Suppose we divide 131 repeatedly by 3 instead and make use of the remainders:

131 divided by 3 is 43 with a remainder of 2
43 divided by 3 is 14 with a remainder of 1
14 divided by 3 is 4 with a remainder of 2
4 divided by 3 is 1 with a remainder of 1
1 divided by 3 is 0 with a remainder of 1

The number 131 in the three-based system, then, is made up of the remainders, working from the bottom up, and is 11212.

In similar fashion we can work out what 131 is in the four-based system, the five-based system, and so on. Here is a little table to give you the values of 131 up through the nine-based system:

two-based system	11000001
three-based system	11212
four-based system	2003
five-based system	1011
six-based system	335
seven-based system	245
eight-based system	203
nine-based system	155

You can check these by working through the powers. In the nine-based system, 155 is $1\cdot9^2$ plus $5\cdot9^1$ plus $5\cdot9^0$. Since 9^2 is 81, 9^1 is 9, and 9^0 is 1, we have 81 plus 45 plus 5, or 131. In the six-based system, 335 is $3\cdot6^2$ plus $3\cdot6^1$ plus $5\cdot6^0$. Since 6^2 is 36, 6^1 is 6, and 6^0 is 1, we have 108 plus 18 plus 5, or 131. In the four-based system, 2003 is $2\cdot4^3$ plus $0\cdot4^2$ plus $0\cdot4^1$ plus $3\cdot4^0$, and since 4^3 is 64, 4^2 is 16, 4^1 is 4, and 4^0 is 1, we have 128 plus 0 plus 0 plus 3, or 131.

The others you can work out for yourself if you choose.

But is there any point to stopping at a nine-based system? Can there be a ten-based system? Well, suppose we write 131 in the ten-based system by dividing it through by tens:

131 divided by 10 is 13 with a remainder of 1
13 divided by 10 is 1 with a remainder of 3
1 divided by 10 is 0 with a remainder of 1

And therefore 131 in the ten-based system is 131.

In other words, our ordinary numbers are simply the ten-based system, working on a series of powers of 10: 10^0, 10^1, 10^2, 10^3, and so on. The number 131 is equal to $1\cdot10^2$ plus $3\cdot10^1$ plus $1\cdot10^0$. Since 10^2 is 100, 10^1 is 10, and 10^0 is 1, this means we have 100 plus 30 plus 1, 131.

There is nothing basic or fundamental about ordinary numbers then. They are based on the powers of 10 because we have ten fingers and counted on our fingers to begin with, but the powers of any other number will fulfill all the mathematical requirements.

Thus we can go on to an eleven-based system and a

twelve-based system. Here, one difficulty arises. The number of digits (counting zero) that is required for any system is equal to the number used as base.

In the two-based system, we need two different digits, 0 and 1. In the three-based system, we need three different digits, 0, 1, and 2. In the familiar ten-based system, we need, of course, ten different digits, 0, 1, 2, 3, 4, 5, 6, 7, 8, and 9.

It follows, then, that in the eleven-based system we will need eleven different digits and in the twelve-based system twelve different digits. Let's write @ for the eleventh digit and # for the twelfth. In ordinary ten-based numbers, @ is 10 and # is 11.

Thus, 131 in the eleven-based system is:

131 divided by 11 is 11 with a remainder of 10 (@)
11 divided by 11 is 1 with a remainder of 0
1 divided by 11 is 0 with a remainder of 1

so that 131 in the eleven-based system is 10@.
And in the twelve-based system:

131 divided by 12 is 10 with a remainder of 11 (#)
10 divided by 12 is 0 with a remainder of 10 (@)

so that 131 in the twelve-based system is @#.

And we can go up and up and up and have a 4,583-based system if we wanted (but with 4,583 different digits, counting the zero).

Now all the number systems may be valid, but which system is most convenient? As one goes to higher and higher bases, numbers become shorter and shorter. Though 131 is 11000001 in the two-based system, it is 131 in the ten-based system and @# in the twelve-based system. It moves from eight digits to three digits to two digits. In fact, in a 131-based system (and higher) it would be down to a single digit. In a way, this represents increasing convenience. Who needs long numbers?

However, the number of different digits used in constructing numbers goes up with the base and this is an increasing inconvenience. Somewhere there is an intermediate base in which the number of different digits isn't

COMPUTERS

Computers have a bad press these days. They are supposed to be soulless and dehumanizing. But what do people expect? They insist on populating the world by the billions. They insist on a government that spends hundreds of billions. (Sure they do. Every single person in the United States is for less government spending except where that hurts his way of life; and every cut damages the livelihood of millions so there are no cuts.) They insist on big business, big science, big armies, and everything else, and things have grown so complicated that none of it is possible without computers.

Sure, computers make humorous mistakes, but that's not the computer. It's the human being who programmed it or operated it. If you can't make your check stubs

balance, do you blame the number system or your own inability to add? (The number system? Well, then, I suppose you can blame computers, too.)

Dehumanizing? I suspect the same complaint was made by some proto-Sumerian architect who got sick and tired of the knotted ropes that the young apprentices were carrying about to measure the distances on the temple under construction. An architect should use his mind and eyes, he would say, and not depend on soulless mechanical contrivances.

Actually, people who say nasty things about computers are only indulging in a pseudo-intellectual cheap-shot. There's no way of removing them from society without disaster, and if all the computers went on strike for twenty-four hours, you would experience what one means by a completely stalled nation.

It is safe to complain about our modern technology while taking full advantage of it. Costs nothing.

IBM Corporation from the Granger Collection

too high and the number of digits in the usual numbers we use isn't too great.

Naturally it would seem to us that the ten-based system is just right. Ten different digits to memorize doesn't seem too high a price to pay for using only four digit combinations to make up any number under ten thousand.

Yet the twelve-based system has been touted now and then. Four digit combinations in the twelve-based system will carry one up to a little over twenty thousand, but that seems scarcely sufficient recompense for the task of learning to manipulate two extra digits. (School children would have to learn such operations as @ plus 5 is 13 and # times 4 is 38.)

But here another point arises. When you deal with any number system, you tend to talk in round numbers: 10, 100, 1000, and so on. Well, 10 in the ten-based system is evenly divisible by 2 and 5 and that is all. On the other hand, 10 in the twelve-based system (which is equivalent to 12 in the ten-based system) is evenly divisible by 2, 3, 4, and 6. This means that a twelve-based system would be more adaptable to commercial transactions and, indeed, the twelve-based system is used every time things are sold in dozens (12's) and grosses (144's) for 12 is 10 and 144 is 100 in the twelve-based system.

In this age of computers, however, the attraction is toward a two-based system. And while a two-based system is an uncomfortable and unaesthetic mélange of 1's and 0's, there is a compromise possible.

A two-based system is closely related to an eight-based system, for 1000 on the two-based system is equal to 10 on the eight-based system, or, if you'd rather, 2^3 equals 8^1. We could therefore set up a correspondence as follows:

TWO-BASED SYSTEM	EIGHT-BASED SYSTEM
000	0
001	1
010	2
011	3
100	4
101	5
110	6
111	7

This would take care of *all* the digits (including zero) in the eight-based system and *all* the three-digit combinations (including 000) in the two-based system.

Therefore any two-based number could be broken up into groups of three digits (with zeros added to the left if necessary) and converted into an eight-based number by using the table I've just given you. Thus, the two-based number 111001000010100110 could be broken up as 111,-001,000,010,100,110 and written as the eight-based number, 710246. On the other hand, the eight-based number 33574 can be written as the two-based number 0110111-01111100 almost as fast as one can write, once one learns the table.

In other words, if we switched from a ten-based system to an eight-based system, there would be a much greater understanding between ourselves and our machines and who knows how much faster science would progress.

Of course, such a switch isn't practical, but just think—Suppose that, originally, primitive man had learned to count on his eight fingers only and had left out those two awkward and troublesome thumbs.

3 EXCLAMATION POINT!

IT IS A SAD thing to be unrequitedly in love, I can tell you. The truth is that I love mathematics and mathematics is completely indifferent to me.

Oh, I can handle the elementary aspects of math all right but as soon as subtle insights are required, she goes in search of someone else. She's not interested in me.

I know this because every once in a while I get all involved with pencil and paper, on the track of some great mathematical discovery and so far I have obtained only two kinds of results: 1) completely correct findings that are quite old, and 2) completely new findings that are quite wrong.

For instance (as an example of the first class of results), I discovered, when I was very young, that the sums of successive odd numbers were successive squares. In other words: $1=1$; $1+3=4$; $1+3+5=9$; $1+3+5+7=16$, and so on. Unfortunately, Pythagoras knew this too in 500 B.C., and I suspect that some Babylonian knew it in 1500 B.C.

An example of the second kind of result involves Fermat's Last Theorem.* I was thinking about it a couple

---

* I'm not going to discuss that here. Suffice it to say now that it is the most famous unsolved problem in mathematics.

of months ago when a sudden flash of insight struck me and a kind of luminous glow irradiated the interior of my skull. *I was able to prove the truth of Fermat's Last Theorem in a very simple way.*

When I tell you that the greatest mathematicians of the last three centuries have tackled Fermat's Last Theorem with ever increasingly sophisticated mathematical tools and that all have failed, you will realize what a stroke of unparalleled genius it was for me to succeed with nothing more than ordinary arithmetical reasoning.

My delirium of ecstasy did not completely blind me to the fact that my proof depended upon one assumption which I could check very easily with pencil and paper. I went upstairs to my study to carry that check through—stepping very carefully so as not to jar all that brilliance inside my cranium.

You guessed it, I'm sure. My assumption proved to be quite false inside of a few minutes. Fermat's Last Theorem was not proven after all; and my radiance paled into the light of ordinary day as I sat at my desk, disappointed and miserable.

Now that I have recovered completely, however, I look back on that episode with some satisfaction. After all, for five minutes, I was *convinced* that I was soon to be recognized as the most famous living mathematician in the world, and words cannot express how wonderful that felt while it lasted!

On the whole, though, I suppose that true old findings, however minor, are better than new false ones, however major. So I will trot out for your delectation, a little discovery of mine which I made just the other day but which, I am certain, is over three centuries old in reality.

However, I've never seen it anywhere, so until some Gentle Reader writes to tell me who first pointed it out and when, I will adopt the discovery as the Asimov Series.

First, let me lay the groundwork.

We can begin with the following expression; $(1+1/n)^n$ where n can be set equal to any whole number. Suppose we try out a few numbers.

If $n=1$, the expression becomes $(1+\frac{1}{1})^1=2$. If $n=2$, the expression becomes $(1+\frac{1}{2})^2$ or $(\frac{3}{2})^2$ or $\frac{9}{4}$ or 2.25. If $n=3$, the expression becomes $(1+\frac{1}{3})^3$ or $(\frac{4}{3})^3$ or $\frac{64}{27}$ or about 2.3704.

We can prepare Table 1 of the value of the expression for a selection of various values of n:

TABLE 1   *The Approach to* e

n	$(1+1/n)^n$
1	2
2	2.25
3	2.3704
4	2.4414
5	2.4888
10	2.5936
20	2.6534
50	2.6915
100	2.7051
200	2.7164

As you see, the higher the value of n, the higher the value of the expression $(1+1/n)^n$. Nevertheless, the value of the expression increases more and more slowly as n increases. When n doubles from 1 to 2, the expression increases in value by 0.25. When n doubles from 100 to 200, the expression increases in value only by 0.0113.

The successive values of the expression form a "converging series" which reaches a definite limiting value. That is, the higher the value of n, the closer the value of the expression comes to a particular limiting value without ever quite reaching it (let alone getting past it).

The limiting value of the expression $(1+1/n)^n$ as n grows larger without limit turns out to be an unending decimal, which is conventionally represented by the symbol e.

It so happens that the quantity e is extremely important to mathematicians and they have made use of computers to calculate its value to thousands of decimal places. Shall we make do with 50? All right. The value of e is: 2.7182-818284590452353602874713526624977572470936 9995...

You may wonder how mathematicians compute the limit of the expression to so many decimal places. Even when I carried n up to 200 and solved for $(1+\frac{1}{200})^{200}$, I only got e correct to two decimal places. Nor can I reach higher values of n. I solved the equation for $n=200$ by the use of five-place logarithm tables—the best available in

my library—and those aren't accurate enough to handle
values of n over 200 in this case. In fact, I don't trust my
value for $n=200$.

Fortunately, there are other ways of determining e.
Consider the following series: $2+\frac{1}{2}+\frac{1}{6}+\frac{1}{24}+\frac{1}{120}+\frac{1}{720}$ . . .

There are six members in this series of numbers as far
as I've given it above, and the successive sums are:

$2=$	2
$2+\frac{1}{2}=$	2.5
$2+\frac{1}{2}+\frac{1}{6}=$	2.6666 . . .
$2+\frac{1}{2}+\frac{1}{6}+\frac{1}{24}=$	2.7083333 . . .
$2+\frac{1}{2}+\frac{1}{6}+\frac{1}{24}+\frac{1}{120}=$	2.7166666 . . .
$2+\frac{1}{2}+\frac{1}{6}+\frac{1}{24}+\frac{1}{120}+\frac{1}{720}=$	2.71805555 . . .

In other words, by a simple addition of six numbers, a
process for which I don't need a table of logarithms at
all, I worked out e correct to three decimal places.

If I add a seventh number in the series, then an eighth,
and so on, I could obtain e correct to a surprising number
of additional decimal places. Indeed, the computer which
obtained the value of e to thousands of places made use
of the series above, summing thousands of fractions in the
series.

But how does one tell what the next fraction in the
series will be? In a useful mathematical series, there
should be some way of predicting every member of the
series from the first few. If I began a series as follows:
$\frac{1}{2}+\frac{1}{3}+\frac{1}{4}+\frac{1}{5}$ . . . you would, without trouble continue
onward . . . $\frac{1}{6}+\frac{1}{7}+\frac{1}{8}$ . . . Similarly, if a series began
$\frac{1}{2}+\frac{1}{4}+\frac{1}{8}+\frac{1}{16}$, you would be confident in continuing . . .
$\frac{1}{32}+\frac{1}{64}+\frac{1}{128}$ . . .

In fact, an interesting parlor game for number-minded
individuals would be to start a series and then ask for the
next number. As simple examples consider:

$$2, 3, 5, 7, 11 \ldots$$
$$2, 8, 18, 32, 50 \ldots$$

Since the first series is the list of primes, the next number is obviously 13. Since the second series consists of
numbers that are twice the list of successive squares, the
next number is 72.

But what are we going to do with a series such as:
$2+\frac{1}{2}+\frac{1}{6}+\frac{1}{24}+\frac{1}{120}+\frac{1}{720}$ . . . What is the next number?
If you know, the answer is obvious, but if you *hadn't* known, would you have been able to see it? And if you *don't* know, can you see it?

Just briefly, I am going to introduce a drastic change of subject.

Did any of you ever read Dorothy Sayers' *Nine Tailors?* I did, many years ago. It is a murder mystery, but I remember nothing of the murder, of the characters, of the action, of anything at all but for one item. That one item involves "ringing the changes."

Apparently (I slowly gathered as I read the book) in ringing the changes, you begin with a series of bells tuned to ring different notes, with one man at the rope of each bell. The bells are pulled in order: do, re, mi, fa, and so on. Then, they are pulled again, in a different order. Then, they are pulled again in a still different order. Then, they are pulled again—

You keep it up until all the possible orders (or "changes") in which the bells may be rung *are* rung. One must follow certain rules in doing so, such that no one bell, for instance, can be shifted more than one unit out of its place in the previous change. There are different patterns of shifting the order in the various kinds of change-ringing and these patterns are interesting in themselves. However, all I am dealing with here are the total number of possible changes connected with a fixed number of bells.

Let's symbolize a bell by an exclamation point (!) to represent its clapper, so that we can speak of one bell as 1!, two bells as 2! and so on.

No bells at all can be rung in one way only—by not ringing—so 0!=1. One bell (assuming bells *must* be rung if they exist at all) can only be rung in one way—bong—so 1!=1. Two bells, *a* and *b*, can clearly be rung in two ways, *ab* and *ba*, so 2!=2.

Three bells, *a*, *b*, and *c*, can be rung in six ways: *abc*, *acb*, *bac*, *bca*, *cab*, and *cba*, and no more, so 3!=6. Four bells, *a*, *b*, *c*, and *d*, can be rung in just twenty-four different ways. I won't list them all, but you can start with *abcd*, *abdc*, *acbd*, and *acdb* and see how many more changes you can list. If you can list twenty-five different and distinct orders of writing four letters, you have shaken the very foundations of mathematics, but I don't expect you will be able to do it. Anyway, $4!=24$.

Similarly (take my word for it for just a moment), five bells can be rung in 120 different changes and six bells in 720, so that $5!=120$ and $6!=720$.

By now I think you've caught on. Suppose we look again at the series that gives us our value of e: $2+\frac{1}{2}+\frac{1}{6}+\frac{1}{24}+\frac{1}{120}+\frac{1}{720}$ . . . and write it this way:

$$e=\frac{1}{0!}+\frac{1}{1!}+\frac{1}{2!}+\frac{1}{3!}+\frac{1}{4!}+\frac{1}{5!}+\frac{1}{6!} \ldots$$

Now we know how to generate the fractions next in line. They are . . . $+\frac{1}{7!}+\frac{1}{8!}+\frac{1}{9!}$ and so on forever.

To find the values of fractions such as $\frac{1}{7!}$, $\frac{1}{8!}$, and $\frac{1}{9!}$, you must know the value of 7!, 8!, and 9! and to know that you must figure out the number of changes in a set of seven bells, eight bells, and nine bells.

Of course, if you're going to try to list all possible changes and count them, you'll be at it all day; and you'll get hot and confused besides.

Let's search for a more indirect method, therefore.

We'll begin with four bells, because fewer bells offer no problem. Which bell shall we ring first? Any of the four, of course, so we have four choices for first place. For each one of these four choices, we can choose any of three bells (any one, that is, except the one already chosen for first place) so that for the first two places in line we have 4×3 possibilities. For each of these we can choose either of the two remaining bells for third place, so that for the first three places, we have $4\times3\times2$ possibilities. For each of these possibilities there remains only one bell for fourth place, so for all four places there are $4\times3\times2\times1$ arrangements.

We can say then, that $4!=4\times3\times2\times1=24$.

If we work out the changes for any number of bells, we will reach similar conclusions. For seven bells, for instance, the total number of changes is $7\times6\times5\times4\times3\times2\times1=5,040$. We can say, then, that $7!=5,040$.

(The common number of bells used in ringing the changes is seven; a set termed a "peal." If all seven bells are rung through once in six seconds, then a complete set of changes—5,040 of them—requires eight hours, twenty-four minutes . . . And ideally, it should be done without a mistake. Ringing the changes is a serious thing.)

CHURCH BELLS

Bells, which I use to illustrate factorial numbers in this essay, are common to a wide variety of cultures. In our own, they are most associated with churches, and in the days before modern timepieces, they were the universal method of apprising the population of the time, calling people to prayers, for instance. (I was in Oxford, England, one Sunday morning in 1974 when the bells started pealing—and kept on pealing. The din was indescribable and as Robert Heinlein once said, "If a nightclub made half that much noise they would shut it down as a public nuisance.")

Bells were also used to sound the alarm in case of fire, of an enemy approach, and so on. They were also rung during thunderstorms to keep off the lightning. Since church towers are usually the tallest structures in the towns of medieval and early modern towers, they were often struck by lightning and the bell ringing did nothing to prevent it. In fact, many bell ringers were killed by lightning.

As for change ringing, the "nine tailors" I mention in the article is by no means maximum. As many as twelve bells are used in change ringing, and changes rung on that many bells is called a "maximus."

Well it might be, since nothing but partial changes can be rung on twelve bells. A complete change in which every possible permutation of twelve bells is carried through in order would involve 479,001,600 different ringings of each bell. Where a "minimus," involving four bells, can be put through a complete change in thirty seconds, a "maximus" would require about forty years!

Change ringing is associated particularly with the Church of England and was originally a gentleman's recreation. Thus, Lord Peter Wimsey pulls a mean bell in The Nine Tailors.

Culver Pictures, Inc.

Actually, the symbol "!" does not really mean "bell." (That was just an ingenious device of mine to introduce the matter.) In this case it stands for the word "factorial." Thus, 4! is "factorial four" and 7! is "factorial seven."

Such numbers represent not only changes that can be rung in a set of bells, but the number of orders in which the cards can be found in a shuffled deck, the number of orders in which men can be seated at a table, and so on.

I have never seen any explanation for the term "factorial" but I can make what seems to me a reasonable stab at explaining it. Since the number $5,040 = 7 \times 6 \times 5 \times 4 \times 3 \times 2 \times 1$, it can be evenly divided by each number from 1 to 7 inclusive. In other words, each number from 1 to 7 is a factor of 5,040; why not, therefore, call 5,040, "factorial seven."

And we can make it general. All the integers from 1 to n are factors of $n!$. Why not call $n!$ "factorial n" therefore.

We can see, now, why the series used to determine e is such a good one to use.

The values of the factorial numbers increase at a tremendous rate, as is clear from the list in Table 2 of values up to merely 15!

TABLE 2	The Factorials
0!	1
1!	1
2!	2
3!	6
4!	24
5!	120
6!	720
7!	5,040
8!	40,320
9!	362,880
10!	3,628,800
11!	39,916,800
12!	479,001,600
13!	6,227,020,800
14!	87,178,291,200
15!	1,307,674,368,000

As the values of the factorials zoom upward, the value of fractions with successive factorials in the denominator must zoom downward. By the time you reach $\frac{1}{6!}$, the value is only $\frac{1}{720}$, and by the time you reach $\frac{1}{15!}$, the value is considerably less than a trillionth.

Each such factorial-denominatored fraction is larger than the remainder of the series all put together. Thus $\frac{1}{15!}$ is larger than $\frac{1}{16!}+\frac{1}{17!}+\frac{1}{18!}$ . . . and so on and so on forever, all put together. And this preponderance of a particular fraction over all later fractions combined increases as one goes along the series.

Therefore suppose we add up all the terms of the series through $\frac{1}{14!}$. The value is short of the truth by $\frac{1}{15!}+\frac{1}{16!}+\frac{1}{17!}+\frac{1}{18!}$ etc, etc. We might, however, say the value is short of the truth by $\frac{1}{15!}$ because the remainder of the series is insignificant in sum compared to $\frac{1}{15!}$. The value of $\frac{1}{15!}$ is less than a trillionth. It is, in other words, less than 0.000000000001, and the value of *e* you obtain by summing a little over a dozen fractions is correct to eleven decimal places.

Suppose we summed all the series up to $\frac{1}{999!}$ (by computer, of course). If we do that, we are $\frac{1}{1000!}$ short of the true answer. To find out how much that is, we must have some idea of the value of 1000!. We might determine that by calculating $1000\times999\times998$ . . . and so on, but don't try. It will take forever.

Fortunately, there exist formulas for calculating out large factorials (at least approximately) and there are tables which give the logarithms of these large factorials. Thus, *log* 1000!=2567.6046442. This means that 1000! $=4.024\times10^{2567}$, or (approximately) a 4 followed by 2,567 zeroes. If the series for *e* is calculated out to $\frac{1}{999!}$, the value will be short of the truth by only $1/(4\times10^{2567})$ and you will have *e* correct to 2,566 decimal places. (The best value of *e* I know of was calculated out to no less than 60,000 decimal places.)

Let me digress once again to recall a time I had personal use for moderately large factorials. When I was in the Army, I went through a period where three fellow sufferers and myself played bridge day and night until one of the others broke up the thing by throwing down his hand and saying, "We've played so many games, the same hands are beginning to show up."

I was terribly thankful, for that gave me something to think about.

Each order of the cards in a bridge deck means a possible different set of bridge hands. Since there are fifty-two cards, the total number of arrangements is 52!. However, within any individual hand, the arrangement doesn't matter. A particular set of thirteen cards received by a particular player is the same hand whatever its arrangement. The total number of arrangements of the thirteen cards of a hand is 13! and this is true for each of four hands. Therefore the total number of bridge-hand combinations is equal to the total number of arrangements divided by the number of those arrangements that don't matter, or:

$$\frac{52!}{(13!)^4}$$

I had no tables handy, so I worked it out the long way but that didn't bother me. It took up my time and, for my particular tastes, was much better than a game of bridge. I have lost the original figures long since, but now I can repeat the work with the help of tables.

The value of 52! is, approximately, 8.066×10^{67}. The value of 13! (as you can see in the table of factorials I gave above) is approximately 6.227×10^9 and the fourth power of that value is about 1.5×10^{39}. If we divide 8.066×10^{67} by 1.5×10^{39}, we find that the total number of different bridge games possible is roughly 5.4×10^{28} or 54,000,000,000,000,000,000,000,000,000 or 54 octillion.

I announced this to my friends. I said, "The chances are not likely that we are repeating games. We could play a trillion games a second for a billion years, without repeating a single game."

My reward was complete incredulity. The friend who had originally complained said, gently, "But, pal, there are only fifty-two cards, you know," and he led me to a quiet corner of the barracks and told me to sit and rest awhile.

Actually, the series used to determine the value of e is only a special example of a general case. It is possible to show that:

$$e^x = x^0/0! + x^1/1! + x^2/2! + x^3/3! + x^4/4! + x^5/5! \ldots$$

Since $x^0 = 1$, for any value of x, and 0! and 1! both equal 1, the series is usually said to start: $e^x = 1 + x + x^2/2! + x^3/3!$

. . . but I prefer my version given above. It is more symmetrical and beautiful.

Now e itself can be expressed as e^1. In this case, the x of the general series becomes 1. Since 1 to any power equals 1, then x^2, x^3, x^4 and all the rest become 1 and the series becomes:

$e^1 = 1/0! + 1/1! + 1/2! + 1/3! + 1/4! + 1/5! \ldots$ which is just the series we've been working with earlier.

But now let's take up the reciprocal of e; or, in other words, $1/e$. Its value to fifteen decimal places is 0.367879-441171442 . . .

It so happens that $1/e$ can be written as e^{-1}, which means that in the general formula for e^x, we can substitute -1 for x.

When -1 is raised to a power, the answer is $+1$ if the power is an even one, and -1 if it is an odd one. In other words: $(-1)^0 = 1$, $(-1)^1 = -1$, $(-1)^2 = +1$, $(-1)^3 = -1$, $(-1)^4 = +1$, and so on forever.

If, in the general series, then, x is set equal to -1, we have:

$e^{-1} = (-1)^0/0! + (-1)^1/1! + (-1)^2/2! + (-1)^3/3! + (-1)^4/4! \ldots$ or $e^{-1} = 1/0! + (-1)/1! + 1/2! + (-1)/3! + 1/4! + (-1)/5! \ldots$ or $e^{-1} = 1/0! - 1/1! + 1/2! - 1/3! + 1/4! - 1/5! + 1/6! - 1/7! \ldots$

In other words, the series for $1/e$ is just like the series for e except that all the even terms are converted from additions to subtractions.

Furthermore, since $1/0!$ and $1/1!$ both equal 1, the first two terms in the series for $1/e - 1/0! - 1/1! -$ are equal to $1 - 1 = 0$. They may therefore be omitted and we may conclude that

$e^{-1} = 1/2! - 1/3! + 1/4! - 1/5! + 1/6! - 1/7! + 1/8! - 1/9! + 1/10!$, and so on forever.

And now, at last, we come to my own personal discovery! As I looked at the series just given above for e^{-1}, I couldn't help think that the alternation between plus and minus is a flaw in its beauty. Could there not be any way in which it could be expressed with pluses only or with minuses only?

Since an expression such as $-1/3! + 1/4!$ can be converted into $- (1/3! - 1/4!)$, it seemed to me I could write the following series:

$e^{-1} = 1/2! - (1/3! - 1/4!) - (1/5! - 1/6!) - (1/7! - 1/8!) \ldots$ and so on.

PLAYING CARDS

It is because of the rapid increase in the factorial num-bers that it is possible to play an infinite number of games (infinite with respect to the limited human life span) with a mere fifty-two cards.

Indeed, the only other common deck is the pinochle deck in which there are only the ace, king, queen, jack, ten, and nine, and where each suit is duplicated. With eight kinds of each of six kinds of cards, you have only forty-eight cards. This involves a lower factorial, and the duplication of suits also cuts into the number of different hands possible. This means there are only 1/312,000,000 times as many different hands with a pinochle deck as with an ordinary deck, but the smaller number is still enough to supply no fear of duplications in the course of dedicated playing of the game of pinochle.

Somehow one gets the feeling that card games, which are so ubiquitous in the present-day world, must be an ancient, even a prehistoric pastime, but not so. They are a medieval invention, probably originating in the Far East and reaching Europe in the 1200s. They may have been brought west by Marco Polo or by gypsies or by Arab conquerors; no one really knows.

Odder still, two of the properties of playing cards, which we take quite for granted now, are even more recent modifications. One is the presence of the small index in the upper left and lower right corners so that we can identify a card when only a small part is exposed, as in the illustration. The other is the up-and-down rotational symmetry so that the card is right-side-up either way. If you were to try to play cards without these modifications, you would be appalled by the inconvenience.

Cards, incidentally, may have been used for fortune-telling (the tarot deck) before they were used for games of chance.

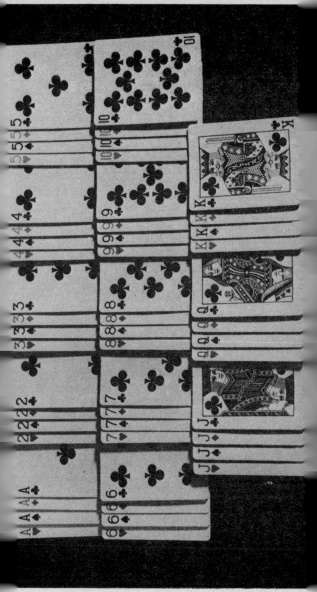

Now we have only minus signs, but we also have parentheses, which again offer an aesthetic flaw.

So I considered the contents of the parentheses. The first one contains $1/3! - 1/4!$ which equals $1/(3 \times 2 \times 1) - 1/(4 \times 3 \times 2 \times 1)$. This is equal to $(4-1)/(1 \times 3 \times 2 \times 1)$, or to $3/4!$. In the same way, $1/5! - 1/6! = 5/6!$; $1/7! - 1/8! = 7/8!$ and so on.

I was astonished and inexpressibly delighted for now I had the Asimov Series which goes:

$e^{-1} = 1/2! - 3/4! - 5/6! - 7/8! - 9/10!$ . . . and so on forever.

I am certain that this series is at once obvious to any real mathematician and I'm sure it has been described in texts for three hundred years—but I've never seen it and until someone stops me, I'm calling it the Asimov Series.

Not only does the Asimov Series contain only minus signs (except for the unexpressed positive sign before the first term), but it contains all the digits in order. You simply can't ask for anything more beautiful than that. Let's conclude now, by working out just a few terms of the series:

$1/2!$	$= 0.5$
$1/2! - 3/4!$	$= 0.375$
$1/2! - 3/4! - 5/6!$	$= 0.3680555 \ldots$
$1/2! - 3/4! - 5/6! - 7/8!$	$= 0.3678819 \ldots$

As you see, by adding up only four terms of the series, I get an answer which is only 0.0000025 greater than the truth, an error of 1 part in a bit less than 150,000 or, roughly $1/1500$ of 1 per cent.

So if you think the "Exclamation Point" of the title refers only to the factorial symbol, you are wrong. It applies even more so to my pleasure and astonishment with the Asimov Series.

P.S. To get round the unexpressed positive sign in the Asimov Series some readers (after the first appearance in print of this chapter) suggested the series be written: $-(-1)/0! - 1/2! - 3/4!$ . . . All the terms would then indeed be negative, even the first, but we would have to step outside the realm of the natural numbers to include 0 and -1, which detracts a bit from the austere beauty of the series.

Another suggested alternative is: $1/1! + 2/3! + 4/5! + 6/7! + 8/9!$ . . . which also gives $1/e$. It includes only positive signs which are prettier (in my opinion) than negative signs but, on the other hand, it includes 0.

Still another reader suggested a similar series for *e* itself; one that goes as follows: $\frac{2}{1} + \frac{2}{3} + \frac{6}{5!} + \frac{8}{7!} + \frac{10}{9!}$ . . . The inversion of the order of the natural numbers detracts from its orderliness but it gives it a certain touch of charming grace, doesn't it?

Oh, if only mathematics loved me as I love her!

4 T-FORMATION

I HAVE BEEN accused of having a mad passion for large numbers and this is perfectly true. I wouldn't dream of denying it. However, may I point out that I am not the only one?

For instance, in a book entitled *Mathematics and the Imagination* (published in 1940) the authors, Edward Kasner and James Newman, introduced a number called the "googol," which is good and large and which was promptly taken up by writers of books and articles on popular mathematics.

Personally, I think it is an awful name, but the young child of one of the authors invented it, and what could a proud father do? Thus, we are afflicted forever with that baby-talk number.

The googol was defined as the number 1 followed by a hundred zeros, and so here (unless I have miscounted or the Noble Printer has goofed) is the googol, written out in full:
10,000,000,000,000,000,000,000,000,000,000,000,000,000,
000,000,000,000,000,000,000,000,000,000,000,000,000,
000,000,000,000,000,000,000.

Now this is a pretty clumsy way of writing a googol, but it fits in with our system of numeration, which is based on the number 10. To write large numbers we simply multiply 10's, so that a hundred is ten times ten and is written 100; a thousand is ten times ten times ten and is written 1000 and so on. The number of zeros in the number is equal to the number of tens being multiplied, so that the googol, with a hundred zeros following the 1, is equal to a hundred tens multiplied together. This can also be written as 10^{100}. And since 100 is ten times ten or 10^2, the googol can even be written as 10^{10^2}

Certainly, this form of exponential notation (the little figure in the upper right of such a number is an "exponent") is very convenient, and any book on popular math will define a googol as 10^{100}. However, to anyone who loves large numbers, the googol is only the beginning and even this shortened version of writing large numbers isn't simple enough.*

So I have made up my own system for writing large numbers and I am going to use this chapter as a chance to explain it. (Freeze, everyone! No one's leaving till I'm through.)

The trouble, it seems to me, is that we are using the number 10 to build upon. That was good enough for cave men, I suppose, but we moderns are terribly sophisticated and we know lots better numbers than that.

For instance, the annual budget of the United States of America is in the neighborhood, now, of $100,000,000,000 (a hundred billion dollars). That means 1,000,000,000,-000 (one trillion) dimes.**

Why don't we, then, use the number, one trillion, as a base? To be sure, we can't visualize a trillion, but why should that stop us? We can't even visualize fifty-three. At least if someone were to show us a group of objects and tell us there are fifty-three of them altogether, we couldn't tell whether he were right or wrong without counting them. That makes a trillion no less unreal than fifty-three, for we have to count both numbers and both are equally countable. To be sure, it would take us much longer to count one trillion than to count fifty-three, but

---

* *The proper name for the googol, using American nomenclature, is "ten duotrigintillion," but I dare say, gloomily, that that will never replace "googol."*

[** *This article first appeared in August 1963. Since then the budget has more than tripled and is over three trillion dimes. Aren't we lucky? Incidentally, footnotes added for this collection are in brackets to distinguish them from those present at the time of first appearance.*]

the principle is the same and I, as anyone will tell you, am a man of principle.

The important thing is to associate a number with something physical that can be grasped and this we have done. The number 1,000,000,000,000 is roughly equal to the number of dimes taken from your pocket and mine (mostly mine, I sometimes sullenly think) each year by kindly, jovial Uncle Sam to build missiles and otherwise run the government and the country.

Then, once we have it firmly fixed in our mind as to what a trillion is, it takes very little effort of imagination to see what a trillion trillion is; a trillion trillion trillion, and so on. In order to keep from drowning in a stutter of trillions, let's use an abbreviated system that, as far as I know, is original with me.*

Let's call a trillion T-1; a trillion trillion T-2; a trillion trillion trillion T-3, and form large numbers in this fashion. (And there's the "T-formation" of the title! Surely you didn't expect football?)

Shall we see how these numbers can be put to use? I have already said that T-1 is the number of dimes it takes to run the United States for one year. In that case, T-2 would represent the number of dimes it would take to run the United States for a trillion years. Since this length of time is undoubtedly longer than the United States will endure (if I may be permitted this unpatriotic sentiment) and, in all likelihood, longer than the planet earth will endure, we see that we have run out of financial applications of the Asimovian T-numbers long before we have even reached T-2.

Let's try something else. The mass of any object is proportional to its content of protons and neutrons which, together, may be referred to as nucleons. Now T-1 nucleons make up a quantity of mass far too small to see in even the best optical microscope and even T-2 nucleons make up only 1⅔ grams of mass, or about ¹⁄₁₆ of an ounce.

Now we've got room, it would seem, to move way up the T-scale. How massive, for instance, are T-3 nucleons? Since T-3 is a trillion times as large as T-2, T-3 nucleons

---

* Actually, Archimedes set up a system of numbers based on the myriad, and spoke of a myriad myriad, a myriad myriad myriad and so on. But a myriad is only 10,000 and I'm using 1,000,000,000,000, so I don't consider Archimedes to be affecting my originality. Besides, he only beat me out by less than twenty-two centuries.

have a mass of 1.67 trillion grams, or a little under two million tons. Maybe there's not as much room as we thought.

In fact, the T-numbers build up with breath-taking speed. T-4 nucleons equal the mass of all the earth's ocean, and T-5 nucleons equal the mass of a thousand solar systems. If we insist on continuing upward, T-6 nucleons equal the mass of ten thousand galaxies the size of ours, and T-7 nucleons are far, far more massive than the entire known universe.

Nucleons are not the only subatomic particles there are, of course, but even if we throw in electrons, mesons, neutrinos, and all the other paraphernalia of subatomic structure, we cannot reach T-7. In short, there are far less than T-7 subatomic particles of all sorts in the visible universe.

Clearly, the system of T-numbers is a powerful method of expressing large numbers. How does it work for the googol? Well, consider the method of converting ordinary exponential numbers into T-numbers and vice versa. T-1 is equal to a trillion, or 10^{12}; T-2 is equal to a trillion trillion, or 10^{24}, and so on. Well, then, you need only divide an exponent by 12 to have the numerical portion of a T-number; and you need only multiply the numerical portion of a T-number by 12 to get a ten-based exponent.

If a googol is 10^{100}, then divide 100 by 12, and you see at once that it can be expressed as T-8½. Notice that T-8½ is larger than T-7 and T-7 is in turn far larger than the number of subatomic particles in the known universe. It would take a billion trillion universes like our own to contain a googol of subatomic particles.

What then is the good of googol, if it is too large to be useful in counting even the smallest material objects spread through the largest known volume?

I could answer: For its own sheer, abstract beauty—

But then you would all throw rocks at me. Instead, then, let me say that there are more things to be counted in this universe than material objects.

For instance, consider an ordinary deck of playing cards. In order to play, you shuffle the deck, the cards fall into a certain order, and you deal a game. Into how many different orders can the deck be shuffled? (Since it is impossible to have more essentially different game-situations than there are orders-of-cards in a shuffled deck, this is a question that should interest your friendly neighborhood poker-player.)

The answer is easily found (see Chapter 3) and comes out to about 80,000,000,000,000,000,000,000,000,000,000, 000,000,000,000,000,000,000,000,000,000,000,000, or 8×10^{67}. In T-numbers, this is something like T-5⅔. With an ordinary deck of cards, then, we can count arrangements and reach a value equal to that of the number of subatomic particles in a galaxy, more or less.

If, instead of 52 cards, we played with 70 cards (and this is not unreasonable; canasta, I understand, uses 108 cards), then the number of different orders after shuffling, just tops the googol mark.

So when it comes to analyzing card games (let alone chess, economics, and nuclear war), numbers like the googol and beyond are met with.

Mathematicians, in fact, are interested in many varieties of numbers (with and without practical applications) in which vastnesses far, far beyond the googol are quickly reached.

Consider Leonardo Fibonacci, for instance, the most accomplished mathematician of the Middle Ages. (He was born in Pisa, so he is often called Leonardo of Pisa.) About 1200, when Fibonacci was in his prime, Pisa was a great commercial city, engaged in commerce with the Moors in North Africa. Leonardo had a chance to visit that region and profit from a Moorish education.

The Moslem world had by that time learned of a new system of numeration from the Hindus. Fibonacci picked it up and in a book, *Liber Abaci*, published in 1202, introduced these "Arabic numerals" and passed them on to a Europe still suffering under the barbarism of the Roman numerals (see Chapter 1). Since Arabic numerals are only about a trillion times as useful as Roman numerals, it took a mere couple of centuries to convince European merchants to make the change.

In this same book Fibonacci introduces the following problem: "How many rabbits can be produced from a single pair in a year if every month each pair begets a new pair, which from the second month on become productive, and no deaths occur?" (It is also assumed that each pair consists of a male and female and that rabbits have no objection to incest.)

In the first month we begin with a pair of immature rabbits, and in the second month we still have one pair, but now they are mature. By the third month they have produced a new pair, so there are two pairs, one mature, one immature. By the fourth month the immature pair has become mature and the first pair has produced another immature pair, so there are three pairs, two mature and one immature.

You can go on if you wish, reasoning out how many pairs of rabbits there will be each month, but I will give you the series of numbers right now and save you the trouble. It is:

$$1, 1, 2, 3, 5, 8, 13, 21, 34, 55, 89, 144$$

At the end of the year, you see, there would be 144 pairs of rabbits and that is the answer to Fibonacci's problem.

The series of numbers evolved out of the problem is the "Fibonacci series" and the individual numbers of the series are the "Fibonacci numbers." If you look at the series, you will see that each number (from the third member on) is the sum of the two preceding numbers.

This means we needn't stop the series at the twelfth Fibonacci number (F_{12}). We can construct F_{13} easily enough by adding F_{11} and F_{12}. Since 89 and 144 are 233, that is F_{13}. Adding 144 and 233 gives us 377 or F_{14}. We can continue with F_{15} equal to 610, F_{16} equal to 987, and so on for as far as we care to go. Simple arithmetic, nothing more than addition, will give us all the Fibonacci numbers we want.

To be sure, the process gets tedious after a while as the Fibonacci numbers stretch into more and more digits and the chances of arithmetical error increase. One arithmetical error anywhere in the series, if uncorrected, throws off all the later members of the series.

But why should anyone want to carry the Fibonacci sequence on and on and on into large numbers? Well, the series has its applications. It is connected with cumulative growth, as the rabbit problem shows, and, as a matter of fact, the distribution of leaves spirally about a lengthening stem, the scales distributed about a pine cone, the seeds distributed in the sunflower center, all have an arrangement related to the Fibonacci series. The series is also re-

lated to the "golden section," which is important to art
and aesthetics as well as to mathematics.

But beyond all that, there are always people who are
fascinated by large numbers. (I can't explain the fascination but believe me it exists.) And if fascination falls short
of working away night after night with pen and ink, it is
possible, these days, to program a computer to do the
work, and get large numbers that it would be impractical
to try to work out in the old-fashioned way.

The October 1962 issue of *Recreational Mathematics
Magazine* * lists the first 571 Fibonacci numbers as worked
out on an IBM 7090 computer. The fifty-fifth Fibonacci
number passes the trillion mark, so that we can say that
F_{55} is greater than T-1.

From that point on, every interval of fifty-five or so
Fibonacci numbers (the interval slowly lengthens) passes
another T-number. Indeed, F_{481} is larger than a googol. It
is equal to almost one and a half googols, in fact.

Those multiplying rabbits, in other words, will quickly
surpass any conceivable device to encourage their multiplication. They will outrun any food supply that can be
dreamed up, any room that can be imagined. There might
be only 144 at the end of a year, but there would be nearly
50,000 at the end of two years, 15,000,000 at the end of
three years, and so on. In thirty years there would be more
rabbits than there are subatomic particles in the known
universe, and in forty years there would be more than a
googol of rabbits.

To be sure, human beings do not multiply as quickly
as Fibonacci's rabbits, and old human beings do die.
Nevertheless, the principle remains. What those rabbits
can do in a few years, we can do in a few centuries or
millenniums. Soon enough. Think of that when you tend
to minimize the population explosion.

For the fun of it, I would like to write F_{571}, which is the
largest number given in the chapter. (There will be larger
numbers later, but I will not write them out!) Anyway,
F_{571} is: 9604120061892255382394288336092486502610 4
9174118770678168222647890290143783084788641925 89

---

* *This is a fascinating little periodical which I heartily recommend to
any nut congruent to myself.*

08418525433163764618300807 4629. This vast number is
not quite equal to T-10.*

For another example of large numbers, consider the
primes. These are numbers like 7, or 641, or 5237, which
can be divided evenly only by themselves and 1. They have
no other factors. You might suppose that as one goes
higher and higher in the scale of numbers, the primes
gradually peter out because there would be more and more
smaller numbers to serve as possible factors.

This, however, does not happen, and even the ancient
Greeks knew that. Euclid was able to prove quite simply
that if all the primes are listed up to a "largest prime," it
is always possible to construct a still larger number which
is either prime itself or has a prime factor that is larger
than the "largest prime." It follows then there is no such
thing as a "largest prime" and the number of primes is
infinite.

Yet even if we can't work out a largest prime, there is
an allied problem. What is the largest prime we know? It
would be pleasant to point to a large number and say:
"This is a prime. There are an infinite number of larger
primes, but we don't know which numbers they are. This
is the largest number we *know* to be a prime."

Once that is done, you see, then some venturesome
amateur mathematician may find a still larger prime.

Finding a really large prime is by no means easy.
Earlier, for instance, I said that 5237 is prime. Suppose
you doubted that, how would you check me? The only
practical way is to try all the prime numbers smaller than
the square root of 5237 and see which, if any, are factors.
This is tedious but possible for 5237. It is simply impractical for really large numbers—except for computers.

Mathematicians have sought formulas, therefore, that
would construct primes. It might not give them every
prime in the book, so that it could not be used to test a
given number for prime-hood. However, it could construct
primes of any desired size, and after that the task of

* *Since this was written, the editor of* Recreational Mathematics *wrote to
say that he had new Fibonacci numbers, up to F_{1000}. This F_{1000} with 209
digits, is something over T-17. [Eleven years have passed since this footnote first appeared, but I have heard nothing more. I'm sure that new
Fibonacci numbers have been worked out but, alas, it is difficult to keep
up with everything. Things get past me.]*

LEONARDO FIBONACCI

Leonardo Fibonacci was born in Pisa about 1170 and he died about 1230. As I said in this essay, his greatest achievement was in popularizing the Arabic numerals in his book Liber Abaci. *In this, he had been anticipated by the English scholar Adelard of Bath (tutor of Henry II before that prince had succeeded to the throne) a century earlier. It was Fibonacci's book, however, that made the necessary impression.*

But why did he call it Liber Abaci, *or* Book of the Abacus? *Because, oddly enough, the use of Arabic numerals was implicit in the "abacus," a computing device that dates back to Babylonia and the earliest days of history.*

The abacus, in its simplest form, is most easily visualized as a series of wires on each of which ten counters are strung. There is room on the wire to move one or more of the counters to the right or left.

. .If you want to add five and four, for instance, you move five counters leftward, then four more, and count all you have moved—nine. If you want to add five and eight, you move five counters, but only have five more, not eight more, to move. You move the five, convert the ten counters into one counter in the wire above, then move the remaining three. The counters in the wire above are "tens," so you have one ten and three ones for a total of thirteen.

The wires represent, successively, units, tens, hundreds, thousands, and so on, and Arabic numerals, in essence, give the number of counters moved in each of the wires. The manipulations required in the abacus are those required in Arabic numerals. What was needed was a special symbol for a wire in which no counters were moved. This was zero, 0, and Arabic numerals were in business.

The Granger Collection

finding a record-high prime would become trivial and could be abandoned.

However, such a formula has never been found. About 1600, a French friar named Marin Mersenne proposed a formula of partial value which would occasionally, but not always, produce a prime. This formula is 2^p-1, where p is itself a prime number. (You understand, I hope, that 2^p represents a number formed by multiplying p two's together, so that 2^8 is $2\times2\times2\times2\times2\times2\times2\times2$, or 256.)

Mersenne maintained that the formula would produce primes when p was equal to 2, 3, 5, 7, 13, 17, 19, 31, 67, 127, or 257. This can be tested for the lower numbers easily enough. For instance, if p equals 3, then the formula becomes $2^3 - 1$, or 7, which is indeed prime. If p equals 7, then 2^7-1 equals 127, which is prime. You can check the equation for any of the other values of p you care to.

The numbers obtained by substituting prime numbers for p in Mersenne's equation are called "Mersenne numbers" and if the number happens to be prime it is a "Mersenne prime." They are symbolized by the capital letter M and the value of p. Thus M_3 equals 7; M_7 equals 127, and so on.

I don't know what system Mersenne used to decide what primes would yield Mersenne primes in his equation, but whatever it was, it was wrong. The Mersenne numbers M_2, M_3, M_5, M_7, M_{13}, M_{17}, M_{19}, M_{31}, and M_{127} are indeed primes, so that Mersenne had put his finger on no less than nine Mersenne primes. However, M_{67} and M_{257}, which Mersenne said were primes, proved on painstaking examination to be no primes at all. On the other hand, M_{61}, M_{89}, and M_{107}, which Mersenne did not list as primes, are primes, and this makes a total of twelve Mersenne primes.

In recent years, thanks to computer work, eight more Mersenne primes have been located (according to the April 1962 issue of *Recreational Mathematics*). These are M_{521}, M_{607}, M_{1279}, M_{2203}, M_{2281}, M_{3217}, M_{4253}, and M_{4423}. What's more, since that issue, three even larger Mersenne primes have been discovered by Donald B. Gillies of the University of Illinois. These are M_{9689}, M_{9941}, and M_{11213}.

The smallest of these newly discovered Mersenne primes, M_{521}, is obtained by working out the formula $2^{521} - 1$. You take 521 two's, multiply them together, and subtract one. The result is far, far higher than a googol. In fact, it is higher than T-13.

Not to stretch out the suspense, the largest known Mersenne prime, M_{11213}, and, I believe, the largest prime known at present, has 3375 digits and is therefore just about T-281¼. The googol, in comparison to that, is a trifle so small that there is no reasonable way to describe its smallness.

The Greeks played many games with numbers, and one of them was to add up the factors of particular integers. For instance, the factors of 12 (not counting the number itself) are 1, 2, 3, 4, and 6. Each of these numbers, but no others, will go evenly into 12. The sum of these factors is 16, which is greater than the number 12 itself, so that 12 is an "abundant number."

The factors of 10, on the other hand, are 1, 2, and 5, which yield a sum of 8. This is less than the number itself, so that 10 is a "deficient number." (All primes are obviously badly deficient.)

But consider 6. Its factors are 1, 2, and 3, and this adds up to 6. When the factors add up to the number itself, that number is a "perfect number."

Nothing has ever come of the perfect numbers in two thousand years, but the Greeks were fascinated by them, and those of them who were mystically inclined revered them. For instance, it could be argued (once Greek culture had penetrated Judeo-Christianity) that God had created the world in six days because six is a perfect number. (Its factors are the first three numbers, and not only is their sum six, but their product is also six, and God couldn't be expected to resist all that.)

I don't know whether the mystics also made a point of the fact that the lunar month is just a trifle over twenty-eight days long, since 28, with factors of 1, 2, 4, 7, and 14 (which add up to 28), is another perfect number. Alas, the days of the lunar month are actually 29½ and the mystics may have been puzzled over this slipshod arrangement on the part of the Creator.

But how many of these wonderful perfect numbers are there? Considering that by the time you reach 28, you have run into two of them, you might think there were many. However, they are rare indeed; far rarer than almost any other well-known kind of number. The third perfect number is 496, and the fourth is 8128, and

MARIN MERSENNE

Marin Mersenne was born near the French town of Oizé on September 8, 1588. Mersenne was a schoolfellow of the great mathematician René Descartes. Whereas Descartes, for some reason, joined the army, for which he was singularly ill adapted, Mersenne entered the Church, joining the Minim Friars in 1611. Within the Church, he did yeoman work for science, of which he was an ardent exponent. He defended Descartes's philosophy against clerical critics, translated some of the works of Galileo, and defended him, too.

Mersenne's chief service to science was the unusual one of serving as a channel for ideas. In the seventeenth century, long before scientific journals, international conferences, and even before the establishment of scientific academies, Mersenne was a one-man connecting link among the scientists of Europe. He wrote voluminous letters to regions as distant as Constantinople, informing one correspondent of the work of another, making suggestions arising out of his knowledge of the work of many, and constantly urging others to follow this course of copious intercommunication.

He opposed mystical doctrines such as astrology, alchemy, and divination; and strongly supported experimentation. As a practical example of this belief, he suggested to Christiaan Huygens the ingenious notion of timing bodies rolling down inclined planes by the use of a pendulum. This had not occurred to Galileo, who had first worked out the principle of the pendulum, but who timed his rolling bodies by using water dripping out of a can with a hole in the bottom. Huygens took the suggestion and it came to fruition in the form of the pendulum clock, the first timepiece that was useful to science.

Mersenne died in Paris on September 1, 1648.

MARIN MERSENNE
Religieux de l'Ordre des Minimes, Thologi.
Philosophe et Mathematicien celebre né a
Oyse au M. une Mort a Paris 1648. âgé de 60 ans.

The Granger Collection

throughout ancient and medieval times, those were the only perfect numbers known.

The fifth perfect number was not discovered until about 1460 (the name of the discoverer is not known) and it is 33,550,336. In modern times, thanks to the help of the computer, more and more perfect numbers have been discovered and the total now is twenty. The twentieth and largest of these is a number with 2663 digits, and this is almost equal to T-222.

But in a way, I have been unfair to Kasner and Newman. I have said they invented the googol and I then went on to show that it was easy to deal with numbers far higher than the googol. However, I should also add they invented another number, far, far larger than the googol. This second number is the "googolplex," which is defined as equal to 10^{googol}. The exponent, then, is a 1 followed by a hundred zeros, and I could write that, but I won't, instead, I'll say that a googolplex can be written as:

$$10^{10^{100}} \text{ or even } 10^{10^{10^2}}$$

The googol itself can be written out easily. I did it at the beginning of the article and it only took up a few lines. Even the largest number previously mentioned in this chapter can be written out with ease. The largest Mersenne prime, if written out in full, would take up less than two pages of this book.

The googolplex, however, cannot be written out—literally *cannot*. It is a 1 followed by a googol zeros, and this book will not hold as many as a googol zeros no matter how small, within reason, those zeros are printed. In fact, you could not write the number on the entire surface of the earth, if you made each zero no larger than an atom. In fact, if you represented each zero by a nucleon, there wouldn't be enough nucleons in the entire known universe or in a trillion like it to supply you with sufficient zeros.

You can see then that the googolplex is incomparably larger than anything I have yet dealt with. And yet I can represent it in T-numbers without much trouble.

Consider! The T-numbers go up through the digits, T-1, T-2, T-3, and so on, and eventually reach T-1,000,000,-000,000. (This is a number equivalent to saying "a trillion trillion trillion trillion . . ." and continuing until you have repeated the word *trillion* a trillion times. It will take you

umpty-ump lifetimes to do it, but the principle remains.)
Since we have decided to let a trillion be written as T-1,
the number T-1,000,000,000,000 can be written T-(T-1).

Remember that we must multiply the numerical part
of the T-number by 12 to get a ten-based exponent.
Therefore T-(T-1) is equal to $10^{12,000,000,000,000}$, which is
more than $10^{10^{13}}$

In the same way, we can calculate that T-(T-2) is more
than $10^{10^{25}}$, and if we continue we finally find that T-(T-8)
is nearly a googolplex. As for T-(T-9), that is far larger
than a googolplex; in fact, it is far larger than a googol
googolplexes.

One more item and I am through.

In a book called *The Lore of Large* Numbers, by Philip
J. Davis, a number called "Skewes' number" is given. This
number was obtained by S. Skewes, a South African
mathematician who stumbled upon it while working out a
complex theorem on prime numbers. The number is described as "reputed to be the largest number that has occurred in a mathematical proof." It is given as:

$$10^{10^{10^{34}}}$$

Since the googolplex is only $10^{10^{10^{2}}}$, Skewes' number is
incomparably the greater of the two.

And how can Skewes' number be put into T-formation?
Well, at this point, even I rebel. I'm not going to do it.

I will leave it to you, O Gentle Reader, and I will tell
you this much as a hint. It seems to me to be obviously
greater than T-[T-(T-1)].

From there on in, the track is yours and the road to
madness is unobstructed. Full speed ahead, all of you.

As for me, I shall hang back and stay sane; or, at least,
as sane as I ever am, which isn't much.*

[* *After this article first appeared, I was hounded by readers every now
and then to write an article on Skewes' number. I finally succumbed and
an article on this subject, "Skewered!," was written in 1974. You will
find it as the last chapter in my book* Of Matters Great and Small
(Doubleday, 1975).]

5 VARIETIES OF THE INFINITE

THERE ARE a number of words that publishers like to get into the titles of science-fiction books as an instant advertisement to possible fans casually glancing over a display that these books are indeed science fiction. Two such words are, of course *space* and *time*. Others are *Earth* (capitalized), *Mars, Venus, Alpha Centauri, tomorrow, stars, sun, asteroids,* and so on. And one—to get to the nub of this chapter—is *infinity*.

One of the best s.f. titles ever invented, in my opinion, is John Campbell's *Invaders from the Infinite*. The word *invaders* is redolent of aggression, action, and suspense, while *infinite* brings up the vastness and terror of outer space.

Donald Day's indispensable *Index to the Science Fiction Magazines* lists "Infinite Brain," "Infinite Enemy," "Infinite Eye," "Infinite Invasion," "Infinite Moment," "Infinite Vision," and "Infinity Zero" in its title index, and I am sure there are many other titles containing the word.*

[* *This article first appeared in September 1959 and Donald Day's* Index *only went up to 1950. Since 1950, the popularity of "Infinite" in s.f. titles has declined as the literary sophistication of the field has increased. Yes, I'm sorry.*]

Yet with all this exposure, with all this familiar use, do we know what *infinite* and *infinity* mean? Perhaps not all of us do.

We might begin, I imagine, by supposing that infinity was a large number; a very large number; in fact, the largest number that could exist.

If so, that would at once be wrong, for infinity is not a large number or any kind of number at all; at least of the sort we think of when we say "number." It certainly isn't the largest number that could exist, for there isn't any such thing.

Let's sneak up on infinity by supposing first that you wanted to write out instructions to a bright youngster, telling him how to go about counting the 538 people who had paid to attend a lecture. There would be one particular door through which all the audience would leave in single file. The youngster need merely apply to each person one of the various integers in the proper order: 1, 2, 3, and so on.

The phrase "and so on" implies continuing to count until all the people have left, and the last person who leaves has received the integer 538. If you want to make the order explicit, you might tell the boy to count in the following fashion and then painstakingly list all the integers from 1 to 538. This would undoubtedly be unbearably tedious, but the boy you are dealing with is bright and knows the meaning of a gap containing a dotted line, so you write: "Count thus: 1, 2, 3, . . . , 536, 537, 538." The boy will then understand (or should understand) that the dotted line indicates a gap to be filled by all the integers from 4 to 535 inclusive, in order and without omission.

Suppose you didn't know what the number of the audience was. It might be 538 or 427 or 651. You could instruct the boy to count until an integer had been given to the last man, whatever the man, whatever the integer. To express that symbolically, you could write thus: "Count: 1, 2, 3, . . . , $n-2$, $n-1$, n." The bright boy would understand that n routinely represents some unknown but definite integer.

Now suppose the next task you set your bright youngster was to count the number of men entering a door, filing through a room, out a second door, around the

LARGE NUMBERS

The fact is that in ancient times there was little need for large numbers. The largest number-name used was generally "thousand." If larger numbers were needed, phrases were used (as by us) of tens of thousands, and of hundreds of thousands. In ancient times, one went beyond and spoke of thousands of thousands. The word "million" (from an Italian word meaning "large thousand") for a thousand-thousand was only invented in the late Middle Ages when commerce had revived to the point where thousand-thousands were common enough in bookkeeping to make a special word convenient. (Billions, trillions, etc., followed later, and to this day the use of the larger numbers is unsettled. In the United States, a billion is a thousand million; in Great Britain, a billion is a million million.)

We can see the ancient poverty of names for numbers if we read the Bible. The largest number specifically named in the Bible occurs in 2 Chronicles 14:9 where a battle is described between Ethiopian invaders and the forces of Asa, King of Judah. "And there came out against them Zerah the Ethiopian with an host of a thousand thousand. . . ." Grossly exaggerated, of course, but the only mention of a number as high as a million in the Bible.

Elsewhere, when the need for large numbers is required, only comparisons can be made. Thus, in Genesis 22:17, God promises Abraham (who had just shown himself to be willing to sacrifice his only son to God), "I will multiply thy seed as the stars of the heaven and as the sand which is upon the sea shore." (That almost seems to apply to the illustration, which shows a crowd in Rio de Janeiro protesting the sinking of neutral Brazilian ships shortly before Brazil declared war on Germany and Italy.)

There was even the feeling that there are numbers so enormous that they can't be counted: Thus Solomon speaks of his subjects as "a great people, that cannot be numbered nor counted for multitude" (1 Kings 3:8). In the third century B.C., Archimedes demonstrated, for the first time, that any finite quantity can be numbered easily.

The Granger Collection

building, and through the first door again, the men forming a continuous closed system.

Imagine both marching men and counting boy to be completely tireless and willing to spend an eternity in their activities. Obviously the task would be endless. There would be no last man at all, ever, and there is no last integer at all, ever. (Any integer, however large, even if it consisted of a series of digits stretching in microscopic size from here to the farthest star, can easily be increased by 1.)

How do we write instructions for the precise counting involved in such a task. We can write: "Count thus: 1, 2, 3, and so on endlessly."

The phrase "and so on endlessly" can be written in shorthand, thus, ∞.

The statement "1, 2, 3, . . . , ∞" should be read "one, two, three, and so on endlessly" or "one, two, three, and so on without limit," but it is usually read, "one, two, three, and so on to infinity." Even mathematicians introduce infinity here, and George Gamow, for instance, has written a most entertaining book entitled just that: *One, Two, Three . . . Infinity*.

It might seem that using the word *infinity* is all right, since it comes from a Latin word meaning "endless," but nevertheless it would be better if the Anglo-Saxon were used in this case. The phrase "and so on endlessly" can't be mistaken. Its meaning is clear. The phrase "and so on to infinity," on the other hand, inevitably gives rise to the notion that infinity is some definite, though very huge, integer and that once we reach it we can stop.

So let's be blunt. Infinity is not an integer or any number of a kind with which we are familiar. It is a quality; a quality of endlessness. And any set of objects (numbers or otherwise) that is endless can be spoken of as an "infinite series" or an "infinite set." The list of integers from 1 on upward is an example of an "infinite set."

Even though ∞ is not a number, we can still put it through certain arithmetical operations. We can do that much for any symbol. We can do it for letters in algebra and write $a+b=c$. Or we can do it for chemical formulas and write: $CH_4+3O_2=CO_2+2H_2O$. Or we can do it for abstractions, such as: Man+Woman=Trouble.

The only thing we must remember is that in putting

symbols that are not integers through arithmetical paces, we ought not to be surprised if they don't follow the ordinary rules of arithmetic which, after all, were originally worked out to apply specifically to integers.

For instance, $3-2=1$, $17-2=15$, $4875-2=4873$. In general, any integer, once 2 is subtracted, becomes a different integer. Anything else is unthinkable.

But now suppose we subtract 2 from the unending series of integers. For convenience sake, we can omit the first two integers, 1 and 2, and start the series: 3, 4, 5, and so on endlessly. You see, don't you, that you can be just as endless starting the integers at 3 as at 1, so that you can write: 3, 4, 5, . . . , ∞.

In other words, when two items are subtracted from an infinite set, what remains is still an infinite set. In symbols, we can write this: $\infty - 2 = \infty$. This looks odd because we are used to integers, where subtracting 2 makes a difference. But infinity is not an integer and works by different rules. (This can't be repeated often enough.)

For that matter, if you lop off the first 3 integers or the first 25 or the first 1000000000000, what is left of the series of integers is still endless. You can always start, say, with 1000000000001, 1000000000002, and go on endlessly. So $\infty - n = \infty$, where n represents any integer, however great.

In fact, we can be more startling than that. Suppose we consider only the even integers. We would have a series that would go: 2, 4, 6, and so on endlessly. It would be an infinite series and could therefore be written: 2, 4, 6, . . . , ∞. In the same way, the odd integers would form an infinite series and could be written: 1, 3, 5, . . . , ∞.

Now, then, suppose you went through the series of integers and crossed out every even integer you came to, thus: 1, 2, 3, 4, 5, 6, 7, 8, 9, 10, 11, 12, . . . , ∞. From the infinite series of integers, you would have eliminated an infinite series of even integers and you would have left behind an infinite series of odd integers. This can be symbolized as $\infty - \infty = \infty$.

Furthermore, it could work the other way about. If you started with the even integers only and added one odd integer, or two, or five; or a trillion, you would still merely have an unending series, so that $\infty + n = \infty$. In fact, if you added the unending series of odd integers to the unending series of even integers, you would simply have the unending series of all integers, or: $\infty + \infty = \infty$.

By this point, however, it is just possible that some of you may suspect me of pulling a fast one.

After all, in the first 10 integers, there are 5 even integers and 5 odd ones; in the first 1000 integers, there are 500 even integers and 500 odd integers; and so on. No matter how many consecutive integers we take, half are always even and half are odd.

Therefore, although the series 2, 4, 6, . . . *is* endless, the total can only be half as great as the total of the also endless series 1, 2, 3, 4, 5, 6. . . . And the same is true for the series 1, 3, 5, . . . , which, though endless, is only half as great as the series of all integers.

And so (you might think) in subtracting the set of even integers from the set of all integers to obtain the set of odd integers, what we are doing can be represented as: $\infty - \frac{1}{2}\infty = \frac{1}{2}\infty$. That, you might think with a certain satisfaction, "makes sense."

To answer that objection, let's go back to counting the unknown audience at the lecture. Our bright boy, who has been doing all our counting, and is tired of it, turns to you and asks, "How many seats are there in the lecture hall?" You answer, "640."

He thinks a little and says, "Well, I see that every seat is taken. There are no empty seats and there is no one standing."

You, having equally good eyesight, say, "That's right."

"Well, then," says the boy, "why count them as they leave. We know right now that there are exactly 640 spectators."

And he's correct. If two series of objects (*A* series and *B* series) just match up so that there is one and only one *A* for every *B* and one and only one *B* for every *A*, then we know that the total number of *A* objects is just equal to the total number of *B* objects.

In fact, this is what we do when we count. If we want to know how many teeth there are in the fully equipped human mouth, we assign to each tooth one and only one number (in order) and we apply each number to one and only one tooth. (This is called placing two series into "one-to-one correspondence.") We find that we need only 32 numbers to do this, so that the series 1, 2, 3, . . . ,

30, 31, 32 can be exactly matched with the series one tooth, next tooth, next tooth, . . . , next tooth, next tooth, last tooth.

And therefore, we say, the number of teeth in the fully-equipped human mouth is the same as the number of integers from 1 to 32 inclusive. Or, to put it tersely and succinctly: there are 32 teeth.

Now we can do the same for the set of even integers. We can write down the even integers and give each one a number. Of course, we can't write down all the even integers, but we can write down some and get started anyway. We can write the number assigned to each even integer directly above it, with a double-headed arrow, so:

$$
\begin{array}{ccccccccccc}
1 & 2 & 3 & 4 & 5 & 6 & 7 & 8 & 9 & 10 & \ldots \\
\updownarrow & \updownarrow & \updownarrow & \updownarrow & \updownarrow & \updownarrow & \updownarrow & \updownarrow & \updownarrow & \updownarrow & \\
2 & 4 & 6 & 8 & 10 & 12 & 14 & 16 & 18 & 20 & \ldots
\end{array}
$$

We can already see a system here. Every even integer is assigned one particular number and no other, and you can tell what the particular number is by dividing the even integer by 2. Thus, the even integer 38 has the number 19 assigned to it and no other. The even integer 24618 has the number 12309 assigned to it. In the same way, any given number in the series of all integers can be assigned to one and only one even integer. The number 538 is applied to even integer 1076 and to no other. The number 29999999 is applied to even integer 59999998 and no other; and so on.

Since every number in the series of even integers can be applied to one and only one number in the series of all integers and vice versa, the two series are in one-to-one correspondence and are equal. The number of even integers then is equal to the number of all integers. By a similar argument, the number of odd integers is equal to the number of all integers.

You may object by saying that when all the even integers (or odd integers) are used up, there will still be fully half the series of all integers left over. Maybe so, but this argument has no meaning since the series of even integers (or odd integers) will never be used up.

Therefore, when we say that "all integers" minus "even integers" equals "odd integers," this *is* like saying $\infty - \infty = \infty$, and terms like $\frac{1}{2}\infty$ can be thrown out.

In fact, in subtracting even integers from all integers, we are crossing out every other number and thus, in a way, dividing the series by 2. Since the series is still unending, $\infty / 2 = \infty$ anyway, so what price half of infinity?

Better yet, if we crossed out every other integer in the series of even integers, we would have an unending series of integers divisible by 4; and if we crossed out every other integer in that series, we would have an unending series of integers divisible by 8, and so on endlessly. Each one of these "smaller" series could be matched up with the series of all integers in one-to-one correspondence. If an unending series of integers can be divided by 2 endlessly, and still remain endless, then we are saying that $\infty / \infty = \infty$.

If you doubt that endless series that have been drastically thinned out can be put into one-to-one correspondence with the series of all integers, just consider those integers that are multiples of one trillion. You have: 1,000,000,000,000; 2,000,000,000,000; 3,000,000,000,000; . . . ; ∞. These are matched up with 1, 2, 3, . . . , ∞. For any number in the set of "trillion-integers," say 4,856,000,000,000,000, there is one and only one number in the set of all integers, which, in this case, is 4856. For any number in the set of all integers, say 342, there is one and only one number in the set of "trillion-integers," in this case, 342,000,000,000,000. Therefore, there are as many integers divisible by a trillion as there are integers altogether.

It works the other way around, too. If you place between each number the midway fraction, thus: ½, 1, 1½, 2, 2½, 3, 3½, . . . , ∞, you are, in effect, doubling the number of items in the series and yet this new series can be put into one-to-one correspondence with the set of integers, so that $2\infty = \infty$. In fact, if you keep on doing it indefinitely, putting in all the fourths, then all the eighths, then all the sixteenths, you can still keep the resulting series in one-to-one correspondence with the set of all integers so that $\infty \cdot \infty = \infty^2 = \infty$.

This may seem too much to swallow. How can all the fractions be lined up so that we can be sure that each one is getting one and only one number. It is easy to line up integers, 1, 2, 3, or even integers, 2, 4, 6, or even prime numbers 2, 3, 5, 7, 11. . . . But how can you line up fractions and be sure that all are included, even fancy ones like $\frac{14899}{2725523}$ and $\frac{6894444731}{2}$.

There are, however, several ways to make up an inclusive list of fractions. Suppose we first list all the fractions in which the numerator and denominator add up to 2. There is only one of these: $\frac{1}{1}$. Then list those fractions where the numerator and denominator add up to 3. There are two of these: $\frac{2}{1}$ and $\frac{1}{2}$. Then we have $\frac{3}{1}$, $\frac{2}{2}$, and $\frac{1}{3}$, where the numerator and denominator add up to 4. Then we have $\frac{4}{1}$, $\frac{3}{2}$, $\frac{2}{3}$, and $\frac{1}{4}$. In each group, you see, we place the fractions in the order of decreasing numerator and increasing denominator.

If we make such a list: $\frac{1}{1}$, $\frac{2}{1}$, $\frac{1}{2}$, $\frac{3}{1}$, $\frac{2}{2}$, $\frac{1}{3}$, $\frac{4}{1}$, $\frac{3}{2}$, $\frac{2}{3}$, $\frac{1}{4}$, $\frac{5}{1}$, $\frac{4}{2}$, $\frac{3}{3}$, $\frac{2}{4}$, $\frac{1}{5}$, and so on endlessly we can be assured that any particular fraction, no matter how complicated, will be included if we proceed far enough. The fraction $\frac{14899}{2725523}$ will be in that group of fractions in which the numerator and denominator add up to 2740422, and it will be the 2725523rd of the group. Similarly, $\frac{6894444731}{2}$ will be the second fraction in the group in which the numerator and the denominator add up to 689444475. Every possible fraction will thus have its particular assigned place in the series.

It follows, then, that every fraction has its own number and that no fraction will be left out. Moreover, every number has its own fraction and no number is left out. The series of all fractions is put into a one-to-one correspondence with the series of all integers, and thus the number of all fractions is equal to the number of all integers.

(In the list of fractions above, you will see that some are equal in value. Thus, $\frac{1}{2}$ and $\frac{2}{4}$ are listed as different fractions, but both have the same value. Fractions like $\frac{1}{1}$, $\frac{2}{2}$, and $\frac{3}{3}$ not only have the same value but that value is that of an integer, 1. All this is all right. It shows that the total number of fractions is equal to the total number of integers even though in the series of fractions, the value of each particular fraction, and all integral values as well, is repeated many times; in fact, endlessly.)

By now you may have more or less reluctantly decided that all unendingness is the same unendingness and that "infinity" is "infinity" no matter what you do to it.

Not so!

Consider the points in a line. A line can be marked off

at equal intervals, and the marks can represent points which are numbered 1, 2, 3, and so on endlessly, if you imagine the line continuing endlessly. The midpoints between the integer-points can be marked ½, 1½, 2½, . . . , and when the thirds can be marked and the fourths and the fifths and indeed all the unending number of fractions can be assigned to some particular point.

It would seem then that every point in the line would have some fraction or other assigned to it. Surely there would be no point in the line left out after an unending number of fractions had been assigned to it?

Oh, wouldn't there?

There is a point on the line, you see, that would be represented by a value equal to the square root of two ($\sqrt{2}$). This can be shown as follows. If you construct a square on the line with each side exactly equal to the interval of one integer already marked off on the line, then the diagonal of the square would be just equal to $\sqrt{2}$. If that diagonal is laid down on the line, starting from the zero point, the end of that diagonal coincides with the point on the line which can be set equal to $\sqrt{2}$.

Now the catch is that the value of $\sqrt{2}$ cannot be represented by a fraction; by any fraction; by any conceivable fraction. This was proved by the ancient Greeks and the proof is simple but I'll ask you to take my word for it here to save room. Well, if all the fractions are assigned to various points in the line, at least one point, that which corresponds to $\sqrt{2}$, will be left out.

All numbers which can be represented as fractions are "rational numbers" because a fraction is really the ratio of two numbers, the numerator and the denominator. Numbers which cannot be represented as fractions are "irrational numbers" and $\sqrt{2}$ is by no means the only one of those, although it was the first such to be discovered. Most square roots, cube roots, fourth roots, etc., are irrationals, so are most sines, cosines, tangents, etc., so are numbers involving pi (π), so are logarithms.

In fact, the set of irrational numbers is unending. It can be shown that between any two points represented by rational numbers on a line, however close those two points are, there is always at least one point represented by an irrational number.

Together, the rational numbers and irrational numbers are spoken of as "real numbers." It can be shown that any given real number can be made to correspond to one and only one point in a given line; and that any point in the line can be made to correspond to one and only one real number. In other words, a point in a line which can't be assigned a fraction, can always be assigned an irrational. No point can be missed by both categories.

The series of real numbers and the series of points in a line are therefore in one-to-one correspondence and are equal.

Now the next question is: Can the series of all real numbers, or of all points in a line (the two being equivalent), be set into a one-to-one correspondence with the series of integers. The answer is, *No!*

It can be shown that no matter how you arrange your real numbers or your points, no matter what conceivable system you use, an endless number of either real numbers or points will always be left out. The result is that we are in the same situation as that in which we are faced with an audience in which all seats are taken and there are people standing. We are forced to conclude that there are more people than seats. And so, in the same way, we are forced to conclude that there are more real numbers, or points in a line, than there are integers.

If we want to express the endless series of points by symbols, we don't want to use the symbol ∞ for "and so on endlessly," since this has been all tied up with integers and rational numbers generally. Instead, the symbol *C* is usually used, standing for *continuum,* since all the points in a line represent a continuous line.

We can therefore write the series: Point 1, Point 2, Point 3, . . . , *C*.

Now we have a variety of endlessness that is different and *more intensely endless* than the endlessness represented by "ordinary infinity."

This new and more intense endlessness also has its peculiar arithmetic. For instance, the points in a short line can be matched up one-for-one with the points in a long line, or the points in a plane, or the points in a solid. In fact, let's not prolong the agony, and say at once that there are as many points in a line a millionth of an inch long as there are points in all of space.

About 1895 the German mathematician Georg Cantor worked out the arithmetic of infinity and also set up a

GEORG CANTOR

To designate Cantor by nationality is difficult. He was born in Russia, in Leningrad, in fact (it was called St. Petersburg then), on March 3, 1845. His father had emigrated to Russia from Denmark, however, and then left Russia for Germany when young Georg was only eleven. In addition, the family was of Jewish descent, though his mother was born a Roman Catholic and his father was converted to Protestantism.

Even as a schoolboy Cantor showed talent for mathematics, and eventually (over his father's objections) he made mathematics his profession. In 1867 he obtained his Ph.D. magna cum laude from the University of Berlin. He obtained an academic position at the University of Halle, advancing to a professorial appointment in 1872.

It was in 1874 that Cantor began to introduce his intellect-shaking concepts of infinity. Earlier, Galileo had caught glimpses of it, but Cantor was the first to erect a complete logical structure in which a whole series of transfinite numbers was postulated, representing different orders of infinity, so to speak.

Not much can be done with the different orders in terms of sets that can be described. The set of integers is equal to the first, the set of real numbers is higher, the set of functions is higher still, and there we must stop.

Cantor's views were not accepted by all his colleagues. In particular Leopold Kronecker, who had been one of Cantor's teachers, attacked Cantor's work with great vigor. Inspired by professional jealousy, Kronecker prevented Cantor's advancement, keeping him from a post at the University of Berlin. Cantor's mental health broke in 1884 under the strains of the controversy, and he died in a mental hospital in Halle, Saxony, on January 6, 1918.

The Granger Collection

whole series of different varieties of endlessnesses, which he called "transfinite numbers."

He represented these transfinite numbers by the letter *aleph,* which is the first letter of the Hebrew alphabet and which looks like this: $\aleph$

The various transfinities can be listed in increasing size or, rather, in increasing intensity of endlessness by giving each one a subscript, beginning with zero. The very lowest transfinite would be "aleph-null," then there would be "aleph-one," "aleph-two," and so on, endlessly.

This could be symbolized as: $\aleph_0, \aleph_1, \aleph_2, \ldots, \aleph_\infty$

Generally, whatever you do to a particular transfinite number in the way of adding, subtracting, multiplying, or dividing, leaves it unchanged. A change comes only when you raise a transfinite to a transfinite power equal to itself (not to a transfinite power less than itself). Then it is increased to the next higher transfinite. Thus:

$$\aleph_0^{\aleph_0} = \aleph_1; \quad \aleph_1^{\aleph_1} = \aleph_2; \text{ and so on.}$$

What we usually consider as infinity, the endlessness of the integers, has been shown to be equal to aleph-null. In other words: $\infty = \aleph_0$. And so the tremendous vastness of ordinary infinity turns out to be the very smallest of all the transfinites.

That variety of endlessness which we have symbolized as *C may* be represented by aleph-one so that $C = \aleph_1$, but this has not been proved. No mathematician has yet been able to prove that there is any infinite series which has an endlessness more intense than the endlessness of the integers but less intense than the endlessness of the points in a line. However, neither has any mathematician been able to prove that such an intermediate endlessness does *not* exist.*

If the continuum *is* equal to aleph-one, then we can finally write an equation for our friend "ordinary infinity" which will change it:

$$\infty^\infty = C.$$

Finally, it has been shown that the endlessness of all

[* *Since this article first appeared, it has been shown that the statement C=Aleph-one can be neither proved nor disproved by any method.*]

the curves that can be drawn on a plane is even more intense than the endlessness of points in a line. In other words, there is no way of lining up the curves so that they can be matched one-to-one with the points in a line, without leaving out an unending series of the curves. This endlessness of curves may be equal to aleph-two, but that hasn't been proved yet, either.

And that is all. Assuming that the endlessness of integers is aleph-null, and the endlessness of points is aleph-one, and the endlessness of curves is aleph-two, we have come to the end. Nobody has ever suggested any variety of endlessness which could correspond to aleph-three (let alone to aleph-thirty or aleph-three-million).

As John E. Freund says in his book *A Modern Introduction to Mathematics* * (a book I recommend to all who found this article in the least interesting), "It seems that our imagination does not permit us to count beyond *three* when dealing with infinite sets."

Still, if we now return to the title *Invaders from the Infinite,* I think we are entitled to ask, with an air of phlegmatic calm, "Which infinite? Just aleph-null? Nothing more?"

---

* *New York: Prentice-Hall, 1956.*

Part II

NUMBERS AND
MATHEMATICS

6 A PIECE OF PI

In my essay "Those Crazy Ideas," which appeared in my book *Fact and Fancy* (Doubleday, 1962), I casually threw in a footnote to the effect that $e^{\pi i} = -1$. Behold, a good proportion of the comment which I received thereafter dealt not with the essay itself but with that footnote (one reader, more in sorrow than in anger, proved the equality, which I had neglected to do).

My conclusion is that some readers are interested in these odd symbols. Since I am, too (albeit I am not really a mathematician, or anything else), the impulse is irresistible to pick up one of them, say π, and talk about it in this chapter and the next. In Chapter 8, I will discuss i.

In the first place, what is π? Well, it is the Greek letter *pi* and it represents the ratio of the length of the perimeter of a circle to the length of its diameter. *Perimeter* is from the Greek *perimetron*, meaning "the measurement around," and *diameter* from the Greek *diametron*, meaning "the measurement through." For some obscure reason, while it is customary to use perimeter in the case of polygons, it is also customary to switch to the Latin *circumference* in speaking of circles. That is all right, I suppose (I am no purist), but it obscures the reason for the symbol π.

Back about 1600 the English mathematician William

Oughtred, in discussing the ratio of a circle's perimeter to its diameter, used the Greek letter π to symbolize the perimeter and the Greek letter δ (delta) to symbolize the diameter. They were the first letters, respectively of *perimetron* and *diametron*.

Now mathematicians often simplify matters by setting values equal to unity whenever they can. For instance, they might talk of a circle of unit diameter. In such a circle, the length of the perimeter is numerically equal to the ratio of perimeter to diameter. (This is obvious to some of you, I suppose, and the rest of you can take my word for it.) Since in a circle of unit diameter the perimeter equals the ratio, the ratio can be symbolized by π, the symbol of the perimeter. And since circles of unit diameter are very frequently dealt with, the habit becomes quickly ingrained.

The first top-flight man to use π as the symbol for the ratio of the length of a circle's perimeter to the length of its diameter was the Swiss mathematician Leonhard Euler, in 1737, and what was good enough for Euler was good enough for everyone else.

Now I can go back to calling the distance around a circle the circumference.

But what *is* the ratio of the circumference of a circle to its diameter in actual numbers?

This apparently is a question that always concerned the ancients even long before pure mathematics was invented. In any kind of construction past the hen-coop stage you must calculate in advance all sorts of measurements, if you are not perpetually to be calling out to some underling, "You nut, these beams are all half a foot too short." In order to make the measurements, the universe being what it is, you are forever having to use the value of π in multiplications. Even when you're not dealing with circles, but only with angles (and you can't avoid angles) you will bump into π.

Presumably, the first empirical calculators who realized that the ratio was important determined the ratio by drawing a circle and actually measuring the length of the diameter and the circumference. Of course, measuring the length of the circumference is a tricky problem that can't be handled by the usual wooden foot-rule, which is far too inflexible for the purpose.

What the pyramid-builders and their predecessors prob-

ably did was to lay a linen cord along the circumference
very carefully, make a little mark at the point where the
circumference was completed, then straighten the line and
measure it with the equivalent of a wooden foot-rule.
(Modern theoretical mathematicians frown at this and
make haughty remarks such as "But you are making the
unwarranted assumption that the line is the same length
when it is straight as when it was curved." I imagine the
honest workman organizing the construction of the local
temple, faced with such an objection, would have solved
matters by throwing the objector into the river Nile.)

Anyway, by drawing circles of different size and making enough measurements, it undoubtedly dawned upon
architects and artisans, very early in the game, that the
ratio was always the same in all circles. In other words,
if one circle had a diameter twice as long or 1⅝ as long
as the diameter of a second, it would also have a circumference twice as long or 1⅝ as long. The problem boiled
down, then, to finding not the ratio of the particular circle
you were interested in using, but a universal ratio that
would hold for all circles for all time. Once someone had
the value of π in his head, he would never have to determine the ratio again for any circle.

As to the actual value of the ratio, as determined by
measurement, that depended, in ancient times, on the care
taken by the person making the measurement and on the
value he placed on accuracy in the abstract. The ancient
Hebrews, for instance, were not much in the way of construction engineers, and when the time came for them to
build their one important building (Solomon's temple),
they had to call in a Phoenician architect.

It is to be expected, then, that the Hebrews in describing the temple would use round figures only, seeing no
point in stupid and troublesome fractions, and refusing to
be bothered with such petty and niggling matters when
the House of God was in question.

Thus, in Chapter 4 of 2 Chronicles, they describe a
"molten sea" which was included in the temple and which
was, presumably, some sort of container in circular form.
The beginning of the description is in the second verse of
that chapter and reads: "Also he made a molten sea of ten
cubits from brim to brim, round in compass, and five
cubits the height thereof; and a line of thirty cubits did
compass it round about."

ARCHIMEDES

Archimedes, the son of an astronomer, was the greatest scientist and mathematician of ancient times, and his equal did not arise until Isaac Newton, two thousand years later. Although educated in the great university city of Alexandria, he did his work in his native city of Syracuse in Sicily, where he had been born about 287 B.C. He seems to have been a relative of the Syracusan King, Hieron II, and wealthy enough to carry on his work at leisure.

Archimedes worked out the principle of the lever, and also the principle of buoyancy, which made it possible to tell that a gold crown had been adulterated with copper without destroying the crown. Archimedes saw the principle in a flash while in the bath, and it was on that occasion that he went running through Syracuse in the nude shouting "Eureka, Eureka!" ("I have it! I have it!").

The most fascinating tales about him come toward the end of his long life, when Syracuse deserted its alliance with the Roman Republic and when, in consequence, a Roman fleet laid siege to the city. Archimedes was a one-man defense at the time, thinking up ingenious devices to do damage to the fleet. He is supposed to have constructed large lenses to set fire to the fleet, mechanical cranes to lift the ships and turn them upside down, and so on. In the end, the story goes, the Romans dared not approach the walls too closely and would flee if as much as a rope showed above it.

In 212 B.C the city was taken, however, after a three-year siege. The Roman commander ordered that Archimedes be taken alive, but he was engaged in a mathematical problem at the time, and when a soldier ordered him to come along, he refused to leave his figures in the sand. The soldier killed him.

The Hebrews, you see, did not realize that in giving the diameter of a circle (as ten cubits or as anything else) they automatically gave the circumference as well. They felt it necessary to specify the circumference as thirty cubits and in so doing revealed the fact that they considered π to be equal to exactly 3.

There is always the danger that some individuals, too wedded to the literal words of the Bible, may consider 3 to be the divinely ordained value of π in consequence. I wonder of this may not have been the motive of the simple soul in some state legislature who some years back, introduced a bill which would have made π legally equal to 3 inside the bounds of the state. Fortunately, the bill did not pass or all the wheels in that state (which would, of course, have respected the laws of the state's august legislators) would have turned hexagonal.

In any case, those ancients who were architecturally sophisticated knew well, from their measurements, that the value of π was distinctly more than 3. The best value they had was $2\frac{2}{7}$ (or $3\frac{1}{7}$, if you prefer) which really isn't bad and is still used to this day for quick approximations.

Decimally, $2\frac{2}{7}$ is equal, roughly, to 3.142857 . . . , while π is equal, roughly, to 3.141592. . . . Thus, $2\frac{2}{7}$ is high by only 0.04 per cent or 1 part in 2500. Good enough for most rule-of-thumb purposes.

Then along came the Greeks and developed a system of geometry that would have none of this vile lay-down-a-string-and-measure-it-with-a-ruler business. That, obviously, gave values that were only as good as the ruler and the string and the human eye, all of which were dreadfully imperfect. Instead, the Greeks went about deducing what the value of π must be once the perfect lines and curves of the ideal plane geometry they had invented were taken properly into account.

Archimedes of Syracuse, for instance, used the "method of exhaustion" (a forerunner of integral calculus, which Archimedes might have invented two thousand years before Newton if some kind benefactor of later centuries had only sent him the Arabic numerals via a time machine) to calculate π.

To get the idea, imagine an equilateral triangle with its vertexes on the circumference of a circle of unit diameter. Ordinary geometry suffices to calculate exactly the perimeter of that triangle. It comes out to $3\sqrt{3/2}$, if you are curious, or 2.598076. . . . This perimeter has to be less than that of the circle (that is, than the value of π), again by elementary geometrical reasoning.

Next, imagine the arcs between the vertexes of the triangle divided in two so that a regular hexagon (a six-sided figure) can be inscribed in the circle. Its perimeter can be determined also (it is exactly 3) and this can be shown to be larger than that of the triangle but still less than that of the circle. By proceeding to do this over and over again, a regular polygon with 12, 24, 48 . . . sides can be inscribed.

The space between the polygon and the boundary of the circle is steadily decreased or "exhausted" and the polygon approaches as close to the circle as you wish, though it never really reaches it. You can do the same with a series of equilateral polygons that circumscribe the circle (that lie outside it, that is, with their sides tangent to the circle) and get a series of decreasing values that approach the circumference of the circle.

In essence, Archimedes trapped the circumference between a series of numbers that approached π from below, and another that approached it from above. In this way π could be determined with any degree of exactness, provided you were patient enough to bear the tedium of working with polygons of large numbers of sides.

Archimedes found the time and patience to work with polygons of ninety-six sides and was able to show that the value of π was a little below $22/7$ and a little above the slightly smaller fraction $223/71$.

Now the average of these two fractions is $3123/994$ and the decimal equivalent of that is 3.141851. . . . This is more than the true value of π by only 0.0082 per cent or 1 part in 12,500.

Nothing better than this was obtained, in Europe, at least, until the sixteenth century. It was then that the fraction $355/113$ was first used as an approximation of π. This is really the best approximation of π that can be expressed as a reasonably simple fraction. The decimal value of $355/113$ is 3.14159292 . . . , while the true value of π is 3.14159265. . . . You can see from that that $355/113$ is higher than the true value by only 0.000008 per cent, or by one part in 12,500,000.

Just to give you an idea of how good an approximation $355/113$ is, let's suppose that the earth were a perfect sphere with a diameter of exactly 8000 miles. We could then calculate the length of the equator by multiplying 8000 by π. Using the approximation $355/113$ for π, the answer comes out 25,132.7433 . . . miles. The true value of π would give the answer 25,132.7412 . . . miles. The difference would come to about 11 feet. A difference of 11 feet in calculating the circumference of the earth might well be reckoned as negligible. Even the artificial satellites that have brought our geography to new heights of precision haven't supplied us with measurements within that range of accuracy.

It follows then that for anyone but mathematicians, $355/113$ is as close to π as it is necessary to get under any but the most unusual circumstances. And yet mathematicians have their own point of view. They can't be happy without the true value. As far as they are concerned, a miss, however close, is as bad as a megaparsec.

The key step toward the true value was taken by François Vieta, a French mathematician of the sixteenth century. He is considered the father of algebra because, among other things, he introduced the use of letter symbols for unknowns, the famous x's and y's, which most of us have had, at one time or another in our lives, to face with trepidation and uncertainty.

Vieta performed the algebraic equivalent of Archimedes' geometric method of exhaustion. That is, instead of setting up an infinite series of polygons that came closer and closer to a circle, he deduced an infinite series of fractions which could be evaluated to give a figure for π. The greater the number of terms used in the evaluation, the closer you were to the true value of π.

I won't give you Vieta's series here because it involves square roots and the square roots of square roots and the square roots of square roots of square roots. There is no point in involving one's self in that when other mathematicians derived other series of terms (always an infinite series) for the evaluation of π; series much easier to write.

For instance, in 1673 the German mathematician Gottfried Wilhelm von Leibniz (who first worked out the binary system—see Chapter 2) derived a series which can be expressed as follows:

$$\pi = \tfrac{4}{1} - \tfrac{4}{3} + \tfrac{4}{5} - \tfrac{4}{7} + \tfrac{4}{9} - \tfrac{4}{11} + \tfrac{4}{13} - \tfrac{4}{15} \ldots$$

Being a naïve nonmathematician myself, with virtually no mathematical insight worth mentioning, I thought, when I first decided to write this essay, that I would use the Leibniz series to dash off a short calculation and show you how it would give π easily to a dozen places or so. However, shortly after beginning, I quit.

You may scorn my lack of perseverance, but any of you are welcome to evaluate the Leibniz series just as far as it is written above, to $\tfrac{4}{15}$, that is. You can even drop me a postcard and tell me the result. If, when you finish, you are disappointed to find that your answer isn't as close to π as the value of $\tfrac{355}{113}$, don't give up. Just add more terms. Add $\tfrac{4}{17}$ to your answer, then subtract $\tfrac{4}{19}$, then add $\tfrac{4}{21}$ and subtract $\tfrac{4}{23}$, and so on. You can go on as long as you want to, and if any of you finds how many terms it takes to improve on $\tfrac{355}{113}$, drop me a line and tell me that, too.

Of course, all this may disappoint you. To be sure, the endless series *is* a mathematical representation of the true and exact value of π. To a mathematician, it is as valid a way as any to express that value. But if you want it in the form of an actual number, how does it help you? It isn't even practical to sum up a couple of dozen terms for anyone who wants to go about the ordinary business of living; how, then, can it be possible to sum up an infinite number?

Ah, but mathematicians do not give up on the sum of a series just because the number of terms in it is unending. For instance, the series:

$$\tfrac{1}{2} + \tfrac{1}{4} + \tfrac{1}{8} + \tfrac{1}{16} + \tfrac{1}{32} + \tfrac{1}{64} \ldots$$

can be summed up, using successively more and more terms. If you do this, you will find that the more terms you use, the closer you get to 1, and you can express this in shorthand form by saying that the sum of that infinite number of terms is merely 1 after all.

There is a formula, in fact, that can be used to determine the sum of any decreasing geometric progression, of which the above is an example.

Thus, the series:

$$\tfrac{3}{10} + \tfrac{3}{100} + \tfrac{3}{1000} + \tfrac{3}{10000} + \tfrac{3}{100000} \ldots$$

adds up, in all its splendidly infinite numbers, to a mere, ⅓, and the series:

$$\tfrac{1}{2} + \tfrac{1}{20} + \tfrac{1}{200} + \tfrac{1}{2000} + \tfrac{1}{20000} \ldots$$

adds up to ⁵⁄₉.

To be sure, the series worked out for the evaluation of π are none of them decreasing geometric progressions, and so the formula cannot be used to evaluate the sum. In fact, no formula has ever been found to evaluate the sum of the Leibniz series or any of the others. Nevertheless, there seemed no reason at first to suppose that there might not be some way of finding a decreasing geometric progression that would evaluate π. If so, π would then be expressible as a fraction. A fraction is actually the ratio of two numbers and anything expressible as a fraction, or ratio, is a "rational number," as I explained in the previous chapter. The hope, then, was that π might be a rational number.

One way of proving that a quantity is a rational number is to work out its value decimally as far as you can (by adding up more and more terms of an infinite series, for instance) and then show the result to be a "repeating decimal"; that is, a decimal in which digits or some group of digits repeat themselves endlessly.

For instance, the decimal value of ⅓ is 0.33333333333 . . . , while that of ⅐ is 0.142857 142857 142857 . . . , and so on endlessly. Even a fraction such as ⅛ which seems to "come out even" is really a repeating decimal if you count zeros, since its decimal equivalent is 0.125000-000000. . . . It can be proved mathematically that every fraction, however complicated, can be expressed as a decimal which sooner or later becomes a repeating one. Conversely, any decimal which ends by becoming a repeating one, however involved the repetitive cycle, can be expressed as an exact fraction.

Take any repeating decimal at random, say 0.37373737-

373737. . . . First, you can make a decreasing geometrical progression out of it by writing it as:

$$\tfrac{37}{100} + \tfrac{37}{10000} + \tfrac{37}{1000000} + \tfrac{37}{100000000} \cdots$$

and you can then use the formula to work out its sum, which comes out to $\tfrac{37}{99}$. (Work out the decimal equivalent of that fraction and see what you get.)

Or suppose you have a decimal which starts out non-repetitively and then becomes repetitive, such as 15.216-55555555555. . . . This can be written as:

$$15 + \tfrac{216}{1000} + \tfrac{5}{10000} + \tfrac{5}{100000} + \tfrac{5}{1000000} \cdots$$

From $\tfrac{5}{10000}$ on, we have a decreasing geometric progression and its sum works out to be $\tfrac{5}{9000}$. So the series becomes a finite one made out of exactly three terms and no more, and can be summed easily:

$$15 + \tfrac{216}{1000} + \tfrac{5}{9000} = \tfrac{136949}{9000}$$

If you wish, work out the decimal equivalent of $\tfrac{136949}{9000}$ and see what you get.

Well, then, if the decimal equivalent of π were worked out for a number of decimal places and some repetition were discovered in it, however slight and however complicated, provided it could be shown to go on endlessly, a new series could be written to express its exact value. This new series would conclude with a decreasing geometric progression which could be summed. There would then be a finite series and the true value of π could be expressed not as a series but as an actual number.

Mathematicians threw themselves into the pursuit. In 1593 Vieta himself used his own series to calculate π to seventeen decimal places. Here it is, if you want to stare at it: 3.14159265358979323. As you see, there are no apparent repetitions of any kind.

Then in 1615 the German mathematician Ludolf von Ceulen used an infinite series to calculate π to thirty-five places. He found no signs of repetitiveness, either. However, this was so impressive a feat for his time that he won a kind of fame, for π is sometimes called "Ludolf's number" in consequence, at least in German textbooks.

And then in 1717 the English mathematician Abraham

Sharp went Ludolf's several better by finding π to seventy-two decimal places. Still no sign of repeating.

But shortly thereafter, the game was spoiled.

To prove a quantity is rational, you have to present the fraction to which it is equivalent and display it. To prove it is irrational, however, you need not necessarily work out a single decimal place. What you must do is to *suppose* that the quantity can be expressed by a fraction, p/q, and then demonstrate that this involves a contradiction, such as that p must at the same time be even and odd. This would prove that no fraction could express the quantity, which would therefore be irrational.

Exactly this sort of proof was developed by the ancient Greeks to show that the square root of 2 was an irrational number (the first irrational ever discovered). The Pythagoreans were supposed to have been the first to discover this and to have been so appalled at finding that there could be quantities that could not be expressed by any fraction, however complicated, that they swore themselves to secrecy and provided a death penalty for snitching. But like all scientific secrets, from irrationals to atom bombs, the information leaked out anyway.

Well, in 1761 German physicist and mathematician Johann Heinrich Lambert finally proved that π was irrational. Therefore, no pattern at all was to be expected, no matter how slight and no matter how many decimal places were worked out. The true value can *only* be expressed as an infinite series.

Alas!

But shed no tears. Once π was proved irrational, mathematicians were satisfied. The problem was over. And as for the application of π to physical calculations, that problem was over and done with, too. You may think that sometimes in very delicate calculations it might be necessary to know π to a few dozen or even to a few hundred places, but not so! The delicacy of scientific measurements is wonderful these days, but still there are few that approach, say, one part in a billion, and for anything that accurate which involves the use of π, nine or ten decimal places would be ample.

For example, suppose you drew a circle ten billion miles across, with the sun at the center, for the purpose of enclosing the entire solar system, and suppose you

wanted to calculate the length of the circumference of this
circle (which would come to over thirty-one billion miles)
by using $^{355}\!/_{113}$ as the approximate value of π. You would
be off by less than three thousand miles.

But suppose you were so precise an individual that you
found an error of three thousand miles in 31,000,000,000
to be insupportable. You might then use Ludolf's value of
π to thirty-five places. You would then be off by a distance
that would be equivalent to a millionth of the diameter of
a proton.

Or let's take a *big* circle, say the circumference of the
known universe. Suppose large radio telescopes under construction can receive signals from a distance as great as
40,000,000,000 light-years. A circle about a universe with
such a radius would have a length of, roughly, 150,000,-
000,000,000,000,000,000 (150 sextillion) miles. If the
length of this circumference were calculated by Ludolf's
value of π to thirty-five places, it would be off by less than
a millionth of an inch.

What can one say then about Sharp's value of π to
seventy-two places?

Obviously, the value of π, as known by the time its irra-
tionality was proven, was already far beyond the accuracy
that could conceivably be demanded by science, now or
in the future.

And yet with the value of π no longer needed for scientists, past what had already been determined, people nevertheless continued their calculations through the first half
of the nineteenth century.

A fellow called George Vega got π to 140 places, another called Zacharias Dase did it to 200 places, and someone called Recher did it to 500 places.

Finally, in 1873 William Shanks reported the value of
π to 707 places, and that, until 1949, was the record—and
small wonder. It took Shanks fifteen years to make the
calculation and, for what that's worth, no signs of any
repetitiveness showed up.

We can wonder about the motivation that would cause
a man to spend fifteen years on a task that can serve no
purpose. Perhaps it is the same mental attitude that will
make a man sit on a flagpole or swallow goldfish in order
to "break a record." Or perhaps Shanks saw this as his one
road to fame.

If so, he made it. Histories of mathematics, in among

their descriptions of the work of men like Archimedes, Fermat, Newton, Euler, and Gauss, will also find room for a line to the effect that William Shanks in the years preceding 1873 calculated π to 707 decimal places. So perhaps he felt that his life had not been wasted.

But alas, for human vanity—

In 1949 the giant computers were coming into their own, and occasionally the young fellows at the controls, full of fun and life and beer, could find time to play with them.

So, on one occasion, they pumped one of the unending series into the machine called ENIAC and had it calculate the value of π. They kept it at the task for seventy hours, and at the end of that time they had the value of π (shades of Shanks!) to 2035 places.*

And to top it all off for poor Shanks and his fifteen wasted years, an error was found in the five hundred umpty-umpth digit of Shanks' value, so that all the digits after that, well over a hundred, were *wrong!*

And of course, in case you're wondering, and you shouldn't, the values as determined by computers showed no signs of any repetitiveness either.

---

* By 1955 a faster computer calculated π to 10,017 places in thirty-three hours and, actually, there are interesting mathematical points to be derived from studying the various digits of π [and it's possible that more has been done since, but I haven't kept track].

7 TOOLS OF THE TRADE

THE PREVIOUS chapter does not conclude the story of π. As the title stated, it was only a piece of π. Let us therefore continue onward.

The Greek contribution to geometry consisted of idealizing and abstracting it. The Egyptians and Babylonians solved specific problems by specific methods but never tried to establish general rules.

The Greeks, however, strove for the general and felt that mathematical figures had certain innate properties that were eternal and immutable. They felt also that a consideration of the nature and relationships of these properties was the closest man could come to experiencing the sheer essence of beauty and divinity. (If I may veer away from science for a moment and invade the sacred precincts of the humanities, I might point out that just this notion was expressed by Edna St. Vincent Millay in a famous line that goes: "Euclid alone has looked on Beauty bare.")

Well, in order to get down to the ultimate bareness of Beauty, one had to conceive of perfect, idealized figures made up of perfect idealized parts. For instance, the ideal line consisted of length and nothing else. It had neither

EUCLID

After the death of Alexander the Great, various of his generals seized control of the ancient world. One of them, Ptolemy, established a dynasty that was to rule over Egypt for three centuries. He converted his capital at Alexandria into the greatest intellectual center of ancient times, and one of the first luminaries to work there was the mathematician Euclid.

Very little is known about Euclid's personal life. He was born about 325 B.C., we don't know where, and the time and place of his death are unknown.

His name is indissolubly linked to geometry, for he wrote a textbook (Elements) on the subject that has been standard, with some modifications, of course, ever since. It went through more than a thousand editions after the invention of printing, and he is undoubtedly the most successful textbook writer of all time.

And yet, as a mathematician, Euclid's fame is not due to his own research. Few of the theorems in his textbook are his own. What Euclid did, and what made him great, was to take all the knowledge accumulated in mathematics to his time and codify it into a single work. In doing so, he evolved, as a starting point, a series of axioms and postulates that were admirable for their brevity and elegance.

In addition to geometry, his text took up ratio and proportion and what is now known as the theory of numbers. He made optics a part of geometry, too, by dealing with light rays as though they were straight lines.

One story told about him involves King Ptolemy who was studying geometry and who asked if Euclid couldn't make his demonstrations a little easier to follow. Euclid said, uncompromisingly, "There is no royal road to geometry."

The Granger Collection

thickness nor breadth nor anything, in fact, but length. Two ideal lines, ideally and perfectly straight, intersected at an ideal and perfect point, which had no dimensions at all, only position. A circle was a line that curved in perfectly equal fashion at all points; and every point on that curve was precisely equally distant from a particular point called the center of the circle.

Unfortunately, although one can imagine such abstractions, one doesn't usually communicate them as abstractions alone. In order to explain the properties of such figures (and even in order to investigate them on your own) it is helpful, almost essential in fact, to draw crass, crude, and ungainly approximations in wax, on mud, on blackboard, or on paper, using a pointed stick, chalk, pencil, or pen. (Beauty must be swathed in drapery in mathematics, alas, as in life.)

Furthermore, in order to prove some of the ineffably beautiful properties of various geometrical figures, it was usually necessary to make use of more lines than existed in the figure alone. It might be necessary to draw a new line through a point and make it parallel or, perhaps, perpendicular to a second line. It might be necessary to divide a line into equal parts, or to double the size of an angle.

To make all this drawing as neat and as accurate as possible, instruments must be used. It follows naturally, I think, once you get into the Greek way of thinking, that the fewer and simpler the instruments used for the purpose, the closer the approach to the ideal.

Eventually, the tools were reduced to an elegant minimum of two. One is a straightedge for the drawing of straight lines. This is not a ruler, mind you, with inches or centimeters marked off on it. It is an unmarked piece of wood (or metal or plastic, for that matter) which can do no more than guide the marking instrument into the form of a straight line.

The second tool is the compass, which, while most simply used to draw circles, will also serve to mark off equal segments of lines, will draw intersecting arcs that mark a point that is equidistant from two other points, and so on.

I presume most of you have taken plane geometry and have utilized these tools to construct one line perpendicular to another, to bisect an angle, to circumscribe a circle about a triangle, and so on. All these tasks and an infinite number of others can be performed by using the straight-edge and compass in a finite series of manipulations.

By Plato's time, of course, it was known that by using more complex tools, certain constructions could be simplified; and, in fact, that some constructions could be performed which, until then, could not be performed by straightedge and compass alone. That, to the Greek geometers, was something like shooting a fox or a sitting duck, or catching fish with worms, or looking at the answers in the back of the book. It got results but it just wasn't the gentlemanly thing to do. The straightedge and compass were the only "proper" tools of the geometrical trade.

Nor was it felt that this restriction to the compass and straightedge unduly limited the geometer. It might be tedious at times to stick to the tools of the trade; it might be easier to take a short cut by using other devices; but surely the straightedge and compass alone could do it all, if you were only persistent enough and ingenious enough.

For instance, if you are given a line of a fixed length which is allowed to represent the numeral 1, it is possible to construct another line, by compass and straightedge alone, exactly twice that length to represent 2, or another line to represent 3 or 5 or 500 or ½ or ⅓ or ⅕ or ⅗ or 2⅗ or 27¹⁰⁄₂₃. In fact, by using compass and straightedge only, any rational number (i.e., any integer or fraction) could be duplicated geometrically. You could even make use of a simple convention (which the Greeks never did, alas) to make it possible to represent both positive and negative rational numbers.

Once irrational numbers were discovered, numbers for which no definite fraction could be written, it might seem that compass and straightedge would fail, but even then they did not.

For instance, the square root of 2 has the value 1.414214 . . . and on and on without end. How, then, can you construct one line which is 1.414214 . . . times as long as another when you cannot possibly ever know exactly how many times as long as you want it to be.

Actually, it's easy. Imagine a given line from point A to point B. (I can do this without a diagram, I think, but if you feel the need you can sketch the lines as you read. It won't be hard.) Let this line, AB, represent L.

Next, construct a line at B, perpendicular to AB. Now you have two lines forming a right angle. Use the compass to draw a circle with its center at *B*, where the two lines meet, and passing through *A*. It will cut the perpendicular line you have just drawn at a point we can call *C*. Because of the well-known properties of the circle, line *BC* is exactly equal to line *AB*, and is also 1.

Finally, connect points *A* and *C* with a third straight line.

That line, *AC*, as can be proven by geometry, is exactly $\sqrt{2}$ times as long as either *AB* or *BC*, and therefore represents the irrational quantity $\sqrt{2}$.

Don't, of course, think that it is now only necessary to measure *AC* in terms of *AB* to obtain an exact value of $\sqrt{2}$. The construction was drawn by imperfect instruments in the hands of imperfect men and is only a crude approximation of the ideal figures they represent. It is the ideal line represented by *AC* that is $\sqrt{2}$, and not *AC* itself in actual reality.

It is possible, in similar fashion, to use the straightedge and compass to represent an infinite number of other irrational quantities.

In fact, the Greeks had no reason to doubt that any conceivable number at all could be represented by a line that could be constructed by use of straightedge and compass alone in a finite number of steps. And since all constructions boiled down to the construction of certain lines representing certain numbers, it was felt that anything that could be done with any tool could be done by straightedge and compass alone. Sometimes the details of the straightedge and compass construction might be elusive and remain undiscovered, but eventually, the Greeks felt, given enough ingenuity, insight, intelligence, intuition, and luck, the construction could be worked out.

For instance, the Greeks never learned how to divide a circle into seventeen equal parts by straightedge and compass alone. Yet it could be done. The method was not discovered until 1801, but in that year, the German mathematician Karl Friedrich Gauss, then only twenty-four, managed it. Once he divided the circle into seventeen parts, he could connect the points of division by a straightedge to form a regular polygon of seventeen sides (a "septendecagon"). The same system could be used to construct a regular polygon of 257 sides, and an infinite number of other polygons with still more sides, the number of sides possible being calculated by a formula which I won't give here.

If the construction of a simple thing like a regular septendecagon could elude the great Greek geometers and yet be a perfectly soluble problem in the end, why could not any conceivable construction, however puzzling it might seem, yet prove soluble in the end.

As an example, one construction that fascinated the Greeks was this: Given a circle, construct a square of the same area.

This is called "squaring the circle."

There are several ways of doing this. Here's one method. Measure the radius of the circle with the most accurate measuring device you have—say, just for fun, that the radius proves to be one inch long precisely. (This method will work for a radius of any length, so why not luxuriate in simplicity.) Square that radius, leaving the value still 1, since 1×1 is 1, thank goodness, and multiply that by the best value of π you can find. (Were you wondering when I'd get back to π?) If you use 3.1415926 as your value of π, the area of the circle proves to be 3.1415926 square inches.

Now, take the square root of that, which is 1.7724539 inches, and draw a straight line exactly 1.7724539 inches long, using your measuring device to make sure of the length. Construct a perpendicular at each end of the line, mark off 1.7724539 inches on each perpendicular, and connect those two points.

Voilà! You have a square equal in area to the given circle. Of course, you may feel uneasy. Your measuring device isn't infinitely accurate and neither is the value of π which you used. Does not this mean that the squaring of the circle is only approximate and not exact?

Yes, but it is not the details that count but the principle. We can *assume* the measuring device to be perfect, and the value of π which was used to be accurate to an infinite number of places. After all, this is just as justifiable as assuming our actual drawn lines to represent ideal lines, considering our straightedge perfectly straight and our compass to end in two perfect points. In principle, we have indeed perfectly squared the circle.

Ah, but we have made use of a measuring device, which is not one of the only two tools of the trade allowed a

KARL FRIEDRICH GAUSS

Gauss, the son of a gardener, was born in Braunschweig, Germany, on April 30, 1777. He was an infant prodigy in mathematics who remained a prodigy all his life. He was capable of great feats of memory and of mental calculation. At the age of three, he was already correcting his father's sums. His unusual mind was recognized and he was educated at the expense of Duke Ferdinand of Brunswick. In 1795 Gauss entered the University of Göttingen.

While still in his teens he made a number of remarkable discoveries, including the "method of least squares," which could determine the best curve fitting a group of as few as three observations. While still in the university, he demonstrated a method for constructing an equilateral polygon of seventeen sides and, more important, showed which polygons would not be so constructed— the first demonstration of a mathematical impossibility.

In 1799 Gauss proved the fundamental theorem of algebra, that every algebraic equation has a root in the form of a complex number, and in 1801 he went on to prove the fundamental theorem of arithmetic, that every natural number can be represented as the product of primes in one and only one way.

All this required intense concentration. There is a story that when he was told in 1807 that his wife was dying, he looked up from the problem that was engaging him and muttered, "Tell her to wait a moment till I'm through."

His agile mind never seemed to cease. At the age of sixty-two he taught himself Russian. Personal tragedy dogged him, though. Each of his two wives died young, and only one of his six children survived him. He died in Göttingen on February 23, 1855.

gentleman geometer. That marks you as a cad and bounder and you are hereby voted out of the club.

Here's another method of squaring the circle. What you really need, assuming the radius of your circle to represent 1, is another straight line representing $\sqrt{\pi}$. A square built on such a line would have just the area of a unit-radius circle. How to get such a line? Well, if you could construct a line equal to π times the length of the radius, there are known methods, using straightedge and compass alone, to construct a line equal in length to the square root of that line, hence representing the $\sqrt{\pi}$, which we are after.

But it is simple to get a line that is π times the radius. According to a well-known formula, the circumference of the circle is equal in length to twice the radius times π. So let us imagine the circle resting on a straight line and let's make a little mark at the point where the circle just touches the line. Now slowly turn the circle so that it moves along the line (without slipping) until the point you have marked makes a complete circuit and once again touches the line. Make another mark where it again touches. Thus, you have marked off the circumference of the circle on a straight line and the distance between the two marks is twice π.

Bisect that marked-off line by the usual methods of straightedge and compass geometry and you have a line representing π. Construct the square root of that line and you have $\sqrt{\pi}$.

Voilà! By that act, you have, in effect, squared the circle.

But no. I'm afraid you're still out of the club. You have made use of a rolling circle with a mark on it and that comes under the heading of an instrument other than the straightedge and compass.

The point is that there are any number of ways of squaring the circle, but the Greeks were unable to find any way of doing it with straightedge and compass alone in a finite number of steps. (They spent I don't know how many man-hours of time searching for a method, and looking back on it, it might all seem an exercise in futility now, but it wasn't. In their search, they came across all sorts of new curves, such as the conic sections, and new theorems, which were far more valuable than the squaring of the circle would have been.)

Although the Greeks failed to find a method, the search continued and continued. People kept on trying and trying and trying and trying—

And now let's change the subject for a while.

Consider a simple equation such as $2x-1=0$. You can see that setting $x=\frac{1}{2}$ will make a true statement out of it, for $2(\frac{1}{2})-1$ is indeed equal to zero. No other number can be substituted for x in this equation and yield a true statement.

By changing the integers in the equation (the "coefficients" as they are called) x can be made to equal other specific numbers. For instance, in $3x-4=0$, x is equal to $\frac{4}{3}$; and in $7x+2=0$, $x=-\frac{2}{7}$. In fact, by choosing the coefficients appropriately, you can have as a value of x any positive or negative integer or fraction whatever.

But in such an "equation of the first degree," you can only obtain rational values for x. You can't possibly have an equation of the form $(Ax+B=0)$, where A and B are rational, such that x will turn out to be equal to $\sqrt{2}$, for instance.

The thing to do is to try a more complicated variety of equation. Suppose you try $x^2-2=0$, which is an "equation of the second degree" because it involves a square. If you solve for x you'll find the answer, $\sqrt{2}$, when substituted for x will yield a true statement. In fact, there are two possible answers, for the substitution of $-\sqrt{2}$ for x will also yield a true statement.

You can build up equations of the third degree, such as $Ax^3+Bx^2+Cx+D=0$, or of the fourth degree (I don't have to give any more examples, do I?), or higher. Solving for x in each case becomes more and more difficult, but will give solutions involving cube roots, fourth roots, and so on.

In any equation of this type (a "polynomial equation") the value of x can be worked out by manipulating the coefficients. To take the simplest case, in the general equation of the first degree: $Ax+B=0$, the value of x is $-B/A$. In the general equation of the second degree: $Ax^2+Bx+C=0$, there are two solutions. One is

$$\frac{-B+\sqrt{B^2-4AC}}{2A} \text{ and the other is} \frac{-B-\sqrt{B^2-4AC}}{2A}.$$

Solutions get progressively more complicated and eventually, for equations of the fifth degree and higher, no general solution can be given, although specific solutions can still be worked out. The principle remains, however, that in all polynomial equations, the value of x can be expressed by use of a finite number of integers involved in a finite number of operations, these operations consisting of addition, subtraction, multiplication, division, raising to a power ("involution"), and extracting roots ("evolution").

These operations are the only ones used in ordinary algebra and are therefore called "algebraic operations." Any number which can be derived from the integers by a finite number of algebraic operations in any combination is called an "algebraic number." To put it in reverse, any algebraic number is a possible solution for some polynomial equation.

Now it so happens that the geometric equivalent of all the algebraic operations, except the extraction of roots higher than the square root, can be performed by straightedge and compass alone. If a given line represents 1, therefore, it follows that a line representing *any* algebraic number that involves no root higher than the square root can be constructed by straightedge and compass in a finite number of manipulations.

Since π does not seem to contain any cube roots (or worse), is it possible that it can be constructed by straightedge and compass? That might be if algebraic numbers included *all* numbers. But do they? Are there numbers which cannot be solutions to any polynomial equation, and are therefore not algebraic?

To begin with, all possible rational numbers can be solutions to equations of the first degree, so all rational numbers are algebraic numbers. Then, certainly some irrational numbers are algebraic numbers, for it is easy to write equations for which $\sqrt{2}$ or $\sqrt[3]{15}-3$ are solutions.

But can there be irrational numbers which will not serve as a solution to a single one of the infinite number of different polynomial equations in each of all the infinite number of degrees possible?

In 1844 the French mathematician Joseph Liouville finally found a way of showing that such nonalgebraic numbers did exist. (No, I don't know how he did it, but if any reader thinks I can understand the method, and I must warn him not to overestimate me, he is welcome to send it in.)

However, having proved that nonalgebraic numbers existed, Liouville could still not find a specific example. The nearest he came was to show that a number represented by the symbol e could not serve as the root for any conceivable equation of the second degree.

(At this point I am tempted to launch into a discussion of the number e because, as I said at the start of the previous chapter, there is the famous equation $e^{\pi i} = -1$. But I'll resist temptation because, for one thing, I had some things to say about e in Chapter 3.)

Then, in 1873, the French mathematician Charles Hermite worked out a method of analysis that showed that e could not be the root of any conceivable equation of any conceivable degree and hence was actually not an algebraic number. It was, in fact, what is called a "transcendental number," one which transcends (that is, goes beyond) the algebraic operations and cannot be produced from the integers by any finite number of those operations. (That is, $\sqrt{2}$ is irrational but can be produced by a single algebraic operation, taking the square root of 2. The value of e, on the other hand, can only be calculated by the use of infinite series involving an infinite number of additions, divisions, subtractions, and so on.)

Using the methods developed by Hermite, the German mathematician Ferdinand Lindemann in 1882 proved that π, too, was a transcendental number.

This is crucial for the purposes of this chapter, for it meant that a line segment equivalent to π cannot be built up by the use of the straightedge and compass alone in a finite number of manipulations. *The circle cannot be squared by straightedge and compass alone.* It is as impossible to do this as to find an exact value for $\sqrt{2}$, or to find an odd number that is an exact multiple of 4.

One odd point about transcendental numbers—

They were difficult to find, but now that they have been, they prove to be present in overwhelming numbers. Practically any expression that involves either e or π is transcendental, provided the expression is not arranged so that the e or π cancel out. Practically all expressions involving logarithms (which involve e) and practically all expressions involving trigonometric functions (which involve π)

are transcendental. Expressions involving numbers raised to an irrational power, such as $x^{\sqrt{2}}$, are transcendental.

In fact, if you refer back to Chapter 5, you will understand me when I say that it has been proved that the algebraic numbers can be put into one-to-one correspondence with the integers, but the transcendental numbers cannot.

This means that the algebraic numbers, although infinite, belong to the lowest of the transfinite numbers, $\aleph_0$, while the transcendental numbers belong, at the least, to the next higher transfinite, $\aleph_1$. There are thus infinitely more transcendental numbers than there are algebraic numbers.

To be sure, the fact that the transcendentality of π is now well established and has been for nearly a century doesn't stop the ardent circle-squarers, who continue to work away desperately with straightedge and compass and continue to report solutions regularly.

So if *you* know a way to square the circle by straightedge and compass alone, I congratulate you, but you have a fallacy in your proof somewhere. And it's no use sending it to me, because I'm a rotten mathematician and couldn't possibly find the fallacy, but I tell you anyway, it's there.

8 THE IMAGINARY THAT ISN'T

WHEN I was a mere slip of a lad and attended college, I had a friend with whom I ate lunch every day. His 11 A.M. class was in sociology, which I absolutely refused to take, and my 11 A.M. class was calculus, which he as steadfastly refused to take—so we had to separate at eleven and meet at twelve.

At it happened, his sociology professor was a scholar who did things in the grand manner, holding court after class was over. The more eager students gathered close and listened to him pontificate for an additional fifteen minutes, while they threw in an occasional log in the form of a question to feed the flame of oracle.

Consequently, when my calculus lecture was over, I had to enter the sociology room and wait patiently for court to conclude.

Once I walked in when the professor was listing on the board his classification of mankind into the two groups of mystics and realists, and under mystics he had included the mathematicians along with the poets and theologians. One student wanted to know why.

"Mathematicians," said the professor, "are mystics because they believed in numbers that have no reality."

Now ordinarily, as a nonmember of the class, I sat in the corner and suffered in silent boredom, but now I rose convulsively, and said, "What numbers?"

The professor looked in my direction and said, "The square root of minus one. It has no existence. Mathematicians call it imaginary. But they believe it has some kind of existence in a mystical way."

"There's nothing mystical about it," I said, angrily. "The square root of minus one is just as real as any other number."

The professor smiled, feeling he had a live one on whom he could now proceed to display his superiority of intellect (I have since had classes of my own and I know exactly how he felt). He said, silkily, "We have a young mathematician here who wants to prove the reality of the square root of minus one. Come, young man, hand me the square root of minus one pieces of chalk!"

I reddened, "Well, now, wait—"

"That's all," he said, waving his hand. Mission, he imagined, accomplished, both neatly and sweetly.

But I raised my voice. "I'll do it. I'll do it. I'll hand you the square root of minus one pieces of chalk, if you hand me a one-half piece of chalk."

The professor smiled again, and said, "Very well," broke a fresh piece of chalk in half, and handed me one of the halves. "Now for your end of the bargain."

"Ah, but wait," I said, "you haven't fulfilled your end. This is one piece of chalk you're handed me, not a one-half piece." I held it up for the others to see. "Wouldn't you all say this was one piece of chalk? It certainly isn't two or three."

Now the professor wasn't smiling. "Hold it. One piece of chalk is a piece of regulation length. You have one that's half the regulation length."

I said, "Now you're springing an arbitrary definition on me. But even if I accept it, are you willing to maintain that this is a one-half piece of chalk and not a 0.48 piece or a 0.52 piece? And can you really consider yourself qualified to discuss the square root of minus one, when you're a little hazy on the meaning of one half?"

But by now the professor had lost his equanimity altogether and his final argument was unanswerable. He said, "Get the hell out of here!" I left (laughing) and thereafter waited for my friend in the corridor.

Twenty years have passed since then and I suppose I ought to finish the argument—

Let's start with a simple algebraic equation such as $x+3=5$. The expression, x, represents some number which, when substituted for x, makes the expression a true equality. In this particular case x must equal 2, since $2+3=5$, and so we have "solved for x."

The interesting thing about this solution is that it is the *only* solution. There is no number but 2 which will give 5 when 3 is added to it.

This is true of any question of this sort, which is called a "linear equation" (because in geometry it can be represented as a straight line) or "a polynomial equation of the first degree." No polynomial equation of the first degree can ever have more than one solution for x.

There are other equations, however, which *can* have more than one solution. Here's an example: $x^2-5x+6=0$, where x^2 ("x square" or "x squared") represents x times x. This is called a "quadratic equation," from a Latin word for "square," because it involves x square. It is also called "a polynomial equation of the second degree" because of the little ^{2} in x^2. As for x itself, that could be written x^1 except that the ^{1} is always omitted and taken for granted, and that is why $x+3=5$ is an equation of the first degree.

If we take the equation $x^2-5x+6=0$, and substitute 2 for x, then x^2 is 4, while $5x$ is 10, so that the equation becomes $4-10+6=10$, which is correct, making 2 a solution of the equation.

However, if we substitute 3 for x, then x^2 is 9 and $5x$ is 15, so that the equation becomes $9-15+6=0$, which is also correct, making 3 a second solution of the equation.

Now no equation of the second degree has ever been found which has more than two solutions, but what about polynomial equations of the third degree? These are equations containing x^3 ("x cube" or "x cubed"), which are therefore also called "cubic equations." The expression x^3 represents x times x times x.

The equation $x^3-6x^2+11x-6=0$ has three solutions, since you can substitute 1, 2, or 3 for x in this equation and come up with a true equality in each case. No cubic equation has ever been found with more than three solutions, however.

In the same way polynomial equations of the fourth degree can be constructed which have four solutions but no more; polynomial equations of the fifth degree, which have five solutions but no more; and so on. You might say, then, that a polynomial equation of the nth degree can have as many as n solutions, but never more than n.

Mathematicians craved something even prettier than that and by about 1800 found it. At that time, the German mathematician Karl Friedrich Gauss showed that every equation of the nth degree had exactly n solutions, not only no more, but also no less.

However, in order to make the fundamental theorem true, our notion of what constitutes a solution to an algebraic equation must be drastically enlarged.

To begin with, men accept the "natural numbers" only: 1, 2, 3, and so on. This is adequate for counting objects that are only considered as units generally. You can have 2 children, 5 cows, or 8 pots; while to have 2½ children, 5¼ cows, or 8⅓ pots does not make much sense.

In measuring continuous quantities such as lengths or weights, however, fractions became essential. The Egyptians and Babylonians managed to work out methods of handling fractions, though these were not very efficient by our own standards; and no doubt conservative scholars among them sneered at the mystical mathematicians who believed in a number like 5½, which was neither 5 nor 6.

Such fractions are really ratios of whole numbers. To say a plank of wood is 2⅝ yards long, for instance, is to say that the length of the plank is to the length of a standard yardstick as 21 is to 8. The Greeks, however, discovered that there were definite quantities which could not be expressed as ratios of whole numbers. The first to be discovered was the square root of 2, commonly expressed as $\sqrt{2}$, which is that number which, when multiplied by itself, gives 2. There is such a number but it cannot be expressed as a ratio; hence, it is an "irrational number."

Only thus far did the notion of number extend before modern times. Thus, the Greeks accepted no number smaller than zero. How can there be less than nothing? To them, consequently, the equation $x+5=3$ had no solution. How can you add 5 to any number and have 3 as a result? Even if you added 5 to the smallest number (that is, to zero), you would have 5 as the sum, and if you added 5 to any other number (which would have to be larger than zero), you would have a sum greater than 5.

The first mathematician to break this taboo and make systematic use of numbers less than zero was the Italian, Girolamo Cardano. After all, there *can* be less than nothing. A debt is less than nothing.

If all you own in the world is a two-dollar debt, you have two dollars less than nothing. If you are then given five dollars, you end with three dollars of your own (assuming you are an honorable man who pays his debts). Consequently, in the equation $x+5=3$, x can be set equal to -2, where the minus sign indicates a number less than zero.

Such numbers are called "negative numbers," from a Latin word meaning "to deny," so that the very name carries the traces of the Greek denial of the existence of such numbers. Numbers greater than zero are "positive numbers" and these can be written $+1$, $+2$, $+3$, and so on.

From a practical standpoint, extending the number system by including negative numbers simplifies all sorts of computations; as, for instance, those in bookkeeping.

From a theoretical standpoint, the use of negative numbers means that every equation of the first degree has exactly one solution. No more; no less.

If we pass on to equations of the second degree, we find that the Greeks would agree with us that the equation $x^2-5x+6=0$ has two solutions, 2 and 3. They would say, however, that the equation $x^2+4x-5=0$ has only one solution, 1. Substitute 1 for x and x^2 is 1, while $4x$ is 4, so that the equation becomes $1+4-5=0$. No other number will serve as a solution, as long as you restrict yourself to positive numbers.

However, the number -5 is a solution, if we consider a few rules that are worked out in connection with the multiplication of negative numbers. In order to achieve consistent results, mathematicians have decided that the multiplication of a negative number by a positive number yields a negative product, while the multiplication of a negative number by a negative number yields a positive product.

If, in the equation $x^2+4x-5=0$, -5 is substituted for x, then x^2 becomes -5 times -5, or $+25$, while $4x$ becomes $+4$ times -5, or -20. The equation becomes

$25-20-5=0$, which is true. We would say, then, that there are two solutions to this equation, $+1$ and -5.

Sometimes, a quadratic equation does indeed seem to have but a single root, as, for example, $x^2-6x+9=0$, which will be a true equality if and only if the number $+3$ is substituted for x. However, the mechanics of solution of the equation show that there are actually two solutions, which happen to be identical. Thus, $x^2-6x+9=0$ can be converted to $(x-3)$ $(x-3)=0$ and each $(x-3)$ yields a solution. The two solutions of this equation are, therefore, $+3$ and $+3$.

Allowing for occasional duplicate solutions, are we ready to say then that all second degree equations can be shown to have eactly two solutions if negative numbers are included in the number system?

Alas, no! For what about the equation $x^2+1=0$. To begin with, x^2 must be -1 since substituting -1 for x^2 makes the equation $-1+1=0$, which is correct enough.

But if x^2 is -1, then x must be the famous square root of minus one ($\sqrt{-1}$), which occasioned the set-to between the sociology professor and myself. The square root of minus one is that number which when multiplied by itself will give -1. But there is no such number in the set of positive and negative quantities, and that is the reason the sociology professor scorned it. First, $+1$ times $+1$ is $+1$; secondly, -1 times -1 is $+1$.

To allow any solution at all for the equation $x^2+1=0$, let alone two solutions, it is necessary to get past this roadblock. If no positive number will do and no negative one either, it is absolutely essential to define a completely new kind of number; an imaginary number, if you like; one with its square equal to -1.

We could, if we wished, give the new kind of number a special sign. The plus sign does for positives and the minus sign for negatives; so we could use an asterisk for the new number and say that, *1 ("star one") times *1 was equal to -1.

However, this was not done. Instead, the symbol i (for "imaginary") was introduced by the Swiss mathematician Leonhard Euler in 1777 and was thereafter generally adopted. So we can write $i=\sqrt{-1}$ or $i^2=-1$.

Having defined i in this fashion, we can express the square root of any negative number. For instance, $\sqrt{-4}$ can be written $\sqrt{4}$ times $\sqrt{-1}$, or $2i$. In general, any square root of a negative number, $\sqrt{-n}$, can be written as the square root of the equivalent positive number times the square root of minus one; that is, $\sqrt{-n}=\sqrt{n}\,i$.

In this way, we can picture a whole series of imaginary numbers exactly analogous to the series of ordinary or "real numbers." For 1, 2, 3, 4, . . . , we would have i, $2i$, $3i$, $4i$. . . . This would include fractions, for $\frac{2}{3}$ would be matched by $2\frac{2}{3}i$; $^{15}/_{17}$ by $^{15}/_{17}i$, and so on. It would also include irrationals, for $\sqrt{2}$ would be matched by $\sqrt{2}\,i$ and even a number like π (pi) would be matched by πi.

These are all comparisons of positive numbers with imaginary numbers. What about negative numbers? Well, why not negative imaginaries, too? For -1, -2, -3, -4, . . . , there would be $-i$, $-2i$, $-3i$, $-4i$. . . .

So now we have four classes of numbers: 1) positive real numbers, 2) negative real numbers, 3) positive imaginary numbers, 4) negative imaginary numbers. (When a negative imaginary is multiplied by a negative imaginary, the product is negative.)

Using this further extension of the number system, we can find the necessary two solutions for the equation $x^2+1=0$. They are $+i$ and $-i$. First $+i$ times $+i$ equals -1, and secondly $-i$ times $-i$ equals -1, so that in either case, the equation becomes $-1+1=0$, which is a true equality.

In fact, you can use the same extension of the number system to find all four solutions for an equation such as $x^4-1=0$. The solutions are $+1$, -1, $+i$, and $-i$. To show this, we must remember that any number raised to the fourth power is equal to the square of that number multiplied by itself. That is, n^4 equals n^2 times n^2.

Now let's substitute each of the suggested solutions into the equations so that x^4 becomes successively $(+1)^4$, $(-1)^4$, $(+i)^4$, and $(-i)^4$.

First $(+1)^4$ equals $(+1)^2$ times $(+1)^2$, and since $(+1)^2$ equals $+1$, that becomes $+1$ times $+1$, which is $+1$.

Second, $(-1)^4$ equals $(-1)^2$ times $(-1)^2$, and since $(-1)^2$ also equals $+1$, the expression is again $+1$ times $+1$, or $+1$.

Third, $(+i)^4$ equals $(+i)^2$ times $(+i)^2$ and we have defined $(+i)^2$ as -1, so that the expression becomes -1 times -1, or $+1$.

LEONHARD EULER

Euler, the son of a Calvinist minister, was born in Basel, Switzerland, on April 15, 1707. He received his master's degree at the age of sixteen from the University of Basel.

Euler went to St. Petersburg, Russia, in 1727, for there Catherine I (the widow of Peter the Great) had recently founded the Petersburg Academy and Euler spent much of his life there. In 1735 he lost the sight of his right eye through too-ardent observations of the Sun in an attempt to work out a system of time determination.

In 1741 Euler went to Berlin to head and revivify the decaying Academy of Sciences but didn't get along with the new Prussian King, Frederick II. He returned to St. Petersburg in 1766 and there he died on September 18, 1783.

Euler was the most prolific mathematician of all time, writing on every branch of the subject and being always careful to describe his reasoning and to list the false paths he had followed. He lost the sight of his remaining eye in 1766 but that scarcely seemed to stop him or even slow him down, for he had a phenomenal memory and could keep in mind that which would fill several black- boards. He published eight hundred papers, some of them quite long, and at the time of his death left enough papers behind to keep the printing presses busy for thirty-five years.

Euler published a tremendously successful populariza- tion of science in 1768, one that remained in print for ninety years. He died shortly after working out certain mathematical problems in connection with ballooning, inspired by the successful flight of the Montgolfier broth- ers. He introduced the symbol "e" for the base of natural logarithms, "i" for the square root of minus one, and "f( )" for functions.

LEONARD EULER.

London, Published as the Act directs, Oct.* 13.* 1801. by J. Wilkes.

Fourth, $(-i)^4$ equals $(-i)^2$ times $(-i)^2$, which is also -1 times -1, or $+1$.

All four suggested solutions, when substituted into the equation $x^4-1=0$, give the expression $+1-1=0$, which is correct.

It might seem all very well to talk about imaginary numbers—for a mathematician. As long as some defined quantity can be made subject to rules of manipulation that do not contradict anything else in the mathematical system, the mathematician is happy. He doesn't really care what it "means."

Ordinary people do, though, and that's where my sociologist's charge of mysticism against mathematicians arises.

And yet it is the easiest thing in the world to supply the so-called "imaginary" numbers with a perfectly real and concrete significance. Just imagine a horizontal line crossed by a vertical line and call the point of intersection zero. Now you have four lines radiating out at mutual right angles from that zero point. You can equate those lines with the four kinds of numbers.

If the line radiating out to the right is marked off at equal intervals, the marks can be numbered $+1$, $+2$, $+3$, $+4$, . . . , and so on for as long as we wish, if we only make the line long enough. Between the markings are all the fractions and irrational numbers. In fact, it can be shown that to every point on such a line there corresponds one and only one positive real number, and for every positive real number there is one and only one point on the line.

The line radiating out to the left can be similarly marked off with the negative real numbers, so that the horizontal line can be considered the "real-number axis," including both positives and negatives.

Similarly, the line radiating upward can be marked off with the positive imaginary numbers, and the one radiating downward with the negative imaginary numbers. The vertical line is then the imaginary-number axis.

Suppose we label the different numbers not by the usual signs and symbols, but by the directions in which the lines point. The rightward line of positive real numbers can be called East because that would be its direction of extension on a conventional map. The leftward line of negative real numbers would be West; the upward line of positive imaginaries would be North; and the downward line of negative imaginaries would be South.

Now if we agree that $+1$ times $+1$ equals $+1$, and if we concentrate on the compass signs as I have defined them, we are saying that East times East equals East. Again since -1 times -1 also equals $+1$, West times West equals East. Then, since $+i$ times $+i$ equals -1, and so does $-i$ times $-i$, then North times North equals West and so does South times South.

We can also make other combinations such as -1 times $+i$, which equals $-i$ (since positive times negative yields a negative product even when imaginaries are involved), so that West times North equals South. If we list all the possible combinations as compass points, abbreviating those points by initial letters, we can set up the following system:

E×E=E	E×S=S	E×W=W	E×N=N
S×E=S	S×S=W	S×W=N	S×N=E
W×E=W	W×S=N	W×W=E	W×N=S
N×E=N	N×S=E	N×W=S	N×N=W

There is a very orderly pattern here. Any compass point multiplied by East is left unchanged, so that East as a multiplier represents a rotation of 0°. On the other hand, any compass point multiplied by West is rotated through 180° ("about face"). North and South represent right-angle turns. Multiplication by South results in a 90° clockwise turn ("right face"); while multiplication by North results in a 90° counterclockwise turn ("left face").

Now it so happens that an unchanging direction is the simplest arrangement, so East (the positive real numbers) is easier to handle and more comforting to the soul than any of the others. West (the negative real numbers), which produces an about face but leaves one on the same line at least, is less comforting, but not too bad. North and South (the imaginary numbers), which send you off in a new direction altogether, are least comfortable.

But viewed as compass points, you can see that no set of numbers is more "imaginary" or, for that matter, more "real" than any other.

Now consider how useful the existence of two number axes can be. As long as we deal with the real numbers only, we can move along the real-number axis, backward and forward, one-dimensionally. The same would be true if we used only the imaginary-number axis.

Using both, we can define a point as so far right or left on the real-number axis and so far up or down on the imaginary-number axis. This will place the point somewhere in one of the quadrants formed by the two axes. This is precisely the manner in which points are located on the earth's surface by means of latitude and longitude.

We can speak of a number such as $+5+5i$, which would represent the point reached when you marked off 5 units East followed by 5 units North. Or you can have $-7+6i$ or $+0.5432-9.115i$ or $+\sqrt{2}+\sqrt{3}\,i$.

Such numbers, combining real and imaginary units, are called "complex numbers."

Using both axes, any point in a plane (and not merely on a line) can be made to correspond to one and only one complex number. Again every conceivable complex number can be made to correspond to one and only one point on a plane.

In fact, the real numbers themselves are only special cases of the complex numbers, and so, for that matter, are the imaginary numbers. If you represent complex numbers as all numbers of the form $+a+bi$, then the real numbers are all those complex numbers in which b happens to be equal to zero. And imaginary numbers are all the complex numbers in which a happens to be equal to zero.

The use of the plane of complex numbers, instead of the lines of real numbers only, has been of inestimable use to the mathematician.

For instance, the number of solutions in a polynomial equation is equal to its degree only if complex numbers are considered as solutions, rather than merely real numbers and imaginary numbers. For instance the two solutions of $x^2-1=0$ are $+1$ and -1, which can be written as $+1+0i$ and $-1+0i$. The two solutions of $x^2+1=0$ are $+i$ and $-i$, or $0+i$ and $0-i$. The four solutions of $x^4-1=0$ are all four complex numbers just listed.

In all these very simple cases, the complex numbers contain zeros and boil down to either real numbers or to imaginary numbers. This, nevertheless, is not always so. In the equation $x^3 - 1 = 0$ one solution, to be sure, is $+1 + 0i$ (which can be written simply as $+1$), but the other two solutions are $-\frac{1}{2} + \frac{1}{2}\sqrt{3}\,i$ and $-\frac{1}{2} - \frac{1}{2}\sqrt{3}\,i$.

The Gentle Reader with ambition can take the cube of either of these expressions (if he remembers how to mulitply polynomials algebraically) and satisfy himself that it will come out $+1$.

Complex numbers are of practical importance too. Many familiar measurements involve "scalar quantities" which differ only in magnitude. One volume is greater or less than another; one weight is greater or less than another; one density is greater or less than another. For that matter, one debt is greater or less than another. For all such measurements, the real numbers, either positive or negative, suffice.

However, there are also "vector quantities" which possess both magnitude and direction. A velocity may differ from another velocity not only in being greater or less, but in being in another direction. This holds true for forces, accelerations, and so on.

For such vector quantities, complex numbers are necessary to the mathematical treatment, since complex numbers include both magnitude and direction (which was my reason for making the analogy between the four types of numbers and the compass points).

Now, when my sociology professor demanded "the square root of minus one pieces of chalk," he was speaking of a scalar phenomenon for which the real numbers were sufficient.

On the other hand, had he asked me how to get from his room to a certain spot on the campus, he would probably have been angered if I had said, "Go two hundred yards." He would have asked, with asperity, "In which direction?"

Now, you see, he would have been dealing with a vector quantity for which the real numbers are insufficient. I could satisfy him by saying "Go two hundred yards northeast," which is equivalent to saying "Go $100\sqrt{2}$ plus $100\sqrt{2}\,i$ yards."

Surely it is as ridiculous to consider the square root of minus one "imaginary" because you can't use it to count pieces of chalk as to consider the number 200 as "imaginary" because by itself it cannot express the location of one point with reference to another.

Part III

NUMBERS AND MEASUREMENT

9 FORGET IT!

THE other day I was looking through a new textbook on biology (*Biological Science: An Inquiry into Life,* written by a number of contributing authors and published by Harcourt, Brace & World, Inc., in 1963). I found it fascinating.

Unfortunately, though, I read the Foreword first (yes, I'm one of *that* kind) and was instantly plunged into the deepest gloom. Let me quote from the first two paragraphs:

"With each new generation our fund of science knowledge increases fivefold. . . . At the current rate of scientific advance, there is about four times as much significant biological knowledge today as in 1930, and about sixteen times as much as in 1900. By the year 2000, at this rate of increase, there will be a hundred times as much biology to 'cover' in the introductory course as at the beginning of the century."

Imagine how this affects me. I am a professional "keeper-upper" with science and in my more manic, ebullient, and carefree moments, I even think I succeed fairly well.

Then I read something like the above-quoted passage and the world falls about my ears. I *don't* keep up with science. Worse, I *can't* keep up with it. Still worse, I'm falling farther behind every day.

And finally, when I'm all through sorrowing for myself, I devote a few moments to worrying about the world generally. What is going to become of Homo sapiens? We're going to smarten ourselves to death. After a while, we will all die of pernicious education, with our brain cells crammed to indigestion with facts and concepts, and with blasts of information exploding out of our ears.

But then, as luck would have it, the very day after I read the Foreword to *Bialogical Science* I came across an old, old book entitled *Pike's Arithmetic*. At least that is the name on the spine. On the title page it spreads itself a bit better, for in those days titles were *titles*. It goes "A New and Complete System of Arithmetic Composed for the Use of the Citizens of the United States, by Nicolas Pike, A.M." It was first published in 1785, but the copy I have is only the "Second Edition, Enlarged," published in 1797.

It is a large book of over 500 pages, crammed full of small print and with no relief whatever in the way of illustrations or diagrams. It is a solid slab of arithmetic except for small sections at the very end that introduce algebra and geometry.

I was amazed. I have two children in grade school * (and once I was in grade school myself), and I know what arithmetic books are like these days. They are nowhere near as large. They can't possibly have even one fifth the wordage of Pike.

Can it be that we are leaving anything out?

So I went through Pike and, you know, we *are* leaving something out. And there's nothing wrong with that. The trouble is we're not leaving *enough* out.

On page 19, for instance, Pike devotes half a page to a listing of numbers as expressed in Roman numerals, extending the list to numbers as high as five hundred thousand.

Now Arabic numerals reached Europe in the High Middle Ages, and once they came on the scene the Roman numerals were completely outmoded (see Chapter 1). They lost all possible use, so infinitely superior was the new Arabic notation. Until then who knows how many

---

[* *This article first appeared in March 1964, and time marches on. My younger child is now well along in college.*]

reams of paper were required to explain methods for calculating with Roman numerals. Afterward the same calculations could be performed with a hundredth of the explanation. No knowledge was lost—only inefficient rules.

And yet five hundred years after the deserved death of the Roman numerals, Pike still included them and expected his readers to be able to translate them into Arabic numerals and vice versa even though he gave no instructions for how to manipulate them. In fact, nearly two hundred years after Pike, the Roman numerals are still being taught. My little daughter is learning them now.

But why? Where's the need? To be sure, you will find Roman numerals on cornerstones and gravestones, on clockfaces and on some public buildings and documents, but it isn't used for any need at all. It is used for show, for status, for antique flavor, for a craving for some kind of phony classicism.

I dare say there are some sentimental fellows who feel that knowledge of the Roman numerals is a kind of gateway to history and culture; that scrapping them would be like knocking over what is left of the Parthenon, but I have no patience with such mawkishness. We might as well suggest that everyone who learns to drive a car be required to spend some time at the wheel of a Model-T Ford so he could get the flavor of early cardom.

Roman numerals? Forget it! —And make room instead for new and valuable material.

But do we dare forget things? Why not? We've forgotten much; more than you imagine. Our troubles stem not from the fact that we've forgotten, but that we remember too well; we don't forget enough.

A great deal of Pike's book consists of material we have imperfectly forgotten. That is why the modern arithmetic book is shorter than Pike. And if we could but perfectly forget, the modern arithmetic book could grow still shorter.

For instance, Pike devotes many pages to tables—presumably important tables that he thought the reader ought to be familiar with. His fifth table is labeled "cloth measure."

Did you know that 2¼ inches make a "nail"? Well, they do. And 16 nails make a yard; while 12 nails make an ell.

No, wait awhile. Those 12 nails (27 inches) make a

Flemish ell. It takes 20 nails (45 inches) to make an English ell, and 24 nails (54 inches) to make a French ell. Then, 16 nails plus 1⅝ inches (37⅝ inches) make a Scotch ell.

Now if you're going to be in the business world and import and export cloth, you're going to have to know all those ells—unless you can figure some way of getting the ell out of business.

Furthermore, almost every piece of goods is measured in its own units. You speak of a firkin of butter, a punch of prunes, a fother of lead, a stone of butcher's meat, and so on. Each of these quantities weighs a certain number of pounds (avoirdupois pounds, but there are also troy pounds and apothecary pounds and so on), and Pike carefully gives all the equivalents.

Do you want to measure distances? Well, how about this: 7⁹²⁄₁₀₀ inches make 1 link; 25 links make 1 pole; 4 poles make 1 chain; 10 chains make 1 furlong; and 8 furlongs make 1 mile.

Or do you want to measure ale or beer—a very common line of work in Colonial times. You have to know the language, of course. Here it is: 2 pints make a quart and 4 quarts make a gallon. Well, we still know that much anyway.

In Colonial times, however, a mere gallon of beer or ale was but a starter. That was for infants. You had to know how to speak of man-sized quantities. Well, 8 gallons made a firkin—that is, it makes "a firkin of ale in London." It takes, however, 9 gallons to make "a firkin of beer in London." The intermediate quantity, 8½ gallons, is marked down as "a firkin of ale or beer"—presumably outside the environs of London where the provincial citizens were less finicky in distinguishing between the two.

But we go on: 2 firkins (I suppose the intermediate kind, but I'm not sure) make a kilderkin asd 2 kilderkins make a barrel. Then 1½ barrels make 1 hogshead; 2 barrels make a puncheon; and 3 barrels make a butt.

Have you got all that straight?

But let's try dry measure in case your appetite has been sharpened for something still better.

Here, 2 pints make a quart and 2 quarts make a pottle. (No, not bottle, *pottle*. Don't tell me you've never heard of a pottle!) But let's proceed.

Next, 2 pottles make a gallon, 2 gallons make a peck, and 4 pecks make a bushel. (Long breath now.) Then 2 bushels make a strike, 2 strikes make a coom, 2 cooms make a quarter, 4 quarters make a chaldron (though in the demanding city of London, it takes 4½ quarters to make a chaldron). Finally, 5 quarters make a wey and 2 weys make a last.

I'm not making this up. I'm copying it right out of Pike, page 48.

Were people who were studying arithmetic in 1797 expected to memorize all this? Apparently, yes, because Pike spends a lot of time on compound addition. That's right, *compound* addition.

You see, the addition you consider addition is just "simple addition." Compound addition is something stronger and I will now explain it to you.

Suppose you have 15 apples, your friend has 17 apples, and a passing stranger has 19 apples and you decide to make a pile of them. Having done so, you wonder how many you have altogether. Preferring not to count, you draw upon your college education and prepare to add $15+17+19$. You begin with the units column and find that $5+7+9=21$. You therefore divide 21 by 10 and find the quotient is 2 plus a remainder of 1, so you put down the remainder, 1, and carry the quotient 2 into the tens col----

I seem to hear loud yells from the audience. "What is all this?" comes the fevered demand. "Where does this 'divide by 10' jazz come from?"

Ah, Gentle Readers, but this is exactly what you do whenever you add. It is only that the kindly souls who devised our Arabic system of numeration based it on the number 10 in such a way that when any two-digit number is divided by 10, the first digit represents the quotient and the second the remainder.

For that reason, having the quotient and remainder in our hands without dividing, we can add automatically. If the units column adds up to 21, we put down 1 and carry 2; if it had added up to 57, we would have put down 7 and carried 5, and so on.

The only reason this works, mind you, is that in adding a set of figures, each column of digits (starting from the right and working leftward) represents a value ten times

THE YARDSTICK

The yardstick is one of those accompaniments of life that we tend to take for granted. Few people have any idea how difficult it was to produce one and how many subtle concepts had to be embraced before the yardstick became possible.

The natural manner of measuring lengths in early times was to use various portions of the body for the purpose. We still talk of "hands" in measuring the heights of horses, and of a "span" for the length represented by the outstretched fingers. A "cubit," from a Latin word meaning "elbow," is the distance from fingertips to elbow, and a "yard" (related to "girth") is the distance from fingertips to nose, or the waist measurement of a man.

The trouble with using portions of the body as a measuring device is that the lengths and measurements of those portions varies from person to person. The length from my fingertip to my nose is quite close to a yard, but my waist measurement is distinctly greater than a yard.

It finally occurred to people to establish a "standard yard" and never mind what your own measurements are. According to tradition, a standard yard was originally adjusted to the length from the fingertips of King Henry I of England to his nose. (And the standard foot is supposed to be based on the foot of Charlemagne.)

Naturally, the King of England can't travel from village to village measuring out lengths of cloth from his nose to his fingertips. Instead a stick was held up against him and marks are made at his nose and his fingertips. The distance between the marks is a standard yard. Other sticks can be measured off against that standard and can become secondary standards to be sent to every village for use in checking the activities of the local merchants.

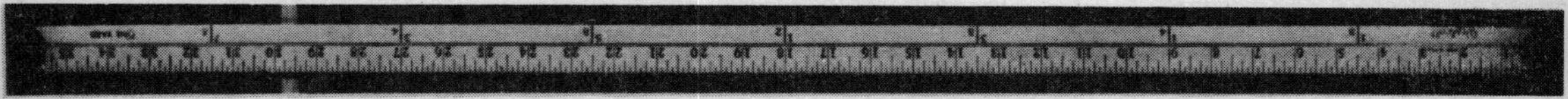

The Granger Collection

as great as the column before. The rightmost column is units, the one to its left is tens, the one to its left is hundreds, and so on.

It is this combination of a number system based on ten and a value ratio from column to column of ten that makes addition very simple. It is for this reason that it is, as Pike calls it, "simple addition."

Now suppose you have 1 dozen and 8 apples, your friend has 1 dozen and 10 apples, and a passing stranger has 1 dozen and 9 apples. Make a pile of those and add them as follows:

1 dozen	8 units
1 dozen	10 units
1 dozen	9 units

Since $8+10+9=27$, do we put down 7 and carry 2? Not at all? The ratio of the "dozens" column to the "units" column is not 10 but 12, since there are 12 units to a dozen. And since the number system we are using is based on 10 and not on 12, we can no longer let the digits do our thinking for us. We have to go long way round.

If $8+10+9=27$, we must divide that sum by the ratio of the value of the columns; in this case, 12. We find that 27 divided by 12 gives a quotient of 2 plus a remainder of 3, so we put down 3 and carry 2. In the dozens column we get $1+1+1+2=5$. Our total therefore is 5 dozen and 3 apples.

Whenever a ratio of other than 10 is used so that you have to make actual divisions in adding, you have "compound addition." You must indulge in compound addition if you try to add 5 pounds 12 ounces and 6 pounds 8 ounces, for there are 16 ounces to a pound. You are stuck again if you add 3 yards 2 feet 6 inches to 1 yard 2 feet 8 inches, for there are 12 inches to a foot, and 3 feet to a yard.

You do the former if you care to; I'll do the latter. First, 6 inches and 8 inches are 14 inches. Divide 14 by 12, getting 1 and a remainder of 2, so you put down 2 and carry 1. As for the feet, $2+2+1=5$. Divide 5 by 3 and get 1 and a remainder of 2, put down 2 and carry 1. In the yards, you have $3+1+1=5$. Your answer, then, is 5 yards 2 feet 2 inches.

Now why on Earth should our unit ratios vary all over the lot, when our number system is so firmly based on 10? There are many reasons (valid in their time) for the use of odd ratios like 2, 3, 4, 8, 12, 16, and 20, but surely we are now advanced and sophisticated enough to use 10 as the exclusive (or nearly exclusive) ratio. If we could do so, we could with much pleasure forget about compound addition—and compound subtraction, compound multiplication, compound division, too. (They also exist, of course.)

To be sure, there are times when nature makes the universal ten impossible. In measuring time, the day and the year have their lengths fixed for us by astronomical conditions and neither unit of time can be abandoned. Compound addition and the rest will have to be retained for such special cases, alas.

But who in blazes says we must measure things in firkins and pottles and Flemish ells? These are purely manmade measurements, and we must remember that measures were made for man and not man for measures.

It so happens that there is a system of measurement based exclusively on ten in this world. It is called the metric system and it is used all over the civilized world except for certain English-speaking nations such as the United States and Great Britain.

By not adopting the metric system, we waste our time for we gain nothing, not one thing, by learning our own measurements. The loss of time (which is expensive indeed) is balanced by not one thing I can imagine. (To be sure, it would be expensive to convert existing instruments and tools but it would have been nowhere nearly as expensive if we had done it a century ago, as we should have.)

There are those, of course, who object to violating our long-used cherished measures. They have given up cooms and chaldrons but imagine there is something about inches and feet and pints and quarts and pecks and bushels that is "simpler" or "more natural" than meters and liters.

There may even be people who find something dangerously foregn and radical (oh, for that vanished word of opprobrium, "Jacobin") in the metric system—yet it was the United States that led the way.

In 1786, thirteen years before the wicked French revolutionaries designed the metric system, Thomas Jefferson (a notorious "Jacobin" according to the Federalists, at least) saw a suggestion of his adopted by the infant United States. The nation established a decimal currency.

What we had been using was British currency, and that is a fearsome and wonderful thing. Just to point out how preposterous it is, let me say that the British people who, over the centuries, have, with monumental patience, taught themselves to endure anything at all provided it was "traditional"—are now sick and tired of their currency and are debating converting it to the decimal system. (They can't agree on the exact details of the change.) *

But consider the British currency as it has been. To begin with, 4 farthings make 1 penny; 12 pennies make 1 shilling, and 20 shillings make 1 pound. In addition, there is a virtual farrago of terms, if not always actual coins, such as ha'pennies and thruppences and sixpences and crowns and half-crowns and florins and guineas and heaven knows what other devices with which to cripple the mental development of the British schoolchild and line the pockets of British tradesmen whenever tourists come to call and attempt to cope with the currency.

Needless to say, Pike gives careful instruction on how to manipulate pounds, shillings, and pence—and very special instructions they are. Try dividing 5 pounds, 13 shillings, 7 pence by 3. Quick now!

In the United States, the money system, as originally established, is as follows: 10 mills make 1 cent; 10 cents make 1 dime; 10 dimes make 1 dollar; 10 dollars make 1 eagle. Actually, modern Americans, in their calculations, stick to dollars and cents only.

The result? American money can be expressed in decimal form and can be treated as can any other decimals. An American child who has learned decimals need only be taught to recognize the dollar sign and he is all set. In the time that he does, a British child has barely mastered the fact that thruppence ha'penny equals 14 farthings.

What a pity that when, thirteen years later, in 1799, the metric system came into being, our original anti-

[* *Since this article was written, the British have carried through the change. When I visited Great Britain in 1974, I was greatly disappointed at not being able to deal with threepences and half crowns. They are also adopting the metric system, leaving the intransigent United States virtually alone in opposition.*]

British, pro-French feelings had not lasted just long enough to allow us to adopt it. Had we done so, we would have been as happy to forget our foolish pecks and ounces, as we are now happy to have forgotten our pence and shillings. (After all, would you like to go back to British currency in preference to our own?)

What I would like to see is one form of money do for all the world. Everywhere. Why not?

I appreciate the fact that I may be accused because of this of wanting to pour humanity into a mold, and of being a conformist. Of course, I am not a conformist (heavens!). I have no objection to local customs and local dialects and local dietaries. In fact, I insist on them for I constitute a locality all by myself. I just don't want to keep provincialisms that were well enough in their time but that interfere with human well-being in a world which is now 90 minutes in circumference.

If you think provincialism is cute and gives humanity color and charm, let me quote to you once more from Pike.

"Federal Money" (dollars and cents) had been introduced eleven years before Pike's second edition, and he gives the exact wording of the law that established it and discusses it in detail—under the decimal system and not under compound addition.

Naturally, since other systems than the Federal were still in us, rules had to be formulated and given for converting (or "reducing") one system to another. Here is the list. I won't give you the actual rules, just the list of reductions that were necessary, exactly as he lists them:

I. To reduce New Hampshire, Massachusetts, Rhode Island, Connecticut, and Virginia currency:

    1. To Federal Money
    2. To New York and North Carolina currency
    3. To Pennsylvania, New Jersey, Delaware, and Maryland currency
    4. To South Carolina and Georgia currency
    5. To English money
    6. To Irish money
    7. To Canada and Nova Scotia currency
    8. To Livres Tournois (French money)
    9. To Spanish milled dollars

II. To reduce Federal Money to New England and Virginia currency.

III. To reduce New Jersey, Pennsylvania, Delaware, and Maryland currency:

    1. To New Hampshire, Massachusetts, Rhode Island, Connecticut, and Virginia currency.
    2. To New York and . . .

Oh, the heck with it. You get the idea.

Can anyone possible be sorry that all that cute provincial flavor has vanished? Are you sorry that every time you travel out of state you don't have to throw yourself into fits of arithmetical discomfort whenever you want to make a purchase? Or into similar fits every time someone from another state invades yours and tries to dicker with you? What a pleasure to have forgotten all that.

Then tell me what's so wonderful about having fifty sets of marriage and divorce laws?

In 1752, Great Britain and her colonies (some two centuries later than Catholic Europe) abandoned the Julian calendar and adopted the astronomically more correct Gregorian calendar (see Chapter 11). Nearly half a century later, Pike was still giving rules for solving complex calendar-based problems for the Julian calendar as well as for the Gregorian. Isn't it nice to have forgotten the Julian calendar?

Wouldn't it be nice if we could forget most of calendrical complications by adopting a rational calendar that would tie the day of the month firmly to the day of the week and have a single three-month calendar serve as a perpetual one, repeating itself over and over every three months? There is a world calendar proposed which would do just this.

It would enable us to do a lot of useful forgetting.

I would like to see the English language come into worldwide use. Not necessarily as the only language or even as the major language. It would just be nice if everyone—whatever his own language was—could also speak English fluently. It would help in communications and perhaps, eventually, everyone would just choose to speak English.

That would save a lot of room for other things.

Why English? Well, for one thing more people speak English as either first or second language than any other language on Earth, so we have a head start. Secondly, far more science is reported in English than in any other language and it is communication in science that is critical today and will be even more critical tomorrow.

To be sure, we ought to make it as easy as possible for people to speak English, which means we should rationalize its spelling and grammar.

English, as it is spelled today, is almost a set of Chinese ideograms. No one can be sure how a word is pronounced by looking at the letters that make it up. How do you pronounce: rough, through, though, cough, hiccough, and lough; and why is it so terribly necessary to spell all those sounds with the mad letter combination "ough"?

It looks funny, perhaps, to spell the words ruff, throo, thoh, cawf, hiccup, and lokh; but we already write hiccup and it doesn't look funny. We spell colour, color, and centre, center, and shew, show and grey, gray. The result looks funny to a Britisher but we are used to it. We can get used to the rest, too, and save a lot of wear and tear on the brain. We would all become more intelligent, if intelligence is measured by proficiency at spelling, and we'll not have lost one thing.

And grammar? Who needs the eternal hair-splitting arguments about "shall" and "will" or "which" and "that"? The uselessness of it can be demonstrated by the fact that virtually no one gets it straight anyway. Aside from losing valuable time, blunting a child's reasoning faculties, and instilling him or her with a ravening dislike for the English language, what do we gain?

If there be some who think that such blurring of fine distinctions will ruin the language, I would like to point out that English, before the grammarians got hold of it, had managed to lose its gender and its declensions almost everywhere except among the pronouns. The fact that we have only one definite article (the) for all genders and cases and times instead of three, as in French (*le, la, les*) or six, as in German (*der, die, das, dem, den, des*) in no way blunts the English language, which remains an admirably flexible instrument. We cherish our follies only because we are used to them, and not because they are not really follies.

AMERICAN BILLS

It is rather heartbreaking that the United States, having started resolutely in the right direction, did not continue.

Immediately after the Reveloutionary War, anti-British feeling was strong enough to cause many Americans to want to do away with anything trivial that would remind them of the hated foe. The "rights of Englishmen" were not trivial, so those were congealed into the Bill of Rights. The system of coinage, however familiar, was trivial.

The key person in this respect was a Pennsylvanian, Gouverneur Morris. He had been a Federalist, an advocate of a strong central government over the quarreling and disunited states who made up what was wrongly called the "United" States immediately after the Revolution. He was a member of the Constitutional Congress and, more than anyone else, is responsible for the actual wording of the Constitution and the casting of it into a clear and simple phraseology, devoid of fustian and melodrama.

It was he, also, who suggested that the United States adopt a new coinage based on a decimal system. The basic unit, the "dollar" (the paper form of which is presented in the illustration, though it scarcely needs it, so familiar is it to all of us), gets its name the long way round. Back about 1500, silver from the silver mines in Joachim's Valley (in what is now northwestern Czechoslovakia) was used to coin ounce-pieces. Joachim's Valley is, in German, Joachimsthal, and the coins were called "Joachminsthalers" or, for short, "thalers," or, in English, "dollars."

In colonial times, Spanish coins of about the value of the well-known dollars existed. The Spaniards called them "pesos", the English "dollars," and the Americans adopted the name and began coining them in 1794.

We must make room for expanding knowledge, or at least make as much room as possible. Surely it is as important to forget the old and useless as it is to learn the new and important.

Forget it, I say, forget it more and more. *Forget it!*

But why am I getting so excited? No one is listening to a word I say.

10 PRE-FIXING IT UP

I GO through life supported and bolstered by many comforting myths, as do all of us. One of my own particularly cherished articles of faith is that there are no arguments against the metric system and that the common units make up an indefensible farrago of nonsense that we keep only out of stubborn folly.

Imagine the sobering effect, then, of having recently come across a letter by a British gentleman who bitterly denounced the metric system as being artificial, sterile, and not geared to human needs. For instance, he said (and I don't quote exactly), if one wants to drink beer, a pint of beer is the thing. A liter of beer is too much and half a liter is too little, but a pint, ah, that's just right.*

As far as I can tell, the gentleman was serious in his provincialism, and in considering that that to which he is accustomed has the force of a natural law. It reminds me of the pious woman who set her face firmly against all foreign languages by holding up her Bible and saying, "If the English language was good enough for the prophet Isaiah, and the apostle Paul, it is good enough for me."

---

* *Before you write to tell me that half a liter is larger than a pint, let me explain that though it is larger than an American pint, it is smaller than a British pint.*

But mainly it reminds me that I want to write an essay on the metric system.

In order to do so, I want to begin by explaining that the value of the system does not lie in the actual size of the basic units. Its worth is this: that it is a logical *system*. The units are sensibly interrelated.

All other sets of measurements with which I am acquainted use separate names for each unit involving a particular type of quantity. In distance, we ourselves have miles, feet, inches, rods, furlongs, and so on. In volume, we have pecks, bushels, pints, drams. In weight, we have ounces, pounds, tons, grains. It is like the Eskimos, who are supposed to have I don't know how many dozens of words for snow, a different word for it when it is falling or when it is lying there, when it is loose or packed, wet or dry, new-fallen or old-fallen, and so on.

We ourselves see the advantage in using adjective-noun combinations. We then have the noun as a general term for all kinds of snow and the adjective describing the specific variety: wet snow, dry snow, hard snow, soft snow, and so on. What's the advantage? First, we see a generalization we did not see before. Second, we can use the same adjectives for other nouns, so that we can have hard rock, hard bread, hard heart, and consequently see a new generalization, that of hardness.

The metric system is the only system of measurement which, to my knowledge, has advanced to this stage.

Begin with an arbitrary measure of length, the meter (from the Latin *metrum* or the Greek *metron*, both meaning "to measure"). Leave that as the generic term for length, so that all units of length are meters. Differentiate one unit of length from another by means of an adjective. That in my opinion, would be fixing it up right.

To be sure, the adjectives in the metric system (lest they get lost by accident, I suppose) are firmly jointed to the generic word and thus become prefixes. (Yes, Gentle Reader, in doing this to the measurement system, they were "pre-fixing it up.")

The prefixes were obtained out of Greek and Latin in accordance with the following little table:

ENGLISH	GREEK	LATIN
thousand	chilioi	mille
hundred	hecaton	centum
ten	deka	decem

Now, if we save the Greek for the large units and the Latin for the small ones, we have:

1 kilometer *	equals	1000	meters
1 hectometer	equals	100	meters
1 dekameter	equals	10	meters
1 meter	equals	1	meter
1 decimeter	equals	0.1	meter
1 centimeter	equals	0.01	meter
1 millimeter	equals	0.001	meter

It doesn't matter how long a meter is; all the other units of length are as defined. If you happen to know the length of the meter in terms of yards or of wavelengths of light or of two marks on a stick, you automatically know the lengths of all the other units. Furthermore, by having all the sub-units vary by powers of ten, it becomes very easy (given our decimal number system) to convert one into another. For instance, I can tell you right off that there are exactly one million millimeters in a kilometer. Now you tell me right off how many inches there are in a mile.

And again, once you have the prefixes memorized, they will do for *any* type of measurement. If you are told that a "poise" is a measure of viscosity, it doesn't matter how large a unit it is or how it is related to other sorts of units or even what, exactly, viscosity is. Without knowing anything at all about it, you still know that a centipoise is equal to a hundredth of a poise, that a hectare is a hundred ares, that a decibel is a tenth of a bel; and even that a "kilobuck" is equal to a thousand dollars.**

In one respect and, to my mind, in only one were the French scientists who established the metric system in 1795 shortsighted. They did not go past the thousand mark in their prefix system.

---

* *The Greek* ch *has the guttural German* ch *sound. The French, who invented the metric system, have no such sound in their language and used k instead as the nearest approach. That is why* chilioi *becomes* kilo. *Since we don't have the guttural* ch *either, this suits us fine.*

** *If anyone wants to write that a millipede is a thousandth of a pede and that one centipede equals ten millipedes, by all means, do—but I won't listen.*

Perhaps they felt that once a convenient basic unit was selected for some measurable quantity, then a sub-unit a thousand times larger would be the largest useful one, while a sub-unit a thousandth as large would be the smallest. Or perhaps they were influenced by the fact that there is no single word in Latin for any number higher than a thousand. (Words like *million* and *billion* were invented in the late middle ages and in early modern times.)

The later Greeks, to be sure, used *myrias* for ten thousand, so it is possible to say "myriameter" for ten thousand meters, but this is hardly ever used. People say "ten kilometers" instead.

The net result, then, is that the metric system as organized originally offers prefixes that cover only six orders of magnitude. The largest unit, "kilo," is one million (10^6) times as great as the smallest unit "milli," and it is the exponent, 6, that marks the orders of magnitude.

Scientists could not, however, stand still for this. Six orders of magnitude may do for everyday life, but as the advance of instrumentation carried science into the very large and very small in almost every field of measurement, the system simply had to stretch.

Unofficial prefixes came into use for units above the kilo and below the milli and of course that meant the danger of nonconformity (which is a bad thing in scientific language). For instance, what we call a "Bev" (billion electron-volts), the British call a "Gev" (giga-electron-volts).

In 1958, then, an extended set of prefixes, at intervals of three orders of magnitude, was agreed upon by the International Committee on Weights and Measures in Paris. Here they are, with a couple of the older ones thrown in for continuity:

SIZE	PREFIX	GREEK ROOT
trillion (10^{12})	tera-	teras ("monster")
billion (10^9)	giga-	gigas ("giant")
million (10^6)	mega-	megas ("great")
thousand (10^3)	kilo-	
one (10^0)		
thousandth (10^{-3})	milli-	
millionth (10^{-6})	micro-	mikros ("small")
billionth (10^{-9})	nano-	nanos ("dwarf")
trillionth (10^{-12})	pico-	

The prefix *pico-* does not have a Greek root.

Well, then, we have a "picometer" as a trillionth of a meter, a "nanogram" as a billionth of a gram, a "gigasecond" as a billion seconds, and a "teradyne" as a trillion dynes. Since the largest unit, the tera, is 10^{24} times the smallest unit, the pico, the metric system now stretches not merely over 6, but over a full 24 orders of magnitude.

In 1962 *femto-* was added for a quadrillionth (10^{-15}) and *atto-* for a quintillionth (10^{-18}). Neither prefix has a Greek root.* This extends the metric system over 30 orders of magnitude.

Is this too much? Have we overdone it, perhaps? Well, let's see.

The metric unit of length is the meter. I won't go into the story of how it was fixed at its precise length, but that precise length in terms of familiar units is 1.093611 yards or 39.37 inches.

A kilometer, naturally, is a thousand times that, or 1093.6 yards, which comes out to 0.62137 mile. We won't be far off if we call a kilometer ⅝ of a mile. A mile is sometimes said to equal "twenty city blocks"; that is, the distance between, let us say, 59th Street and 79th Street in Manhattan. If so, a kilometer would represent 12½ city blocks, or the distance from halfway between 66th and 67th streets to 79th Street.

For a megameter we increase matters three orders of magnitude and it is equal to 621.37 miles. This is a convenient unit for planetary measurements. The air distance from Boston, Massachusetts, to San Francisco, California, is just about 4⅓ megameters. The diameter of the earth is 12¾ megameters and the circumference of the earth is about 40 megameters. And finally, the moon is 380 megameters from the earth.

Passing on to the gigameter, we have a unit 621,370 miles long, and this comes in handy for the nearer portions of the solar system. Venus at its closest is 42 gigameters away and Mars can approach us as closely as 58 gigameters. The sun is 145 gigameters from the earth and Jupiter, at its closest, is 640 gigameters distant; at its farthest, 930 gigameters away.

[* *I did not give the non-Greek roots when this article first appeared in November 1962, but I will now. Pico is from the Spanish word for "small." Femto and atto are from the Danish words for "fifteen" and "eighteen" respectively.*]

ANDROMEDA GALAXY

The Andromeda Galaxy, mentioned briefly in this article, has one unusual distinction. It is the farthest object that can be seen with the unaided eye—so if anyone asks you how far you can see (with glasses on, if you're near-sighted), tell him 2,300,000 light-years.

The Andromeda looks like a faint, fuzzy object of about the fourth magnitude. It is not likely to be noticed by a casual sky-gazer, but it was noted in the star maps of some of the Arab astronomers of the Middle Ages. The first to describe it among our Western astronomers was the German observer Simon Marius, in 1612.

In the next century, a French observer, Charles Messier, was interested in recording all the permanently fuzzy objects in the sky so that they not be mistaken for comets. (Messier was interested in comets.) The Andromeda was thirty-first on his list, and its alternate name, still often used, is M31.

In the simple telescopes of the 1700s, the Andromeda looked like a whirling cloud of gas, and the French astronomer Pierre Simon de Laplace thought that was indeed what it was. In a popular book on astronomy he wrote in the early 1800s, he made the suggestion in an appendix. Stars like our Sun and the planets that accompany them originated out of a whirling, condensing cloud of gas like that of the Andromeda. The Andromeda was then called Andromeda Nebula (from the Latin word for "cloud"), and Laplace's suggestion has always been called the "nebular hypothesis."

In recent years a vastly more sophisticated form of the nebular hypothesis has come to be accepted as the origin of the solar system, but the Andromeda is no cloud of gas. It is a collection of stars as large as, or larger than, our own Milky Way Galaxy, and farther beyond are billions of other galaxies.

The Granger Collection

Finally, by stretching to the limit of the newly extended metric system, we have the terameter, equal to 621,370,000 miles. This will allow us to embrace the entire solar system. The extreme width of Pluto's orbit, for instance, is not quite 12 terameters.

The solar system, however, is just a speck in the Galaxy. For measuring distances to the stars, the two most common units are the light-year and the parsec, and both are outside the metric system. What's more, even the new extension of the system can't reach them. The light-year is the distance that light travels in one year. This is about 5,880,000,000,000 miles or 9450 terameters. The parsec is the distance at which a star would appear to us to have a parallax of one second of arc (*par*allax-*sec*ond, get it), and that is equal to 3.26 light-years, or about 30,000 terameters.

Even these nonmetric units err on the small side. If one were to draw a sphere about the solar system with a radius of one parsec, not a single known star would be found within that sphere. The nearest stars, those of the Alpha Centauri system, are about 1.3 parsecs away. There are only thirty-three stars, out of a hundred billion or so in the Galaxy, closer to our sun than four parsecs, and of these only seven are visible to the naked eye.

There are many stars beyond this—far beyond this. The Galaxy as a whole has a diameter which is, at its longest, 30,000 parsecs. Of course, we might use the metric prefixes and say that the diameter of the Galaxy is 30 kiloparsecs.

But then the Galaxy is only a speck in the entire universe. The nearest extragalactic structures are the Magellanic Clouds, which are 50 kiloparsecs away, while the nearest full-size galaxy to our own is Andromeda, which is 700 kiloparsecs away. And there are hundreds of billions of galaxies beyond at a distance of many megaparsecs.

The farthest galaxies that have been made out have distances estimated at about two billion parsecs, which would mean that the entire visible universe, as of now, has a diameter of about 4 gigaparsecs.*

[* Since this article was written, quasars have been detected at distances of 4 gigaparsecs so the visible universe has a diameter of 8 gigaparsecs.]

Suppose, now, we consider the units of length in the other direction—toward the very small.

A micrometer is a good unit of length for objects visible under the ordinary optical microscope. The body cells, for instance, average about 4 micrometers in diameter. (A micrometer is often called a "micron.")

Drop down to the nanometer (often called a "millimicron") and it can be conveniently used to measure the wavelengths of visible light. The wavelength of the longest red light is 760 nanometers, while that of the shortest violet light is 380 nanometers. Ultraviolet light has a range of wavelengths from 380 nanometers down to 1 nanometer.

Shrinking the metric system still further, we have the picometer, or a trillionth of a meter. Individual atoms have diameters of from 100 to 600 picometers. And soft gamma rays have wavelengths of about 1 picometer.

The diameter of subatomic particles and the wavelengths of the hard gamma rays go well below the picometer level, however, reaching something like 1 femtometer.

The full range of lengths encountered by present-day science, from the diameter of the known universe at one extreme, to the diameter of a subatomic particle at the other, covers a range of 41 orders of magnitude. In other words, it would take 10^{41} protons laid side by side to stretch across the known universe.

What about mass?

The fundamental unit of mass in the metric system is the gram, a word derived from the Greek *gramma*, meaning a letter of the alphabet.* It is a small unit of weight, equivalent to $\frac{1}{28.35}$ ounces. A kilogram, or a thousand grams, is equal to 2.205 pounds, and a megagram is therefore equal to 2205 pounds.

The megagram is almost equal to the long ton (2240 pounds) in our own units, so it is sometimes called the "metric ton" or the "tonne." The latter gives it the French spelling, but doesn't do much in the way of differentiating the pronunciation, so I prefer metric ton.

---

* *The Greeks marked small weights with letters of the alphabet to indicate their weight, for they used letters to represent numbers, too.*

A gigagram is 1000 metric tons and a teragram is 1,000,000 metric tons and this is large enough by commercial standards. These don't even begin, however, to scratch the surface astronomically. Even a comparatively small body like the moon has a mass equal to 73 trillion teragrams. The earth is 81 times more massive and has a mass of nearly 6 quadrillion teragrams. And the sun, a merely average star, has a mass 330,000 times that of the earth.

Of course, we might use the sun itself as a unit of weight. For instance the Galaxy has a total mass equal to 150,000,000,000 times that of the sun, and we could therefore say that the mass of the Galaxy is equal to 150 gigasuns. Since it is also estimated that in the known universe there are *at least* 100,000,000,000 galaxies, then, assuming ours to be of average mass, that would mean a minimum total mass of the universe equal to 15,000,000,-000 terasuns or 100 gigagalaxies.

Suppose, now, we work in the other direction.

A milligram, or a thousandth of a gram, represents a quantity of matter easily visible to the naked eye. A drop of water would weigh about 50 milligrams.

Drop to a microgram, or a millionth of a gram, and we are in the microscopic range. An amoeba would weigh in the neighborhood of five micrograms.

The cells of our body are considerably smaller and for them we drop down to the nanogram, or a billionth of a gram. The average liver cell has a weight of about two nanograms.

Below the cells are the viruses, but even if we drop to the picogram, a trillionth of a gram, we do not reach that realm. The tobacco-mosaic virus, for instance, weighs only 66 attograms.

Nor is that particularly near the bottom of the scale. There are molecules far smaller than the smallest virus, and the atoms that make up the molecules and the particles that make up the atom. Consider the following table:

	WEIGHT IN ATTOGRAMS
hemoglobin molecule	0.1
uranium atom	0.0004
proton	0.00000166
electron	0.0000000009

All told, the range in mass from the electron to the minimum total mass of the known universe covers 83 orders of magnitude. In other words, it would take 10^{83} electrons to make a heap as massive as the total known universe.

In some ways, time (the third of the types of measurement I am considering) possesses the most familiar units, because that is the one place where the metric system introduced no modification at all. We still have the second, the minute, the hour, the day, the year, and so on.

This means, too, that the units of time are the only ones used by scientists that lack a systematic prefix system. The result is that you cannot tell, offhand, the number of seconds in a week or the number of minutes in a year or the number of days in fifteen years. Neither can scientists.

The fundamental unit of time is the second and we could, if we wished, build the metric prefixes on those as follows:

1 second	equals	1	second
1 kilosecond	equals	16⅔	minutes
1 megasecond	equals	11⅔	days
1 gigasecond	equals	32	years
1 terasecond	equals	32,000	years

It is sobering to think that I have lived only a little over 1¼ gigaseconds *; that civilization has existed for at most about 250 gigaseconds; and that man-like creatures may not have existed for more than 18 teraseconds altogether. Still, that doesn't make much of an inroad into geologic time and even less of an inroad into astronomic time.

The solar system has been in existence for about 150,000 teraseconds and may well remain in existence without major change for 500,000 additional teraseconds. The smaller the star, the more carefully it hoards its fuel supply and a red dwarf may last without undue change for as long as 3,000,000 teraseconds. As for the total age of the universe, past and future, I say nothing. There is

[* *Since this article first appeared, my age has increased to 1¾ giga-seconds, alas, but never mind, it's better than the alternative.*]

AMOEBA

The amoeba is a one-celled animal and in usually considered the most primitive of the type. It has no fixed shape as other one-celled animals ("protozoa") have but can bulge at any point to form a "pseudopod" (Greek for "false foot"). It moves by means of these pseudopods and that is considered the most primitive form of animal locomotion.

The fact that its shape is not fixed, but is changeable, is the basis of its name, which is from the Greek word for "change." The particular species of amoeba we commonly mean when the name is used without qualification is "Amoeba proteus" which is found on decaying organic matter in streams and ponds. The word "proteus" is the name of a Greek demigod who could change his shape at will.

There are numerous other species of amoeba, some of which are parasitic, and six of which can parasitize man. One of them, Entamoeba histolytica *("amoeba-within; cell-dissolving"), causes amoebic dysentery.*

Although the amoeba is mentioned in the article as the type of small organism, it is not (as also indicated) a small cell. The amoeba must, within its single cell, include all the machinery for the essential functions of life. A human cell, far more specialized, can afford to be smaller. Thus, an amoeba has 2,400 times the volume of a typical body cell and about 25,000 times the volume of the smallest human cell, the spermatozoon.

The smallest free-living cells are the bacteria, and the amoeba has 210,000,000 times the volume of the smallest bacteria.

The smallest objects that can be considered alive (although they function only within cells they parasitize) are the viruses. The amoeba has 2,400,000,000,000 the volume of the smallest virus. The amoeba is as large to that smallest virus as we are to the amoeba.

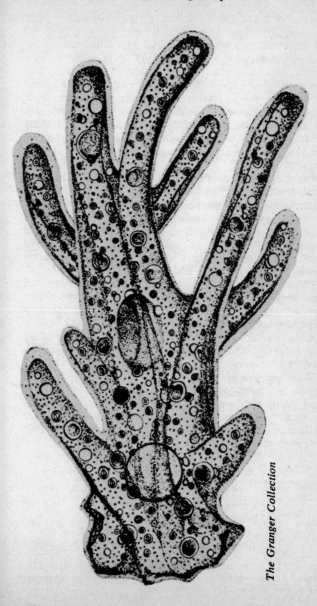

The Granger Collection

no way of estimating, and the continuous-creation boys consider its lifetime to be eternal.*

I have one suggestion to make for astronomic time, however (a suggestion which I don't think is particularly original with me). The sun, according to reasonable estimates, revolves about the galactic center once every 200,000,000 years. This we could call a "galactic year" or, better, a "gal-year." (An ugly word, but never mind!) One galyear is equal to 6250 teraseconds. On the other hand, a "picogalyear" is equal to 1 hour and 45 minutes.

If we stick to galyears then, the entire fossil record covers at most only 3 galyears; the total life of the solar system thus far is only 25 galyears; and the total life of a red dwarf as a red dwarf is perhaps 500 galyears.

But now I've got to try the other direction, too, and see what happens for small units of time. Here at least there are no common units to confuse us. Scientists have therefore been able to use *millisecond* and *microsecond* freely, and now they can join to that *nanosecond, picosecond, femtosecond,* and *attosecond*.

These small units of time aren't very useful in the macroscopic world. When a Gagarin or a Glenn circles the earth at 5 miles a second, he travels less than 9 yards in a millisecond and less than a third of an inch in a microsecond. The earth itself, moving at a velocity of 18½ miles a second in its travels about the sun, moves only a little over an inch in a microsecond.

In other words, at the microsecond level, ordinary motion is frozen out. However, the motion of light is more rapid than any ordinary motion, while the motion of some speeding subatomic particles is nearly as rapid as that of light. Therefore, let's consider the small units of time in terms of light.

DISTANCE COVERED BY LIGHT

1 second	186,200	miles
1 millisecond	186	miles
1 microsecond	327	yards
1 nanosecond	1	foot
1 picosecond	1/80	inch

[* *Since this article was written, the continuous creation theory has about been wiped out, and it isn't likely that the Universe, in its present form, at least, is eternal.*]

Now, you may think that at picosecond levels subatomic motion and even light-propagation is "frozen." After all, I dismissed earth's motion as "frozen" when it moved an inch. How much more so, then, when thousandths of an inch are in question.

However, there is a difference. The earth, in moving an inch, moves 1/500,000,000 of its own diameter. A speeding subatomic particle moving at almost the speed of light for a distance 1/80 of an inch moves 120,000,000,000 times its own diameter. To travel a hundred and twenty billion times its own diameter, the earth would have to keep on going for 1,500,000 years. For Gagarin or Glenn to have traveled for a hundred and twenty billion times their own diameter, they would have had to stay in orbit a full year.

A subatomic particle traveling 1/80 of an inch is therefore anything but "frozen," and has time to make a fabulous number of collisions with other subatomic particles or to undergo internal changes. As an example, neutral pions break down in a matter of 0.1 femtosecond after formation.

What's more, the omega-meson breaks down in something like 0.0001 attosecond or, roughly, the time it would take light to cross the diameter of an atomic nucleus and back.

The entire range of time, then, from the lifetime of an omega-meson to that of a red-dwarf star covers a range of 40 orders of magnitude. In other words, during the normal life of a red dwarf, some 10^{40} omega-mesons have time to come into existence and break down, one after the other.

To summarize, the measurable lengths cover a range of 41 order of magnitude, the measurable masses 83 orders of magnitude, and the measurable times 40 orders of magnitude. Clearly, we are not overdoing it in expanding the metric system from 6 to 30 orders of magnitude.

Part IV

NUMBERS AND
THE CALENDAR

11 THE
DAYS OF
OUR YEARS

A GROUP of us meet for an occasional evening of talk and nonsense, followed by coffee and doughnuts and one of the group scored a coup by persuading a well-known entertainer to attend the session. The well-known entertainer made one condition, however. He was not to entertain, or even be asked to entertain. This was agreed to.*

Now there arose a problem. If the meeting were left to its own devices, someone was sure to begin badgering the entertainer. Consequently, other entertainment had to be supplied, so one of the boys turned to me and said, "Say, you know what?"

I knew what and I objected at once. I said, "How can I stand up there and talk with everyone staring at this other fellow in the audience and wishing *he* were up there instead? You'd be throwing me to the wolves!"

But they all smiled very toothily and told me about the wonderful talks I give. (Somehow everyone quickly discovers the fact that I soften into putty as soon as the flattery is turned on.) In no time at all, I agreed to be

---

[* *I didn't name the entertainer when this article first appeared in August 1964, because I thought he wouldn't want me to. I was wrong, because when I met him again months later and asked for his autograph, he wrote "To Isaac, with best wishes, from a well-known entertainer."*]

thrown to the wolves. Surprisingly, it worked, which speaks highly for the audience's intellect—or perhaps their magnanimity.

As it happened, the meeting was held on "leap day" and so my topic of conversation was ready-made and the gist of it went as follows:

I suppose there's no question but that the earliest unit of time-telling was the day. It forces itself upon the awareness of even the most primitive of humanoids. However, the day is not convenient for long intervals of time. Even allowing a primitive lifespan of thirty years, a man would live some 11,000 days and it is very easy to lose track among all those days.

Since the Sun governs the day-unit, it seems natural to turn to the next most prominent heavenly body, the Moon, for another unit. One offers itself at once, ready-made— the period of the phases. The Moon waxes from nothing to a full Moon and then to nothing in a definite period of time. This period of time is called the "month" in English (clearly from the word "moon") or more specifically, the "lunar month," since we have other months, representing periods of time slightly shorter or slightly longer than the one that is strictly tied to the phases of the moon.

The lunar month is roughly equal to 29½ days. More exactly, it is equal to 29 days, 12 hours, 44 minutes, 2.8 seconds, or 29.5306 days.

In pre-agricultural times, it may well have been that no special significance attached itself to the month, which remained only a convenient device for measuring moderately long periods of time. The life expectancy of primitive man was probably something like 350 months, which is a much more convenient figure than that of 11,000 days.

In fact, there has been speculation that the extended lifetimes of the patriarchs reported in the fifth chapter of the Book of Genesis may have arisen out of a confusion of years with lunar months. For instance, suppose Methuselah had lived 969 lunar months. This would be just about 79 years, a very reasonable figure. However, once that got twisted to 969 years by later tradition we gained the "old as Methuselah" bit.

However, I mention this only in passing, for this idea

is not really taken seriously by any biblical scholars. It is much more likely that these lifetimes are a hangover from Babylonian tradition about the times before the Flood. . . . But I am off the subject.

It is my feeling that the month gained a new and enhanced importance with the introduction of agriculture. An agricultural society was much more closely and precariously tied to the seasons than a hunting or herding society was. Nomads could wander in search of grain or grass but farmers had to stay where they were and hope for rain. To increase their chances, farmers had to be certain to sow at a proper time to take advantage of seasonal rains and seasonal warmth; and a mistake in the sowing period might easily spell disaster. What's more, the development of agriculture made possible a denser population, and that intensified the scope of the possible disaster.

Man had to pay attention, then, to the cycle of seasons, and while he was still in the prehistoric stage he must have noted that those seasons came full cycle in roughly twelve months. In other words, if crops were planted at a particular time of the year and all went well, then if twelve months were counted from the first planting and crops were planted again, all would again go well.

Counting the months can be tricky in a primitive society, especially when a miscount can be ruinous, so it isn't surprising that the count was usually left in the hands of a specialized caste, the priesthood. The priests could not only devote their time to accurate counting, but could also use their experience and skill to propitiate the gods. After all, the cycle of the seasons was by no means as rigid and unvarying as was the cycle of day and night or the cycle of the phases of the moon. A late frost or a failure of rain could blast that season's crops, and since such flaws in weather were bound to follow any little mistake in ritual (at least so men often believed), the priestly functions were of importance indeed.

It is not surprising then, that the lunar month grew to have enormous religious significance. There were new Moon festivals and special priestly proclamations of each one of them, so that the lunar month came to be called the "synodic month."

The cycle of seasons is called the "year" and twelve lunar months therefore make up a "lunar year." The use

THE CRESCENT MOON

The crescent Moon, which marked the beginning of the month in ancient times, together with the remaining phases of the Moon, was responsible for the birth of astronomy, for surely the regularly changing shape of the Moon was the first object in the sky that roused man's curiosity. The necessities and value of calendar-making must have urged man on to develop mathematics and religion out of the lunar cycle.

There was something else, too. . . .

The ancient Greek philosophers found it aesthetically satisfying to divide the Universe into two parts: the Earth and the heavenly bodies. To do so, they sought for fundamental differences in properties. Thus: The heavenly bodies were all luminous, while the earth was nonluminous.

The Moon, however, had to be an exception to this general rule. The relationship of the phases of the Moon to the relative positions of the Moon and Sun made it clear even in ancient times that the Moon shone only by reflected sunlight. That meant that, of its own, the Moon was as dull and nonluminous as the Earth.

What's more, when the Moon is in its crescent phase and is just a thin sliver of curling light, as in the illustration, the rest of the Moon is sometimes seen shining with a dim ruddy light of its own. Galileo pointed out that from the Moon, the Earth was seen in the full phase and that the Moon was shining dimly in Earthlight. Earth, too, reflected light and was as luminous as the Moon.

Then, too, the ancient Greeks had already determined the distance of the Moon quite accurately, and it could be seen to be a world of some two thousand miles in diameter to appear to be as large as it seemed from that distance. In short, thanks to the Moon, naked-eye astronomy sufficed to establish the doctrine of "plurality of worlds," for if the Moon was a world so might many other heavenly bodies be.

of lunar years in measuring time is referred to as the use of a "lunar calendar." The only important group of people in modern times, using a strict lunar calendar, are the Mohammedans. Each of the Mohammedan years is made up of 12 months which are, in turn, usually made up of 29 and 30 days in alternation.

Such months average 29.5 days, but the length of the true lunar month is, as I've pointed out, 29.5306 days. The lunar year built up out of twelve 29.5-day months is 354 days long, whereas twelve lunar months are actually 354.37 days long.

You may say "So what" but don't. A true lunar year should always start on the day of the new Moon. If, however, you start one lunar year on the new Moon and then simply alternate 29-day and 30-day months, the third year will start the day before the new Moon, and the sixth year will start two days before the new Moon. To properly religious people, this would be unthinkable.

Now it so happens that 30 true lunar years come out to be almost exactly an even number of days—10,631.016. Thirty years built up out of 29.5-day months come to 10,620 days—just 11 days short of keeping time with the Moon. For that reason, the Mohammedans scatter 11 days through the 30 years in some fixed pattern which prevents any individual years from starting as much as a full day ahead or behind the New Moon. In each 30-year cycle there are nineteen 354-day years and eleven 355-day years, and the calendar remains even with the Moon.

An extra day, inserted in this way to keep the calendar even with the movements of a heavenly body, is called an "intercalary day"; a day inserted "between the calendar," so to speak.

The lunar year, whether it is 354 or 355 days in length, does not, however, match the cycle of the seasons. By the dawn of historic times the Babylonian astronomers had noted that the Sun moved against the background of stars. This passage was followed with absorption because it grew apparent that a complete circle of the sky by the Sun matched the complete cycle of the seasons closely. (This apparent influence of the stars on the seasons probably started the Babylonian fad of astrology —which is still with us today.)

The Sun makes its complete cycle about the zodiac in roughly 365 days, so that the lunar year is about 11 days shorter than the season-cycle, or "solar-year." Three lunar years fall 33 days, or a little more than a full month, behind the season-cycle.

This is important. If you use a lunar calendar and start it so that the first day of the year is planting time, then three years later you are planting a month too soon, and by the time a decade has passed you are planting in midwinter. After 33 years the first day of the year is back where it is supposed to be, having traveled through the entire solar year.

This is exactly what happens in the Mohammedan year. The ninth month of the Mohammedan year is named Ramadan, and it is especially holy because it was the month in which Mohammed began to receive the revelation of the Koran. In Ramadan, therefore, Moslems abstain from food and water during the day-light hours. But each year, Ramadan falls a bit earlier in the cycle of the seasons, and at 3-year intervals it is to be found in the hot season of the year; at this time abstaining from drink is particularly wearing, and Moslem tempers grow particularly short.

The Mohammedan years are numbered from the Hegira; that is, from the date when Mohammed fled from Mecca to Medina. That event took place in A.D. 622. Ordinarily, you might suppose, therefore, that to find the number of the Mohammendan year, one need only subtract 622 from the number of the Christian year. This is not quite so, since the Mohammedan year is shorter than ours. I write this chapter in A.D. 1964 and it is now 1342 solar years since the Hegira. However, it is 1384 lunar years since the Hegira, so that, as I write, the Moslem year is A.H. 1384.

I've calculated that the Mohammedan year will catch up to the Christian year in about nineteen millennia. The year A.D. 20,874 will also be A.H. 20,874, and the Moslems will then be able to switch to our year with a minimum of trouble.

But what can we do about the lunar year in order to make it keep even with the seasons and the solar year? We can't just add 11 days at the end, for then the next year would not start with the new Moon and to the ancient Babylonians, for instance, a new Moon start was essential.

However, if we start a solar year with the new Moon and wait, we will find that the twentieth solar year thereafter starts once again on the day of the new Moon. You see, 19 solar years contain just about 235 lunar months.

Concentrate on those 235 lunar months. That is equivalent to 19 lunar years (made up of 12 lunar months each) plus 7 lunar months left over. We could, then, if we wanted to, let the lunar years progress as the Mohammedans do, until 19 such years had passed. At this time the calendar would be exactly 7 months behind the seasons, and by adding 7 months to the 19th year (a 19th year of 19 months—very neat) we could start a new 19-year cycle, exactly even with both the Moon and the seasons.

The Babylonians were unwilling, however, to let themselves fall 7 months behind the season. Instead, they added that 7-month discrepancy through the 19-year cycle, one month at a time and as nearly evenly as possible. Each cycle had twelve 12-month years and seven 13-month years. The "intercalary month" was added in the 3rd, 6th, 8th, 11th, 14th, 17th, and 19th year of each cycle, so that the year was never more than about 20 days behind or ahead of the Sun.

Such a calendar, based on the lunar months, but gimmicked so as to keep up with the Sun, is a "lunar-solar calendar."

The Babylonian lunar-solar calendar was popular in ancient times since it adjusted the seasons while preserving the sanctity of the Moon. The Hebrews and Greeks both adopted this calendar and, in fact, it is still the basis for the Jewish calendar today. The individual dates in the Jewish calendar are allowed to fall slightly behind the Sun until the intercalary month is added, when they suddenly shoot slightly ahead of the Sun. That is why holidays like Passover and Yom Kippur occur on different days of the civil calendar (kept strictly even with the Sun) each year. These holidays occur on the same day of the year each year in the Jewish calendar.

The early Christians continued to use the Jewish calendar for three centuries, and established the day of Easter on that basis. As the centuries passed, matters grew somewhat complicated, for the Romans (who were becoming Christian in swelling numbers) were no longer used to a lunar-solar calendar and were puzzled at the erratic jumping about of Easter. Some formula had to be found by which the correct date for Easter could be calculated in advance, using the Roman calendar.

It was decided at the Council of Nicaea, in A.D. 325 (by which time Rome had become officially Christian), that Easter was to fall on the Sunday after the first full Moon after the vernal equinox, the date of the vernal equinox being established as March 21. However, the full Moon referred to is not the actual full Moon, but a fictitious one called the "Paschal Full Moon" ("Paschal" being derived from *Pesach,* which is the Hebrew word for Passover). The date of the Paschal Full Moon is calculated according to a formula involving Golden Numbers and Dominical Letters, which I won't go into.

The result is that Easter still jumps about the days of the civil year and can fall as early as March 22 and as late as April 25. Many other church holidays are tied to Easter and likewise move about from year to year.

Moreover, all Christians have not always agreed on the exact formula by which the date of Easter was to be calculated. Disagreement on this detail was one of the reasons for the schism between the Catholic Church of the West and the Orthodox Church of the East. In the early Middle Ages there was a strong Celtic Church which had its own formula.

Our own calendar is inherited from Egypt, where seasons were unimportant. The one great event of the year was the Nile flood, and this took place (on the average) every 365 days. From a very early date, certainly as early as 2781 B.C., the Moon was abandoned and a "solar calendar," adapted to a constant-length 365-day year, was adopted.

The solar calendar kept to the tradition of 12 months, however. As the year was of constant length, the months were of constant length, too—30 days each. This meant that the new Moon could fall on any day of the month, but the Egyptians didn't care. (A month not based on the Moon is a "calendar month.")

Of course 12 months of 30 days each add up only to 360 days, so at the end of each 12-month cycle, 5 additional days were added and treated as holidays.

The solar year, however, is not exactly 365 days long. There are several kinds of solar years, differing slightly in length, but the one upon which the seasons depend is the "tropical year," and this is about 365¼ days long.

This means that each year, the Egyptian 365-day year falls ¼ day behind the Sun. As time went on the Nile flood occurred later and later in the year, until finally it had made a complete circuit of the year. In 1460 tropical years, in other words, there would be 1461 Egyptian years.

This period of 1461 Egyptian years was called the "Sothic cycle," from Sothis, the Egyptian name for the star Sirius. If, at the beginning of one Sothic cycle, Sirius rose with the Sun on the first day of the Egyptian year, it would rise later and later during each succeeding year until finally, 1461 Egyptian years later, a new cycle would begin as Sothis rose with the Sun on New Year's Day once more.

The Greeks had learned about that extra quarter day as early as 380 B.C., when Eudoxus of Cnidus made the discovery. In 239 B.C. Ptolemy Euergetes, the Macedonian king of Egypt, tried to adjust the Egyptian calendar to take that quarter day into account, but the ultra-conservative Egyptians would have none of such a radical innovation.

Meanwhile, the Roman Republic had a lunar-solar calendar, one in which an intercalary month was added every once in a while. The priestly officials in charge were elected politicians, however, and were by no means as conscientious as those in the East. The Roman priests added a month or not according to whether they wanted a long year (when the other annually elected officials in power were of their own party) or a short one (when they were not). By 46 B.C., the Roman calendar was 80 days behind the Sun.

Julius Caesar was in power then and decided to put an end to this nonsense. He had just returned from Egypt where he had observed the convenience and simplicity of a solar year, and he imported an Egyptian astronomer, Sosigenes, to help him. Together, they let 46 B.C. continue for 445 days so that it was later known as "The Year of Confusion." However, this brought the calendar even with the Sun so that 46 B.C. was the *last* year of confusion.

With 45 B.C. the Romans adopted a modified Egyptian calendar in which the five extra days at the end of the year were distributed throughout the year, giving us our months of uneven length. Ideally, we should have seven 30-day months and five 31-day months. Unfortunately the Romans considered February an unlucky month and shortened it, so that we ended with a silly arrangement of seven 31-day months, four 30-day months, and one 28-day month.

In order to take care of that extra ¼ day, Caesar and Sosigenes established every fourth year with a length of 366 days. (Under the numbering of the years of the Christian era, every year divisible by 4 has the intercalary day—set as February 29. Since 1964 divided by 4 is 491, without a remainder, there is a February 29 in 1964.)

This is the "Julian year," after Julius Caesar. At the Council of Nicaea, the Christian Church adopted the Julian calendar. Christmas was finally accepted as a Church holiday *after* the Council of Nicaea and was therefore given a date in the Julian year. It does not, therefore, bounce about from year to year as Easter does.

The 365-day year is just 52 weeks and 1 day long. This means that if February 6, for instance, is on a Sunday in one year, it is on a Monday the next year, on a Tuesday the year after, and so on. If there were only 365-day years, then any given date would move through the days of the week in steady progression. If a 366-day year is involved, however, that year is 52 weeks and 2 days long, and if February 6 is on Tuesday that year, it is on Thursday the year after. The day has leaped over Wednesday. It is for that reason that the 366-day year is called "leap year" and February 29 is "leap day."

All would have been well if the tropical year were really exactly 365.25 days long; but it isn't. The tropical year is 365 days, 5 hours, 48 minutes, 46 seconds, or 365.24220 days long. The Julian year is, on the average, 11 minutes 14 seconds, or 0.0078 day, too long.

This may not seem much, but it means that the Julian year gains a full day on the tropical year in 128 years. As the Julian year gains, the vernal equinox, falling behind, comes earlier and earlier in the year. At the Council of Nicaea in A.D. 325, the vernal equinox was on March 21. By A.D. 453 it was on March 20, by A.D. 581 on March 19, and so on. By A.D. 1263, in the lifetime of

JULIUS CAESAR

Julius Caesar, for whom the Julian calendar is named, is, of course, far better known among the general public for many other reasons.

He was born in 102 B.C., and he was just about the most remarkable man of ancient times. He was a man of enormous courage, a playboy and wastrel, who, in middle life, turned to leading armies and proved himself to be a great general who never lost a battle. He was a great orator, second only to Cicero among the Romans, and a great writer. And he was a successful politician.

His charm was legendary. In 76 B.C. he set sail for the island of Rhodes in order to study under the best Greek teachers. On the way, he was captured by pirates who held him for ransom of about $100,000 in modern money. While the money was being scraped up by friends and relatives, Caesar charmed his captors and had a great time with them. While they were engaged in friendly conversation, Caesar told them that once he was set free, he would return with a fleet and hang every one of them. The pirates laughed at the joke, and when Caesar was paid for and freed, he did indeed return with a fleet and hang them all.

With the Roman Republic slowly decaying as it proved increasingly difficult to rule the empire it had gathered, Caesar engaged in civil war (in the course of which he entered Egypt and had a famous love affair with Cleopatra) and finally emerged as sole ruler and dictator of the Roman realm.

Here was where his own great failing showed up. He firmly believed an enemy forgiven was an enemy destroyed. He forgave many who had fought on the other side and gave them high positions in the state. They conspired against him, and on March 15, 44 B.C. (the Ides of March), they assassinated him.

Roger Bacon, the Julian year had gained eight days on the Sun and the vernal equinox was on March 13.

Still not fatal, but the Church looked forward to an indefinite future and Easter was tied to a vernal equinox at March 21. If this were allowed to go on, Easter would come to be celebrated in midsummer, while Christmas would edge into the spring. In 1263, therefore, Roger Bacon wrote a letter to Pope Urban IV explaining the situation. The Church, however, took over three centuries to consider the matter.

By 1582 the Julian calendar had gained two more days and the vernal equinox was falling on March 11. Pope Gregory XIII finally took action. First, he dropped ten days, changing October 5, 1852 to October 15, 1582. That brought the calendar even with the Sun and the vernal equinox in 1583 fell on March 21 as the Council of Nicaea had decided it should.

The next step was to prevent the calendar from getting out of step again. Since the Julian year gains a full day every 128 years, it gains three full days in 384 years or, to approximate slightly, three full days in four centuries. That means that every 400 days, three leap years (according to the Julian system) ought to be omitted.

Consider the century years—1500, 1600, 1700, and so on. In the Julian year, all century years are divisible by 4 and are therefore leap years. Every 400 years there are 4 such century years, so why not keep 3 of them ordinary years, and allow only one of them (the one that is divisible by 400) to be a leap year? This arrangement will match the year more closely to the Sun and give us the "Gregorian calendar."

To summarize: Every 400 years, the Julian calendar allows 100 leap years for a total of 146,100 days. In that same 400 years, the Gregorian calendar allows only 97 leap years for a total of 146,097 days. Compare these lengths with that of 400 tropical years, which comes to 146,096.88. Whereas, in that stretch of time, the Julian year had gained 3.12 days on the Sun, the Gregorian year had gained only 0.12 day.

Still, 0.12 day is nearly 3 hours, and this means that in 3400 years the Gregorian calendar will have gained a full day on the Sun. Around A.D. 5000 we will have to consider dropping out one extra leap year.

But the Church had waited a little too long to take action. Had it done the job a century earlier, all western Europe would have changed calendars without trouble. By A.D. 1582, however, much of northern Europe had turned Protestant. These nations would far sooner remain out of step with the Sun in accordance with the dictates of the pagan Caesar, than consent to be corrected by the Pope. Therefore they kept the Julian year.

The year 1600 introduced no crisis. It was a century year but one that was divisible by 400. Therefore, it was a leap year by both the Julian and Gregorian calendars. But 1700 was a different matter. The Julian calendar had it as a leap year and the Gregorian did not. By March 1, 1700, the Julian calendar was going to be an additional day ahead of the Sun (eleven days altogether). Denmark, the Netherlands, and Protestant Germany gave in and adopted the Gregorian calendar.

Great Britain and the American colonies held out until 1752 before giving in. Because of the additional day gained in 1700, they had to drop eleven days and changed September 2, 1752 to September 13, 1752. There were riots all over England as a result, for many people came quickly to the conclusion that they had suddenly been made eleven days older by legislation.

"Give us back our eleven days!" they cried in despair.

(A more rational objection was the fact that although the third quartetr of 1752 was short eleven days, land-lords calmly charged a full quarter's rent.)

As a result of this, it turns out that Washington was not born on "Washington's birthday." He was born on February 22, 1732 on the Gregorian calendar, to be sure, but the date recorded in the family Bible had to be the Julian date, February 11, 1732. When the changeover took place, Washington—a remarkably sensible man— changed the date of his birthday and thus preserved the actual day.

The Eastern Orthodox nations of Europe were more stubborn than the Protestant nations. The years 1800 and 1900 went by. Both were leap years by the Julian calendar, but not by the Gregorian calendar. By 1900, then, the Julian vernal equinox was on March 8 and the Julian calendar was 13 days ahead of the Sun. It was not until after World War I that the Soviet Union, for instance, adopted the Gregorian calendar. (In doing so, the Soviets made a slight modification of the leap year pattern which made matters even more accurate. The Soviet calendar will not gain a day on the Sun until fully 35,000 years pass.)

Some of the Orthodox churches, however, *still* cling to the Julian year, which is why the Orthodox Christmas falls on January 6 on our calendar. It is still December 25 by their calendar.

In fact, a horrible thought occurs to me—

I was myself born at a time when the Julian calendar was still in force in the—ahem—old country.* Unlike George Washington, I never changed the birthdate and, as a result, each year I celebrate my birthday 13 days earlier than I should, making myself 13 days older than I have to be.

And this 13-day older me is in all the records and I can't ever change it back.

Give me back my 13 days! Give me back my 13 days! Give me back . . .

---

* Well, the Soviet Union, if you must know. I came here at the age of 3.

12 BEGIN AT THE BEGINNING

EACH year, another New Year's Day falls upon us; and because my birthday follows hard upon New Year's Day, the beginning of the year is always a doubled occasion for great and somber soul-searching on my part.

Perhaps I can make my consciousness of passing time less poignant by thinking more objectively. For instance, who says the year starts on New Year's Day? What is there about New Year's Day that is different from any other day? What makes January 1 so special?

In fact, when we chop up time into any kind of units, how do we decide with which unit to start?

For instance, let's begin at the beginning (as I dearly love to do) and consider the day itself.

The day is composed of two parts, the daytime * and the night. Each, separately, has a natural astronomic beginning. The daytime begins with sunrise; the night begins with sunset. (Dawn and twilight encroach upon the night but that is a mere detail.)

---

* It is very annoying that "day" means both the sunlit portion of time and the twenty-four-hour period of daytime and night together. This is a completely unnecessary shortcoming of the admirable English language. I understand that the Greek language contains separate words for the two entities. I shall use "daytime" for the sunlit period and "day" for the twenty-four-hour period.

181

In the latitudes in which most of humanity live, however, both daytime and night change in length during the year (one growing longer as the other grows shorter) and there is, therefore, a certain convenience in using daytime plus night as a single twenty-four-hour unit of time. The combination of the two, the day, is of nearly constant duration.

Well, then, should the day start at sunrise or at sunset? You might argue for the first, since in a primitive society that is when the workday begins. On the other hand, in that same society sunset is when the workday ends, and surely an ending means a new beginning.

Some groups made one decision and some the other. The Egyptians, for instance, began the day at sunrise, while the Hebrews began it at sunset.

The latter state of affairs is reflected in the very first chapter of Genesis in which the days of creation are described. In Genesis 1:5 it is written: "And the evening and the morning were the first day." Evening (that is, night) comes ahead of morning (that is, daytime) because the day starts at sunset.

This arrangement is maintained in Judaism to this day, and Jewish holidays still begin "the evening before." Christianity began as an offshoot of Judaism and remnants of this sunset beginning cling even now to some non-Jewish holidays.

The expression Chritmas Eve, if taken literally, is the evening of December 25, but as we all know it really means the evening of December 24—which it would naturally mean if Christmas began "the evening before" as a Jewish holiday would. The same goes for New Year's Eve.

Another familiar example is All Hallows' Eve, the evening of the day before All Hallows' Day, which is given over to the commemoration of all the "hallows" (or "saints"). All Hallows' Day is on November 1, and All Hallows' Eve is therefore on the evening of October 31. Need I tell you that All Hallows' Eve is better known by its familiar contracted form of "Halloween."

As a matter of fact, though, neither sunset nor sunrise is now the beginning of the day. The period from sunrise to sunrise is slightly more than 24 hours for half the year as the daytime periods grow shorter, and slightly less than 24 hours for the remaining half of the year as the daytime periods grow longer. This is also true for the period from sunset to sunset.

Sunrise and sunset change in opposite directions, either approaching each other or receding from each other, so that the middle of daytime (midday) and the middle of night (midnight) remain fixed at 24-hour intervals throughout the year. (Actually, there are minor deviations but these can be ignored.)

One can begin the day at midday and count on a steady 24-hour cycle, but then the working period is split between two different dates. Far better to start the day at midnight when all decent people are asleep; and that, in fact, is what we do.

Astronomers, who are among the indecent minority not in bed asleep at midnight, long insisted on starting their day at midday so as not to break up a night's observation into two separate dates. However, the spirit of conformity was not to be withstood, and in 1925, they accepted the inconvenience of a beginning at midnight in order to get into step with the rest of the world.

All the units of time that are shorter than a day depend on the day and offer no problem. You start counting the hours from the beginning of the day; you start counting the minutes from the beginning of the hours, and so on.

Of course, when the start of the day changed its position, that affected the counting of the hours. Originally, the daytime and the night were each divided into twelve hours, beginning at, respectively, sunrise and sunset. The hours changed length with the change in length of daytime and night so that in June (in the northern hemisphere) the daytime was made up of twelve long hours and the night of twelve short hours, while in December the situation was reversed.

This manner of counting the hours still survives in the Catholic Church as "canonical hours." Thus, "prime" ("one") is the term for 6 A.M. "Tierce" ("three") is 9 A.M., "sext" ("six") is 12 A.M., and "none" ("nine") is 3 P.M. Notice that "none" is located in the middle of the afternoon when the day is warmest. The warmest part of the day might well be felt to be the middle of the day, and the word was somehow switched to the astronomic midday so that we call 12 A.M. "noon."

This older method of counting the hours also plays a part in one of the parables of Jesus (Matt. 20:1-16), in which laborers are hired at various times of the day, up to and including "the eleventh hour." The eleventh hour referred to in the parable is one hour before sunset when the working day ends. For that reason, "the eleventh hour" has come to mean the last moment in which something can be done. The force of the expression is lost on us, however, for we think of the eleventh hour as being either 11 A.M. or 11 P.M., and 11 A.M. is too early in the day to begin a feel panicky, while 11 P.M. is too late—we ought to be asleep by then.

The week originated in the Babylonian calendar where one day out of seven was devoted to rest. (The rationale was that it was an unlucky day.)

The Jews, captive in Babylon in the sixth century B.C., picked up the notion and established it on a religious basis, making it a day of happiness rather than of ill fortune. They explained its beginnings in Genesis 2:2 where, after the work of the six days of creation—"on the seventh day God ended his work which he had made; and he rested on the seventh day."

To those societies which accept the Bible as a book of special significance, the Jewish "sabbath" (from the Hebrew word for "rest") is thus defined as the seventh, and last, day of the week. This day is the one marked Saturday on our calendars, and Sunday, therefore, is the first day of a new week. All our calendars arrange the days in seven columns with Sunday first and Saturday seventh.

The early Christians began to attach special significance to the first day of the week. For one thing, it was the "Lord's day" since the Resurrection had taken place on a Sunday. Then, too, as time went on and Christians began to think of themselves as something more than a Jewish sect, it became important to them to have distinct rituals of their own. In Christian societies, therefore, Sunday, and not Saturday, became the day of rest. (Of course, in our modern effete times, Saturday and Sunday are *both* days of rest, and are lumped together as the "weekend," a period celebrated by automobile accidents.)

The fact that the work week begins on Monday causes a great many people to think of that as the first day of the week, and leads to the following children's puzzle (which I mention only because it trapped me neatly the first time I heard it).

You ask your victim to pronounce t-o, t-o-o, and t-w-o, one at a time, thinking deeply between questions. In each case he says (wondering what's up) "tooooo."

Then you say, "Now pronounce the second day of the week" and his face clears up, for he thinks he sees the trap. He is sure you are hoping he will say "toooosday" like a lowbrow. With exaggerated precision, therefore, he says "tyoosday."

At which you look gently puzzled and say, "Isn't that strange? I always pronounce it Monday."

The month, being tied to the Moon, began, in ancient times, at a fixed phase. In theory, any phase will do. The month can start at each full Moon, or each first quarter, and so on. Actually, the most logical way is to begin each month with the new Moon—that is, on that evening when the first sliver of the growing crescent makes itself visible immediately after sunset. To any logical primitive, a new Moon is clearly being created at that time and the month should start then.

Nowadays, however, the month is freed of the Moon and is tied to the year, which is in turn based on the Sun. In our calendar, in ordinary years, the first month begins on the first day of the year, the second month on the 32nd day of the year, the third month on the 60th day of the year, the fourth month on the 91st day of the year, and so on—quite regardless of the phases of the Moon. (In a leap year, all the months from the third onward start a day late because of the existence of February 29.)

But that brings us to the year. When does that begin and why?

Primitive agricultural societies must have been first aware of the year as a succession of seasons. Spring, summer, autumn, and winter were the morning, midday, evening, and night of the year, as in the case of the day, there seemed two equally qualified candidates for the post of beginning.

The beginning of the work year is the time of spring, when warmth returns to the earth and planting can begin. Should that not also be the beginning of the year in general? On the other hand, autumn marks the end of the work year, with the harvest (it is to be devoutly hoped) safely in hand. With the work year ended, ought not the new year begin?

With the development of astronomy, the beginning of the spring season was associated with the vernal equinox which, on our calendar, falls on March 20, while the beginning of autumn is associated with the autumnal equinox which falls, half a year later, on September 23.

Some societies chose one equinox as the beginning and some the other. Among the Hebrews, both equinoxes came to be associated with a New Year's Day. One of these fell on the first day of the month of Nisan (which comes at about the vernal equinox). In the middle of that month comes the feast of Passover, which is thus tied to the vernal equinox.

Since, according to the Gospels, Jesus' Crucifixion and Resurrection occurred during the Passover season (the Last Supper was a Passover seder), Good Friday and Easter are also tied to the vernal equinox (see Chapter 11).

The Hebrews also celebrated a New Year's Day on the first two days of Tishri (which falls at about the autumnal equinox), and this became the more important of the two occasions. It is celebrated by Jews today as "Rosh Hashonah" ("head of the year"), the familiarly known "Jewish New Year."

A much later example of a New Year's Day in connection with the autumnal equinox came in connection with the French Revolution. On September 22, 1792, the French monarchy was abolished and a republic proclaimed. The Revolutionary idealists felt that since a new epoch in human history had begun, a new calendar was needed. They made September 22 the New Year's Day and established a new list of months. The first month was Vendémiaire, so that September 22 became Vendémiaire 1.

For thirteen years, Vendémiaire 1 continued to be the official New Year's Day of the French Government, but the calendar never caught on outside France or even among the people inside France. In 1806 Napoleon gave up the struggle and officially reinstated the old calendar.

There are two important solar events in addition to the equinoxes. After the vernal equinox, the noonday Sun continues to rise higher and higher until it reaches a maximum height on June 21, which is the summer solstice, and this day, in consequence, has the longest daytime period of the year.

The height of the noonday Sun declines thereafter until it reaches the position of the autumnal equinox. It then continues to decline farther and farther till it reaches a minimum height on December 21, the winter solstice and the shortest daytime period of the year.

The summer solstice is not of much significance. "Midsummer Day" falls at about the summer solstice (the traditional English day is June 24). This is a time for gaiety and carefree joy, even folly. Shakespeare's *A Midsummer Night's Dream* is an example of a play devoted to the kind of not-to-be-taken-seriously fun of the season, and the phrase "midsummer madness" may have arisen similarly.

The winter solstice is a much more serious affair. The Sun is declining from day to day, and to a primitive society, not sure of the invariability of astronomical laws, it might well appear that *this* time, the Sun will continue its decline and disappear forever so that spring will never come again and all life will die.

Therefore, as the Sun's decline slowed from day to day and came to a halt and began to turn on December 21, there must have been great relief and joy which, in the end, became ritualized into a great religious festival, marked by gaiety and licentiousness.

The best-known examples of this are the several days of holiday among the Romans at this season of the year. The holiday was in honor of Saturn (an ancient Italian god of agriculture) and was therefore called the "Saturnalia." It was a time of feasting and of giving of presents; of good will to men, even to the point where slaves were given temporary freedom while their masters waited upon them. There was also a lot of drinking at Saturnalia parties.

In fact, the word "saturnalian" has come to mean dissolute, or characterized by unrestrained merriment.

There is logic, then, in beginning the year at the winter solstice which marks, so to speak, the birth of a new Sun, as the first appearance of a crescent after sunset marks the birth of a new Moon. Something like this may have been in Julius Caesar's mind when he reorganized the Roman calendar and made it solar rather than lunar (see Chapter 11).

NAPOLEON BONAPARTE

Napoleon, who went from Corsican rebel, to French general, to Emperor, to exile, is mentioned briefly in this article as having put an end to the only modern experiment in novel calendars. He was distantly involved in science in other respects.

In 1807, when his conquests brought him to Poland, he expressed surprise that no statue to Copernicus had ever been erected, and one was put up in consequence. When it was, no Catholic priest would agree to officiate on the occasion.

Napoleon patronized scientists such as Lagrange and Laplace, promoted them and honored them. Once, when he was holding British prisoners of war, he released them only after Edward Jenner (the discoverer of vaccination against smallpox) added his name to those petitioning for the release.

When Napoleon invaded Egypt in 1798, he brought a number of scientists with him to investigate its ancient civilization. The Rosetta stone, inscribed in both Greek and Egyptian, was discovered on that occasion, and Egyptian was eventually deciphered so that our knowledge of ancient history was greatly expanded. Once Emperor, Napoleon supported French science vigorously in an attempt to make it compete more successfully with British science. It was similar to the American-Soviet rivalry a century and a half later.

The most famous Napoleonic tale with respect to science was in connection with the astronomer Laplace, who was putting out the first few volumes of his Celestial Mechanics which completed the work of Newton and described the machinery of the Solar system. Napoleon leafed through the book and remarked there was no mention of God. "I had no need of that hypothesis," said Laplace.

The Romans had, traditionally, begun their year on March 15 (the "Ides of March"), which was intended to fall upon the vernal equinox originally but which, thanks to the sloppy way in which the Romans maintained their calendar, eventually moved far out of synchronization with the equinox. Caesar adjusted matters and moved the beginning of the year to January 1 instead, placing it nearly at the winter solstice.

This habit of beginning the year on or about the winter solstice did not become universal, however. In England (and the American colonies) March 25, intended to represent the vernal equinox, remained the official beginning of the year until 1752. It was only then that the January 1 beginning was adopted.

The beginning of a new Sun reflects itself in modern times in another way, too. In the days of the Roman Empire, the rising power of Christianity found its most dangerous competitor in Mithraism, a cult that was Persian in origin and was devoted to sun worship. The ritual centered about the mythological character of Mithras, who represented the Sun, and whose birth was celebrated on December 25—about the time of the winter solstice. This was a good time for a holiday, anyway, for the Romans were used to celebrating the Saturnalia at that time of year.

Eventually, though, Christianity stole Mithraic thunder by establishing the birth of Jesus on December 25 (there is no biblical authority for this), so that the period of the winter solstice has come to mark the birth of both the Son and the Sun. There are some present-day moralists (of whom I am one) who find something unpleasantly reminiscent of the Roman Saturnalia in the modern secular celebration of Christmas.

But where do the years begin? It is certainly convenient to number the years, but where do we start the numbers? In ancient times, when the sense of history was not highly developed, it was sufficient to begin numbering the years with the accession of the local king or ruler. The numbering would begin over again with each new king. Where a city has an annually chosen magistrate, the year might not be numbered at all, but merely identified by the name of the magistrate for that year. Athens named its years by its archons.

When the Bible dates things at all, it does it in this manner. For instance, in II Kings 16:1, it is written: "In the seventeenth year of Pekah the son of Remaliah, Ahaz the son of Jotham king of Judah began to reign." (Pekah was the contemporary king of Israel.)

And in Luke 2:2, the time of the taxing, during which Jesus was born, is dated only as follows: "And this taxing was first made when Cyrenius was governor of Syria."

Unless you have accurate lists of kings and magistrates and know just how many years each was in power and how to relate the list of one region with that of another, you are in trouble, and it is for that reason that so many ancient dates are uncertain—even (as I shall soon explain) a date as important as that of the birth of Jesus.

A much better system would be to pick some important date in the past (preferably one far enough in the past so that you don't have to deal with negative-numbered years before that time) and number of years in progression thereafter, without ever starting over.

The Greeks made use of the Olympian Games for that purpose. This was celebrated every four years so that a four-year cycle was an "Olympiad." The Olympiads were numbered progressively, and the year itself was the 1st, 2nd, 3rd or 4th year of a particular Olympiad.

This is needlessly complicated, however, and in the time following Alexander the Great something better was introduced into the Greek world. The ancient East was being fought over by Alexander's generals, and one of them, Seleucus, defeated another at Gaza. By this victory Seleucus was confirmed in his rule over a vast section of Asia. He determined to number the years from that battle, which took place in the 1st year of the 117th Olympiad. That year became Year 1 of the "Seleucid Era" and later years continued in succession as 2, 3, 4, 5, and so on. Nothing more elaborate than that.

The Seleucid Era was of unusual importance because Seleucus and his descendants ruled over Judea, which therefore adopted the system. Even after the Jews broke free of the Seleucids under the leadership of the Maccabees, they continued to use the Seleucid Era in dating their commercial transactions over the length and breadth of the ancient world. Those commercial records can be tied in with various year-dating systems, so that many of them could be accurately synchronized as a result.

The most important year-dating system of the ancient world ,however, was that of the "Roman Era." This began with the year in which Rome was founded. According to tradition, this was the 4th Year of the 6th Olympiad, which came to be considered as 1 A.U.C. (The abbreviation "A.U.C." stands for "Anno Urbis Conditae"; that is, "The Year of the Founding of the City.")

Using the Roman Era, the Battle of Zama, in which Hannibal was finally defeated, was fought in 553 A.U.C., while Julius Caesar was assassinated in 710 A.U.C., and so on. This system gradually spread over the ancient world, as Rome waxed supreme, and lasted well into early medieval times.

The early Christians, anxious to show that biblical records antedated those of Greece and Rome, strove to begin counting at a date earlier than that of either the founding of Rome or the beginning of the Olympian Games. A Church historian, Eusebius of Caesarea, who lived about 1050 A.U.C., calculated that the Patriarch, Abraham, had been born 1263 years before the founding of Rome. Therefore he adopted that year as his Year 1, so that 1050 A.U.C. became 2313, Era of Abraham.

Once the Bible was thoroughly established as *the* book of the western world, it was possible to carry matters to their logical extreme and date the years from the creation of the world. The medieval Jews calculated that the creation of the world had taken place 3007 years before the founding of Rome, while various Christian calculators chose years varying from 3251 to 4755 years before the founding of Rome. These are the various "Mundane Eras" ("Eras of the World"). The Jewish Mundane Era is used today in the Jewish calendar, so that in September 1964, the Jewish year 5725 began.

The Mundane Eras have one important factor in their favor. They start early enough so that there are very few, if any, dates in recorded history that have to be given negative numbers. This is not true of the Roman Era, for instance. The founding of the Olympian Games, the Trojan War, the reign of David, the building of the Pyramids, all came before the founding of Rome and have to be given negative year numbers.

The Romans wouldn't have cared, of course, for none of the ancients were very chronology conscious, but modern historians would. In fact, modern historians are even worse off than they would have been if the Roman Era had been retained.

About 1288 A.U.C., a Syrian monk named Dionysius Exiguus, working from biblical data and secular records, calculated that Jesus must have been born in 754 A.U.C. This seemed a good time to use as a beginning for counting the years, and in the time of Charlemagne (two and a half centuries after Dionysius) this notion won out.

The year 754 A.U.C. became A.D. 1 (standing for *Anno Domini,* meaning "the year of the Lord"). By this new "Christian Era," the founding of Rome took place in 753 B.C. ("before Christ"). The first year of the first Olympiad was in 776 B.C., the first year of the Seleucid Era was in 312 B.C., and so on.

This is the system used today, and means that all of ancient history from Sumer to Augustus must be dated in negative numbers, and we must forever remember that Caesar was assassinated in 44 B.C. and that the next year is number 43 and not 45.

Worse stiill, Dionysius was wrong in his calculations. Matthew 2:1 clearly states that "Jesus was born in Bethlehem of Judea in the days of Herod the king." This Herod is the so-called Herod the Great, who was born about 681 A.U.C., and was made king of Judea by Mark Antony in 714 A.U.C. He died (and this is known as certainly as any ancient date is known) in 750 A.U.C., and therefore Jesus could not have been born any later than 850 A.U.C.

But 750 A.U.C., according to the system of Dionysius Exiguus, is 4 B.C., and therefore you constantly find in lists of dates that Jesus was born in 4 B.C.; that is, four years before the birth of Jesus.

In fact, there is no reason to be sure that Jesus was born in the very year that Herod died. In Matthew 2:16, it is written that Herod, in an attempt to kill Jesus, ordered all male children of two years and under to be slain. This verse can be interpreted as indicating that Jesus may have been at least two years old while Herod was still alive, and might therefore have been born as early as 6 B.C. Indeed, some estimates have placed the birth of Jesus as early as 17 B.C.

Which forces me to admit sadly that although I love to begin at the beginning, I can't always be sure where the beginning is.

CHARLEMAGNE

Charlemagne is mentioned here as the moving spirit behind the official adoption of the modern Christian era, which the world today almost universally uses in numbering its years.

Under Charlemagne, born in Aachen, Germany, about 742, the Frankish Empire reached its apogee. He ruled over what is now France, Belgium, the Netherlands, Switzerland, most of Germany, most of Italy, and even some of Spain. The Roman Empire in the West was revived (after a fashion), and in 800 he was made Emperor, thus beginning a tradition that was to last just over a thousand years and end in 1806 as a result of Napoleon's conquests in Germany.

Charlemagne's importance in the history of science was that, in the midst of the period known as the Dark Age, he did his best to light the candles once more. He himself was illiterate as was almost everyone but churchmen. In adulthood, however, he managed to learn to read but could not persuade his fingers to learn to make the marks necessary for writing.

He recognized the value of learning in general, too, and in 789 began to establish schools in which the elements of mathematics, grammar, and ecclesiastical subjects could be taught under the over-all guidance of an English scholar named Alcuin.

The result of Charlemagne's efforts is sometimes termed the "Carolingian renaissance." It was a noble effort but a feeble one, and it did not outlast the great Emperor himself. He died in Aachen, January 28, 814, and he was succeeded by his much less talented son, Ludwig, usually referred to as "the Pious" because he was entirely in the hands of the priesthood and could not control his family or the nobility. The coming of the Viking terror completed the disintegration of the abortive renaissance.

Culver Pictures, Inc.

Part V

NUMBERS AND BIOLOGY

13 THAT'S ABOUT THE SIZE OF IT

No matter how much we tell ourselves that quality is what counts, sheer size remains impressive. The two most popular types of animals in any zoo are the monkeys and the elephants, the former because they are embarrassingly like ourselves, the latter simply because they are huge. We laugh at the monkeys but stand in silent awe before the elephant. And even among the monkeys, if one were to place Gargantua in a cage, he would outdraw every other primate in the place. In fact, he did.

This emphasis on the huge naturally makes the human being feel small, even puny. The fact that mankind has nevertheless reached a position of unparalleled domination of the planet is consequently presented very often as a David-and-Goliath saga, with ourselves as David.

And yet this picture of ourselves is not quite accurate, as we can see if we view the statistics properly.

First, let's consider the upper portion of the scale. I've just mentioned the elephant as an example of great size, and this is hallowed by cliché. "Big as an elephant" is a common phrase.

But, of course, the elephant does not set an unqualified record. No land animal can be expected to. On land, an animal must fight gravity, undiluted. Even if it were not a question of lifting its bulk several feet off the ground

199

ELEPHANTS

The most glamorous interconnection of elephant and man came in ancient times when the elephant was used in warfare as the living equivalent of the modern tank. It could carry a number of men, together with important assault weapons. It could do damage on its own, with its trunk, tusks, and legs. Most of all, it represented a fearful psychological hazard to the opposing forces, who could only with difficulty face the giant animals. The greatest defects of the use of elephants lay in the fact that elephants were intelligent enough to run from overwhelming odds, and in their panic (especially if wounded) could prove more damaging to their own side than to the enemy.

The West came across elephants for the first time in 326 B.C. when Alexander the Great defeated the Punjabi King, Porus, despite the latter's use of two hundred elephants. For a century afterward, the monarchs who succeeded Alexander used elephants.

Usually only one side or the other had elephants, but at the Battle of Ipsus in 301 B.C. between rival generals of the late Alexander's army, there were elephants on both sides, nearly three hundred in all. African elephants were sometimes used, though Asian elephants were more common. The African elephants, however, were native to north Africa and were smaller than the Asian elephants. The north African variety is now extinct, and when we speak of African elephants today, we mean those of eastern Africa, which are the giants of the species and the largest land mammal alive. It is the giant African elephant that is shown in the illustration.

The Greek general Pyrrhus brought elephants into southern Italy in 280 B.C. to fight the Romans; but the Romans, though terrified of the beasts, fought resolutely anyway. The last elephant battle was that of Zama, where Hannibal's elephants did not help him defeat the Romans.

The Granger Collection

and moving it more or less rapidly, that fight sets sharp limits to size. If an animal were envisaged as lying flat on the ground, and living out its life as motionlessly as an oyster, it would still have to heave masses of tissue upward with every breath. A beached whale dies for several reasons, but one is that its own weight upon its lungs slowly strangles it to death.

In the water, however, buoyancy largely negates gravity, and a mass that would mean crushing death on land is supported under water without trouble.

For that reason, the largest creatures on earth, present or past, are to be found among the whales. And the species of whale that holds the record is the blue whale or, as it is alternatively known, the sulfur-bottom. One specimen of this greatest of giants has been recorded with a length of 108 feet and a weight of 131¼ tons.*

Now the blue whale, like ourselves, is a mammal. If we want to see how we stand among the mammals, as far as size is concerned, let's see what the other extreme is like.

The smallest mammals are the shrews, creatures that look superficially mouselike, but are not mice or even rodents. Rather, they are insectivores, and are actually more closely related to us than to mice. The smallest full-grown shrew weighs a minimum of 0.052 ounce.

Between these two mammalian extremes stretches a solid phalanx of animals. Below the blue whale are other smaller whales, then creatures such as elephants, walruses, hippopotamuses, down through moose, bears, bison, horses, lions, wolves, beavers, rabbits, rats, mice and shrews. Where in this long list from largest whale to smallest shrew is man?

To avoid any complications, and partly because my weight comes to a good, round figure of two hundred pounds, I will use myself as a measure.**

Now, we can consider man either a giant or a pygmy, according to the frame of reference. Compared to the shrew he is a giant, of course, and compared to the whale

[* *This article first appeared in October 1961. For this new appearance, I have corrected any figures for which I have obtained better values since.*]

[** *In 1964, three years after writing this article, I lost weight and have kept it off ever since. I am now 180 pounds.*]

he is a pygmy. How do we decide which view to give the greater weight?

In the first place, it is confusing to compare tons, pounds and ounces, so let's put all three weights into a common unit. In order to avoid fractions (just at first, anyway) let's consider grams as the common unit. (For your reference, one ounce equals about 28.35 grams, one pound equals about 453.6 grams, and one ton equals about 907,000 grams.)

Now, you see, we can say that a blue whale weighs as much as 120,000,000 grams while a shrew weighs as little as 1.5 grams. In between is man with a weight of 90,700 grams.

We are tens of thousands of grams heavier than a shrew, but a whale is tens of *millions* of grams heavier than a man, so we might insist that we are much more of a pygmy than a giant and insist on retaining the David-and-Goliath picture.

But human sense and judgment do not differentiate by subtraction; they do so by division. The difference between a two-pound weight and a six-pound weight seems greater to us than that between a six-pound weight and a twelve pound weight, even though the difference is only four pounds in the first case and fully six pounds in the latter. What counts, it seems, is that six divided by two is three, while twelve divided by six is only two. Ratio, not difference, is what we are after.

Naturally, it is tedious to divide. An any fourth-grader and many adults will maintain, division comes under the heading of advanced mathematics. Therefore, it would be pleasant if we could obtain ratios by subtraction.

To do this, we take the logarithm of a number, rather than the number itself. For instance, the most common form of logarithms are set up in such a fashion that 1 is the logarithm of 10, 2 is the logarithm of 100, 3 is the logarithm of 1,000 and so on.

If we use the numbers themselves, we would point out an equality of ratio by saying that 1,000/100 is equal to 100/10, which is division. But if we used the logarithms, we could point out the same equality of ratio by saying that 3 minus 2 is equal to 2 minus 1, which is subtraction.

Or, again, 1,000/316 is roughly equal to 316/100. (Check it and see.) Since the logarithm of 1,000 is 3 and the logarithm of 100 is 2, we can set the logarithm of 316 equal to 2.5, and then, using logarithms, we can express the equality of ratio by saying that 3 minus 2.5 is equal to 2.5 minus 2.

So let's give the extremes of mammalian weight in terms of the logarithm of the number of grams. The 120,000,-000-gram blue whale can be represented logarithmically by 8.08, while the 1.5-gram shrew is 0.18. As for the 90,700-gram man, he is 4.96.

As you see, man is about 4.8 logarithmic units removed from the shrew but only about 3.1 logarithmic units removed from the largest whale. We are therefore much more nearly giants than pygmies.

In case you think all this is mathematical folderol and that I am pulling a fast one, what I'm saying is merely equivalent to this: A man is 45,000 times as massive as a shrew, but a blue whale is only 1,300 times as massive as a man. We would seem much larger to a shrew than a whale does to us.

In fact, a mass that would be just intermediate between that of a shrew and a whale would be one with a logarithm that is the arithmetical average of 0.18 and 8.08, or 4.13. This logarithm represents a mass of 13,500 grams, or 30 pounds. By that argument, a medium-sized mammal would be about the size of a four-year-old child, or a dog of moderate weight.

Of course, you might argue that a division into two groups—pygmy and giant—is too simple. Why not a division into three groups—pygmy, moderate, and giant? Splitting the logarithmic range into three equal parts, we would have the pygmies in the range from 0.18 to 2.81, moderates from 2.81 to 5.44, and the giants from 5.44 to 8.08.

Put into common units this would mean that any animal under 1.5 pounds would be a pygmy and any animal over 550 pounds would be a giant. By that line of thinking, the animals between, including man, would be of moderate size. This seems reasonable enough, I must admit, and it seems a fair way of showing that man, if not a pygmy, is also not a giant.

But if we're going to be fair, let's be fair all the way. The David-and-Goliath theme is introduced with respect to man's winning of overlordship on this planet; it is the victory of brains over brawn. But in that case, why consider the whale as the extreme of brawn? Early man never competed with whales. Whales stayed in the ocean and man stayed on land. Our battle was with land creatures only, so let's consider land mammals in setting up our upper limit.

The largest land mammal that ever existed is not alive today. It is the baluchitherium, an extinct giant rhinoceros that stood eighteen feet tall at the shoulder, and must have weighed in the neighborhood of 20 tons.

As you see, the baluchitherium (which means "Baluchi beast," by the way, because its fossils were first found in Baluchistan) has less than one-seventh the mass of a blue whale. The logarithmic value of the baluchitherium's mass in grams stands at 7.26.

(From now on, I will give weights in common units but will follow it with a logarithmic value in parentheses. Please remember that this is the logarithm of the weight in grams every time.)

But, of course, the baluchitherium was extinct before the coming of man and there was no competition with him either. To make it reasonably fair, we must compare man with those creatures that were alive in his time and therefore represented potential competition. The largest mammals living in the time of man are the various elephants. The largest living African elephant may reach a total weight of 10.7 tons (6.99). To be sure, it is possible that man competed with still larger species of elephant now extinct. The largest elephant that ever existed could not have weighed more than 20 tons (7.26).

(Notice, by the way, that an elephant is only about half as heavy as a baluchitherium and has only 5 per cent of the weight of a blue whale. In fact, a full-grown elephant of the largest living kind is only about the weight of a newborn blue whale.)

Nor am I through. In battling other species for world domination, the direct competitors to man were other carnivores. An elephant is herbivorous. It might crush a man to death accidentally, or on purpose if angered, but otherwise it had no reason to harm man. A man does not represent food to an elephant.

A man does represent food to a saber-toothed tiger, however, which, if hungry enough, would stalk, kill and eat a man who was only trying to stay out of the way. *There* is the competition.

Now the very largest animals are almost invariably herbivores. There are more plant calories available than animal calories and a vegetable diet can, on the whole, support larger animals than a meat diet. (Which is not to say that some carnivores aren't much larger than some herbivores.)

To be sure, the largest animal of all, the blue whale, is technically a carnivore. However, he lives on tiny creatures strained out of ocean water, and this isn't so far removed, in a philosophical sense, from browsing on grass. He is not a carnivore of the classic type, the kind with teeth that go snap!

The largest true carnivore in all the history of the earth is the sperm whale (of which Moby Dick is an example). A mature sperm whale, with a large mouth and a handsome set of teeth in its lower jaw, may weigh seventy-five tons (7.83).

But there again, we are not competing with sea creatures. The largest *land* carnivore among the mammals is the great Alaskan bear (also called the Kodiak bear), which occasionally tips the scale at 1,650 pounds (5.87). I don't know of any extinct land carnivore among the mammals that was larger.

Turning to the bottom end of the scale, there we need make no adjustments. The shrew is a land mammal and a carnivore and, as far as I know, is the smallest mammal that ever existed. Perhaps it is the smallest mammal that can possibly exist. The metabolic rate of mammals goes up as size decreases because the surface-to-volume ratio goes up with decreasing size. Some small animals might (and do) make up for that by letting the metabolic rate drop and the devil with it, but a warm-blooded creature cannot. It must keep its temperature high, and, therefore, its metabolism racing (except during temporary hibernations).

A warm-blooded animal the size of a shrew must eat just about constantly to keep going. A shrew starves to death if it goes a couple of hours without eating; it is always hungry and is very vicious and ill-tempered in consequence. No one has ever seen a fat shrew or ever will. (And if anyone wishes to send pictures of the neighbor's wife in order to refute that statement, please don't.)

Now let's take the range of land-living mammalian carnivores and break that into three parts. From 0.18 to

2.08 are the pygmies, from 2.08 to 3.98 the moderates, and from 3.98 to 5.87 the giants. In common units that would mean that any creature under 4¼ ounces is a pygmy, anything from 4¼ ounces to 22 pounds is a moderate, and anything over 22 pounds is a giant.

Among the mammalian land carnivores of the era in which man struggled through first to survival and then to victory, man is a giant. In the David-and-Goliath struggle, one of the Goliaths won.

Of course, some suspicion may be aroused by the fact that I am so carefully specifying mammals throughout. Maybe man is only a giant among mammals, you may think, but were I to broaden the horizon he would turn out to be a pygmy after all.

Well, not so. As a matter of fact, mammals in general are giants among animals. Only one kind of non-mammal can compete (on land) with the large mammals, and they are the reptile monsters of the Mesozoic era—the large group of animals usually referred to in common speech as "the dinosaurs."

The largest dinosaurs were almost the length of the very largest whales, but they were mostly thin neck and thin tail, so that they cannot match those same whales in mass. The bulkiest of the large dinosaurs, the Brachiosaurus, probably weighed as much as 75 tons (7.83). It is the size of the sperm whale, but it is only three-fifths the size of the blue whale. And, as is to be expected, the largest of the dinosaurs were herbivores.

The largest carnivorous dinosaurs were the allosaurs, some of whom may have weighed as much as twenty tons (7.26). An allosaur might weigh as much as a baluchitherium, be twice the weight of the largest elephant and twenty-four times the weight of the poor little Kodiak bear.

The allosaurs were beyond doubt the largest and most fearsome land carnivores that ever lived. They and all their tribe, however, were gone from the earth millions of years before man appeared on the scene.

If we confine ourselves to reptiles alive in man's time, the largest appear to be certain giant crocodiles of Southeast Asia. Unfortunately, reports about the size of such creatures always tend to concentrate on the length rather than the weight (this is even truer of snakes); some are

described as approaching thirty feet in length. I estimate
that such monsters should also approach a maximum of
two tons (6.25) in weight.

I have a more precise figure for the next most massive
group of living reptiles, the turtles. The largest turtle on
record is a marine leatherback with a weight of 1,902
pounds (5.93), or not quite a ton.

To be sure, neither of these creatures is a land animal.
The leatherback is definitely a creature of the sea, while
crocodiles are river creatures. Nevertheless, as far as the
crocodiles are concerned I am inclined not to omit them
from the list of man's competitors. Early civilizations
developed along tropical or subtropical rivers; who is not
aware of the menace of the crocodile of the Nile, for instance? And certainly it is a dangerous creature with a
mouth and teeth that go snap! to end all snaps! (What
jungle movie would omit the terrifying glide and gape of
the crocodile?)

The crocodiles are smaller than the largest land-living
mammals, but the largest of these reptiles would seem
to outweigh the Kodiak bear. However, even if we let
5.93 be the new upper limit of the "land" carnivores,
man would still count as a giant.

If we move to reptiles that are truly of the land, their
inferiority to mammals in point of size is clear. The largest
land reptile is the Galápagos tortoise, which may reach six
hundred pounds (5.42). The largest snake is the reticu-
lated python, which may reach an extreme length of
thirty-three feet. Here again, weights aren't given, as all
the ooh'ing and ah'ing is over the measurement by yardstick. However, I don't see how this can represent a
weight greater than 450 pounds (5.32). Finally, the largest living lizard is the Komodo monitor, which grows to
a maximum length of twelve feet and to a weight of 250
pounds (5.05).

The fishes make a fairly respectable showing. The
largest of all fishes, living or extinct, is the whale shark.
The largest specimens of these are supposed to be as large
and as massive as the sperm whale, though perhaps a forty-
five-ton maximum (7.61) might be more realistic. Again,
these sharks are harmless filterers of sea water. The
largest carnivorous shark is the white shark, which reaches
lengths of thirty-five feet and possibly a weight of twelve
tons (7.03).

Of the bony fishes, the largest (such as the tuna, sword-fish, sunfish, or sturgeon) may tip the scales at as much as three thousand pounds (6.13). All fish, however, are water creatures, of course, and not direct competition for any man not engaged in such highly specialized occupations as pearl-diving.

The birds, as you might expect, make a poorer showing. You can't be very heavy and still fly.

This means that any bird that competes with man in weight must be flightless. The heaviest bird that ever lived was the flightless Aepyornis of Madagascar (also called the elephant bird), which stood ten feet high and may have weighed as much as one thousand pounds (5.66). The largest moas of New Zealand were even taller (twelve feet) but were more lightly built and did not weigh more than five hundred pounds (5.36). In comparison, the largest living bird, the ostrich—still flightless—has a maximum weight of about three hundred fifty pounds (5.20).

When we get to flying birds, weight drops drastically. The albatross has a record wingspread of twelve feet, but wings don't weigh much and even the heaviest flying bird probably does not weigh more than forty pounds (4.26). Even the pteranodon, which was the largest of the extinct flying reptiles, and had a wingspread of up to twenty-five feet, was virtually all wing and no body, and probably weighed less than an albatross.*

To complete the classes of the vertebrates, the largest amphibians are giant salamanders found in Japan, which are up to five feet in length and weigh up to ninety pounds (4.60).

Working in the other direction, we find that the smallest bird, the bee hummingbird of Cuba, is about 0.07 ounce in weight (0.30). (Hummingbirds, like shrews, have to keep eating almost all the time, and starve quickly.)

The cold-blooded vertebrates can manage smaller sizes than any of the warm-blooded mammals and birds, however, since cold blood implies that body temperature can drop to that of the surroundings and metabolism can be lowered to practical levels. The smallest vertebrates of all are therefore certain species of fish. There is a fish of

[* *In 1975 fossils of a flying reptile much larger than the pteranodon were discovered. I suspect it may have weighed as much as fifty pounds.*]

HUMMINGBIRDS

The hummingbirds are the closest that warm-blooded animals can come to filling the environmental niche of insects. Any smaller and the capacity to produce heat by metabolic action could not match the loss of heat through the surface.

As it is the largest hummingbird, the giant hummingbird is about 20 grams (0.7 ounce) in weight, which is rather less than that of the average sparrow, and the smallest is only one-tenth that size. The name of the smallest, the bee hummingbird, emphasizes the similarity to insects. It feeds on nectar and can hover in the air, then dart suddenly in any direction, like an outsize dragonfly.

The eggs laid by the hummingbirds are the smallest of those laid by any bird. It would take 125 of them to weigh as much as a hen's egg and about 18,000 of them to weigh as much as the largest egg of all, that of the extinct giant bird the aepyornis. Still, compared to the size of the hummingbird itself, the eggs are quite large. The two it usually lays weigh up to a tenth that of the mother. (This is not a record, however. The flightless New Zealand bird, the kiwi, lays an egg that is almost a quarter of its own weight, and how it does that without foundering itself will always remain a puzzle to me.)

The hummingbird is the most extravagant energy-user of any living organism. It expends about 10.3 kilocalories per twenty-four-hour period, which means about 5 kilocalories per gram. The human being may expend 2,500 kilocalories in the same period but that is only about 0.035 per gram. Weight for weight, hummingbirds expend nearly 150 times the energy we do. During night, however, hummingbirds become torpid, and both body temperature and metabolic rate drop considerably. The shrew, which in the article shares honors for warm-blooded smallness, has a slightly lower metabolic rate, but is as active by night as by day—no torpidity.

The Bettmann Archive

the goby group in the Philippine Islands that has a length, when full grown, of only three-eighths of an inch. Such a fish weighs $\frac{1}{50}$ of a gram (-2.70), which, as you notice, carries us into negative logarithms.

What about invertebrates?

Well, invertebrates, having no internal skeleton with which to brace their tissues, cannot be expected to grow as large as vertebrates. Only in the water, where they can count on buoyancy, can they make any decent showing at all.

The largest invertebrates of all are to be found among the mollusks. Giant squids with lengths up to fifty-five feet have been actually measured, and lengths up to one hundred feet have been conjectured. Even so, such lengths are illusory, for they include the relatively light tentacles for the most part. The total weight of such creatures is not likely to be much more than two tons (6.26).

Another type of mollusk, the giant clam, may reach a weight of seven hundred pounds (5.50), mostly dead shell, while the largest arthropod is a lobster that weighed in at thirty-four pounds (4.19).

As for the land invertebrates, mass is negligible. The largest land crabs and land snails never match the weights of any but quite small mammals. The same is true of the most successful and important of all the land invertebrates, the insects. The bulkiest insect is the goliath beetle, which can be up to five or six inches in length, with a weight of about 100 grams (2.00).

And the insects, with a top weight just overlapping the bottom of the mammalian scale, are well represented in levels of less and less massive creatures. The bottom is an astonishing one, for there are small beetles called fairy flies that are as small as $\frac{1}{125}$ of an inch in length, full-grown. Such creatures can have weights of no more than 0.000005 grams (-5.30).

Nor is even this the record. Among the various classes of multicelled invertebrates, the smallest of all is Rotifera. Even the largest of these are only one-fifteenth of an inch long, while the smallest are but one three-hundredth of an inch long and may weigh 0.000000006 gram (-8.22). The rotifers, in other words, are to the shrews as the shrews are to the whales. If we go still lower, we will end

TABLE 3   *Sizes*

ANIMAL	CHARACTERISTIC	LOGARITHM OF WEIGHT IN GRAMS
Blue whale	Largest of all animals	8.08
Sperm whale	Largest of all carnivores	7.83
Brachiosaurus	Largest land animal (extinct)	7.83
Whale shark	Largest fish	7.61
Allosaur	Largest land carnivore (extinct)	7.26
Baluchitherium	Largest land mammal (extinct)	7.26
White shark	Largest carnivorous fish	7.03
Elephant	Largest land animal (alive)	6.99
Giant squid	Largest invertebrate	6.26
Crocodile	Largest reptile (alive)	6.25
Sunfish	Largest bony fish	6.13
Leatherback	Largest turtle	5.93
Kodiak bear	Largest land carnivore (alive)	5.87
Aepyornis	Largest bird (extinct)	5.66
Giant clam	Largest gastropod	5.50
Galápagos tortoise	Largest land reptile (alive)	5.42
Reticulated python	Largest snake	5.32
Ostrich	Largest bird (alive)	5.20
Komodo monitor	Largest lizard	5.05
Man		4.96
Giant salamander	Largest amphibian	4.60
Albatross	Largest flying bird	4.26
Lobster	Largest arthropod	4.19
Goliath beetle	Largest insect	2.00
Bee hummingbird	Smallest bird	0.30
Shrew	Smallest mammal	0.18
Goby	Smallest fish and vertebrate	−2.70
Fairy fly	Smallest insect	−5.30
Rotifer	Smallest multicelled creature	−8.22

considering not only man but also the shrew as a giant among living creatures.

But below the rotifers are the one-celled creatures (though, in fact, the larger one-celled creatures are larger than the smallest rotifers and insects), and I will stop here, adding only a summarizing table of sizes.

But if we are to go back to the picture of David and Goliath, and consider man a Goliath, we have some real Davids to consider—rodents, insects, bacteria, viruses. Come to think of it, the returns aren't yet in, and the wise money might be on the real Davids after all.

Part VI

NUMBERS AND ASTRONOMY

14 THE PROTON-RECKONER

THERE is, in my heart, a very warm niche for the mathematician Archimedes.

In fact, if transmigrations of souls were something I believed in, I could only wish that my soul had once inhabited the body of Archimedes, because I feel it would have had a congenial home there.

I'll explain why.

Archimedes was a Greek who lived in Syracuse, Sicily. He was born about 287 B.C. and he died in 212 B.C. His lifetime covered a period during which the great days of Greece (speaking miiltarily and politically) were long since over, and when Rome was passing through its meteoric rise to world power. In fact, Archimedes died during the looting of Syracuse by the conquering Roman army. The period, however, represents the century during which Greek science reached its height—and Archimedes stands at the pinnacle of Greek science.

But that's not why I feel the particular kinship with him (after all, I stand at no pinnacle of any science). It is rather because of a single work of his; one called "Psammites" in Greek, "Arenarius" in Latin, and "The Sand-Reckoner" in English.

It is addressed to Gelon, the eldest son of the Syracusan king, and it begins as follows:

217

"There are some, king Gelon, who think that the number of the sand is infinite in multitude; and I mean by the sand not only that which exists about Syracuse and the rest of Sicily but also that which is found in every region whether inhabited or uninhabited. Again there are some who, without regarding it as infinite, yet think that no number has been named which is great enough to exceed its multitude. And it is clear that they who hold this view, if they imagined a mass made up of sand in other respects as large as the mass of the earth, including in it all the seas and the hollows of the earth filled up to a height equal to that of the highest of the mountains, would be many times further still from recognizing that any number could be expressed which exceeded the multitude of the sand so taken. But I will try to show you by means of geometrical proofs, which you will be able to follow, that of the numbers named by me and given in the work which I sent to Zeuxippus, some exceed not only the number of the mass of sand equal in magnitude to the earth filled up in the way described but also that of a mass equal in magnitude to the universe."

Archimedes then goes on to invent a system for expressing large numbers and follows that system clear up to a number which we would express as $10^{80,000,000,000,000,000,000}$, or nearly $10^{10^{17}}$.

After that, he sets about estimating the size of the universe according to the best knowledge of his day. He also sets about defining the size of a grain of sand. Ten thousand grains of sand, he says, would be contained in a poppy seed, where the poppy seed is $\frac{1}{40}$ of a fingerbreadth in diameter.

Given the size of the universe and the size of a grain of sand, he easily determines how many grains of sand would be required to fill the universe. It works out to a certain figure in his system of numbers, which in *our* system of numbers is equal to 10^{63}.

It's obvious to me (and I say this with all possible respect) that Archimedes was writing one of my science essays for me, and that is why he has wormed his way into my heart.

But let's see what can be done to advance his article further in as close an approach as possible to the original spirit.

The diameter of a poppy seed, says Archimedes, is $\frac{1}{40}$ of a finger-breadth. My own fingers seem to be about 20 millimeters in diameter and so the diameter of a poppy seed would be, by Archimedes' definition, 0.5 millimeter.

If a sphere 0.5 millimeter in diameter will hold 10,000 (10^4) grains of sand and if Archimedes' universe will hold 10^{63} grains of sand, then the volume of Archimedes' universe is 10^{59} times as great as that of a poppy seed. The diameter of the universe would then be $\sqrt[3]{10^{59}}$ times as great as that of a poppy seed. The cube root of 10^{59} is equal to 4.65×10^{19} and if that is multiplied by 0.5 millimeter, it turns out that Archimedes' universe is 2.3×10^{19} millimeters in diameter, or, taking half that value, 1.15×10^{19} millimeters in radius.

This radius comes out to 1.2 light-years. In those days, the stars were assumed to be fixed to a large sphere with the Earth at the center, so that Archimedes was saying that the sphere of the fixed stars was about 1.2 light-years from the Earth in every direction.

This is a very respectable figure for an ancient mathematician to arrive at, at a time when the true distance of the very nearest heavenly body—the Moon—was just in the process of being worked out and when all other distances were completely unknown.

Nevertheless, it falls far short of the truth and even the nearest star, as we now know, is nearly four times the distance from us that Archimedes conceived all the stars to be.

What, then, is the real size of the universe?

The objects in the universe which are farthest from us are the galaxies; and some of them are much farther than others. Early in the twentieth century, it was determined that the galaxies (with a very few exceptions among those closest to us) were all receding from us. Furthermore, the dimmer the galaxy and therefore the farther (presumably), the greater the rate of recession.

In 1929, the American astronomer Edwin Powell Hubble decided that, from the data available, it would seem that there was a linear relationship between speed of recession and distance. In other words, if galaxy 1 were twice as far as galaxy 2, then galaxy 1 would be receding from us at twice the velocity that galaxy 2 would be.

This relationship (usually called Hubble's Law) can be expressed as follows:

$$R = kD \qquad \text{(Equation 1)}$$

where R is the speed of recession of a galaxy, D its distance, and k a constant, which we may call "Hubble's constant."

This is not one of the great basic laws of the universe in which scientists can feel complete confidence. However, in the nearly forty years since Hubble's Law was propounded, it does not seem to have misled astronomers and no observational evidence as to its falsity has been advanced. Therefore, it continues to be accepted.*

One of the strengths of Hubble's Law is that it is the sort of thing that would indeed be expected if the universe as a whole (but not the matter that made it up) were expanding. In that case, every galaxy would be moving away from every other galaxy and from the vantage point of any one galaxy, the speed of recession of the other galaxies would indeed increase linearly with distance. Since the equations of Einstein's General Theory of Relativity can be made to fit the expanding universe (indeed the Dutch astronomer Willem de Sitter suggested an expanding universe years before Hubble's Law was proposed) astronomers are reasonably happy.

But what is the value of Hubble's constant? The first suggestion was that it was equal to five hundred kilometers per second per million parsecs. That would mean that an object a million parsecs away would be receding from us at a speed of five hundred kilometers per second; an object two million parsecs away at a speed of one thousand kilometers per second; an object three million parsecs away at a speed of fifteen hundred kilometers per second, and so on.

This value of the constant, it turned out, was too high by a considerable amount. Current thinking apparently would make its value somewhere between seventy-five and one hundred and seventy-five kilometers per second per million parsecs. Since the size of the constant has been

[* *This article first appeared in January 1966. In the decade since, there has been considerable argument over Hubble's Law, and while it is still accepted by astronomers, my attitude would not be as complacent now as it was then.*]

shrinking as astronomers gain more and more information, I suspect that the lower limit of the current estimate is the most nearly valid value and I will take seventy-five kilometers per second per million parsecs as the value of Hubble's constant.

In that case, how far distant can galaxies exist? If, with every million parsecs, the speed of recession increases by seventy-five kilometers per second, then, eventually, a recession equal to the speed of light (three hundred thousand kilometers per second) will be reached.

And what about galaxies still more distant? If Hubble's Law holds firmly at all distances and if we ignore the laws of relativity, then galaxies still farther than those already receding at the speed of light must be viewed as receding at speeds greater than that of light.

We needn't pause here to take up the question as to whether speeds greater than that of light are possible or not, and whether such beyond-the-limit galaxies can exist or not. It doesn't matter. Light from a galaxy receding from us at a speed greater than light cannot reach us; nor can neutrinos nor gravitational influence nor electromagnetic fields nor anything. Such galaxies cannot be observed in any way and therefore, as far as we are concerned, do not exist, whether we argue according to the Gospel of Einstein or the Gospel of Newton.

We have, then, what we call an Observable Universe. This is not merely that portion of the universe which happens to be observable with our best and most powerful instruments; but that portion of the universe which is all that can be observed even with perfect instruments of infinite power.

The Observable Universe, then, is finite in volume and its radius is equal to that distance at which the speed of recession of a galaxy is three hundred thousand kilometers per second.

Suppose we express Equation 1 as

$$D = R/k \qquad \text{(Equation 2)}$$

set R equal to three hundred thousand kilometers per second and k equal to seventy-five kilometers per second per million parsecs. We can then solve for D and the answer will come out in units of million parsecs.

It turns out, then, that

$$D = 30,000 \div 75 = 4,000 \qquad \text{(Equation 3)}$$

The farthest possible distance from us; or, what amounts to the same thing, the radius of the Observable Universe; is 4,000 million parsecs, or 4,000,000,000 parsecs. A parsec is equal to 3.26 light-years, which means that the radius of the Observable Universe is 13,000,000,000 light-years. This can be called the Hubble Radius.

Astronomers have not yet penetrated the full distance of the Hubble Radius, but they are approaching it. From Mount Palomar comes word that the astronomer Maarten Schmidt has determined that an object identified as 3C9 is receding at a speed of 240,000 kilometers per second, four-fifths the speed of light. That object is, therefore, a little more than ten billion light-years distant, and is the most distant object known.*

As you see, the radius of the Observable Universe is immensely greater than the radius of Archimedes' universe: thirteen billion as compared to 1.2. The ratio is just about ten billion. If the volumes of two spheres are compared, they vary with the cube of the radius. If the radius of the Observable Universe is 10^{10} times that of Archimedes' universe, the volume of the former is $(10^{10})^3$ or 10^{30} times that of the latter.

If the number of sand particles that filled Archimedes' universe is 10^{63}, then the number required to fill the immensely larger volume of the Observable Universe is 10^{93}.

But, after all, why cling to sand grains? Archimedes simply used them in order to fill the greatest possible volume with the smallest possible objects. Indeed, he stretched things a little. If a poppy seed 0.5 millimeter in diameter will hold ten thousand grains of sand, then each grain of sand must be 0.025 millimeter in diameter. These are pretty fine grains of sand, individually invisible to the eye.

We can do better. We know of atoms, which Archimedes did not, and of subatomic particles, too. Suppose we try to search among such objects for the smallest

[* In 1973 an object at a distance of twelve billion light-years was detected.]

possible volume; not merely a volume, but the Smallest Possible Volume.

If it were the smallest possible mass we were searching for, there would be no problem; it would be the rest mass of the electron which is 9.1×10^{-28} grams. No object that has any mass at all has a smaller mass than the electron. (The positron has a mass that is as small, but the positron is merely the electron's anti-particle, the looking-glass version of the electron, in other words.)

There are particles less massive than the electron. Examples are the photon and the various neutrinos, but these all have *zero* rest mass, and do not qualify as an "object that has any mass at all."

Why is this? Well, the electron has one other item of uniqueness. It is the least massive object which can carry an electric charge. Particles with zero rest mass are invariably electrically uncharged, so that the existence of electric charge seems to require the presence of mass—and of mass no smaller than that associated with the electron.

Perhaps electric charge *is* mass, and the electron is nothing but electric charge—whatever that is.

Yet it is possible to have a particle such as the proton, which is 1,836 times as massive as the electron, with an electric charge no greater. Or we can have a particle such as a neutron, which is 1,838 times as massive as an electron and has no charge at all.

We might look at such massive, undercharged particles as consisting of numerous charges of both types, positive and negative, most or all of which cancel one another, leaving one positive charge in excess in the case of the proton, and no uncanceled charge at all in the case of the neutron.

But, then, how can charges cancel each other without, at the same time, cancelling the associated mass? No one knows. The answer to such questions may not come before considerably more is learned about the internal structure of protons and neutrons. We will have to wait.

Now what about volume?

We can talk about the mass of subatomic particles with confidence, but volume is another matter. All particles exhibit wave properties, and associated with all chunks of matter are "matter-waves" of wavelength varying inversely with the momentum of the particles (that is, with the product of their mass and velocity).

The matter-waves associated with electrons have wavelengths of the order of 10^{-8} centimeters, which is about the diameter of an atom. It is therefore unrealistic to talk about the electron as a particle, or to view it as a hard, shiny sphere with a definite volume. Thanks to its wave nature, the electron "smears out" to fill the atom of which it forms a part. Sometimes it is "smeared out" over a whole group of atoms.

Massless particles such as photons and neutrinos are even more noticeably wave-forms in nature and can even less be spoken of as having a volume.

If we move on to a proton, however (or a neutron), we find an object with a mass nearly two thousand times an electron. This means that all other things being equal the wavelength of the matter-wave associated with the proton ought to be about a two-thousandth that associated with the electron.

The matter-waves are drawn in tightly about the proton and its particulate nature is correspondingly enhanced. The proton *can* be thought of as a particle and one *can* speak of it as having a definite volume, one that is much less than the wavelength of the smeared out electron. (To be sure, if a proton could be magnified sufficiently to look at we would find it had a hazy surface with no clear boundary so that its volume would be only approximately "definite.")

Suppose we pass on to objects even more massive than the proton. Would the matter-waves be drawn in still farther and the volume be even less? There are subatomic particles more massive than the proton. All are extremely short-lived, however, and I have come across no estimates of their volumes.

Still, we can build up conglomerations of many protons and neutrons which are stable enough to be studied. These are the various atomic nuclei. An atomic nucleus built up of, say, ten protons and ten neutrons would be twenty times as massive as a single proton and the matter-waves ascociated with the nucleus as a whole would have a wavelength correspondingly shorter. Would this contract the volume of the twenty protons and neutrons to less than that of a single proton?

Apparently not. By the time you reach a body as

massive as the proton, its particular nature is so prominent that it can be treated almost as a tiny billiard ball. No matter how many protons and neutrons are lumped together in an atomic nucleus each individual proton and neutron retains about its original volume. This means that the volume of a proton may well be considered as the smallest volume that has any meaning. That is, you can speak of a volume "half that of a proton" but you will never find anything that will fill that volume without lapping over, either as a particle or a wave.

The sizes of various atomic nuclei have been calculated. The radius of a carbon nucleus, for instance, has been worked out as 3.8×10^{-13} centimeters and that of a bismuth nucleus as about 8×10^{-13} centimeters. If a nucleus is made up of a closely packed sphere of incompressible neutrons or protons then the volume of two such spheres ought to be related as the cube roots of the number of particles. The number of particles in a carbon nucleus is 12 (6 protons and 6 neutrons) and the number in a bismuth nucleus is 209 (83 protons and 126 neutrons). The ratio of the number of particles is 209/12 or 17.4 and the cube root of 17.4 is 2.58. Therefore, the radius of the bismuth nucleus should be 2.58 times that of the carbon nucleus and the actual ratio is 2.1. In view of the uncertainties of measurement, this isn't bad.

Let's next compare the carbon neucleus to a single proton (or neutron). The carbon nucleus has twelve particles and the proton but one. The ratio is 12 and the cube root of that is just about 2.3. Therefore, the radius of the carbon nucleus ought to be about 2.3 times the radius of a proton. We find, then, that the radius of a proton is about 1.6×10^{-13} centimeters.

Now we can line up protons side by side and see how many will stretch clear across the Observable Universe. If we divide the radius of the Observable Universe by the radius of a proton, we will get the answer.

The radius of the Observable Universe is thirteen billion light-years or 1.3×10^{10} light-years, and each light-year is 9.5×10^{17} centimeters long. In centimeters then, the radius of the Observable Universe is 1.23×10^{28}. Divide that by the radius of the proton, which is 1.6×10^{-13} centimeters and you have the answer: 77×10^{40}.

In other words, if anyone ever asks you: "How many

protons can you line up side by side?" you can answer "77,000,000,000,000,000,000,000,000,000,000,-
000,000!" because there is no room to line up any more.

Now for volume. If the proton has a radius of 1.6×10^{-13}
centimeters and it is assumed to be spherical, it has a
volume of 1.7×10^{-40} cubic centimeters, and that is the
Smallest Possible Volume. Again, given a radius of
1.23×10^{28} centimeters for the Observable Universe, its
volume is 7.8×10^{84} cubic centimeters, and that is the
Greatest Possible Volume.

We next suppose that the Greatest Possible Volume is
packed perfectly tightly (leaving no empty spaces) with
objects of the Smallest Possible Volume. If we divided
7.8×10^{84} by 1.7×10^{-40}, we find that the number of protons it takes to fill the Observable Universe is 4.6×10^{124}.

That is the solution (by modern standards) of the
problem that Archimedes proposed for himself in "The
Sand-Reckoner" and, oddly enough, the modern solution
is almost exactly the square of Archimedes' solution.

However, Archimedes need not be abashed at this,
wherever he may be along the Great Blackboard in the
Sky. He was doing more than merely chopping figures to
come up with a large one. He was engaged in demonstrat-
ing an important point in mathematics; that a number
system can be devised capable of expressing any finite
number however large; and this he succeeded perfectly
in doing.

Ah, but I'm not quite done. How many protons are
there *really* in the Observable Universe?

The "cosmic density"—that is, the quantity of matter
in the universe, if all of it were spread out perfectly
evenly—has been estimated at figures ranging from 10^{-30}
to 10^{-29} grams per cubic centimeter. This represents a
high-grade vacuum which shows that there is practically
no matter in the universe. Nevertheless, there are an enormous number of cubic centimeters in the universe and
even "practically no matter" mounts up.

The volume of the Observable Universe, as I said, is
7.8×10^{84} cubic centimeters and if the cosmic density is
equal throughout the universe and not merely in the few
billion light-years nearest ourselves, then the total mass
contained in the Observable Universe is from 7.8×10^{54}
grams to 7.8×10^{55} grams. Let's hit that in between and

say that the mass of the Observable Universe is 3×10^{55} grams. Since the mass of our own Milky Way Galaxy is about 3×10^{44} grams, there is enough mass in the Observable Universe to make up a hundred billion (10^{11}) galaxies like our own.

Virtually all this mass is resident in the nucleons of the Universe, *i.e.*, the protons and neutrons. The mass of the individual proton or neutron is about 1.67×10^{-24}, which means that there are something like 1.8×10^{79} nucleons in the Observable Universe.

As a first approximation we can suppose the universe to be made up of hydrogen and helium only, with ten atoms of the former for each atom of the latter. The nucleus of the hydrogen atom consists of a single proton and the helium atom consists of two protons and two neutrons. In every eleven atoms, then, there is a total of twelve protons and two neutrons. The ratio of protons to neutrons in the universe is therefore six to one or roughly 1.6×10^{79} protons and 0.2×10^{79} neutrons in the universe. (There are thus ten quadrillion times as many protons in the nearly empty Observable Universe as there are sand grains in Archimedes' fully packed universe.)

In addition, each proton is associated with an electron, so that the total number of particles in the Observable Universe (assuming that only protons, neutrons, and electrons exist in significant numbers) is 3.4×10^{79}.

This proton-reckoning in the Observable Universe ignores relativistic effects. The farther away a galaxy is and the more rapidly it recedes from us, the greater the foreshortening it endures because of the Fitzgerald contraction (at least to our own observing eyes).

Suppose a galaxy were at a distance of ten billion light-years and were receding from us at four-fifths the speed of light. Suppose, further, we saw it edge-on so that ordinarily its extreme length in the line of sight would be one hundred thousand light-years. Because of foreshortening, we would observe that length (assuming we could observe it) to be only sixty thousand light-years.

Galaxies still farther away would seem even more foreshortened, and as we approached the Hubble Radius of thirteen billion light-years, where the speed of recession approaches the speed of light, that foreshortening would make the thickness of the galaxies in the line of sight approach zero. We have the picture then, of the neighborhood of the Hubble Radius occupied by paper-thin and paper-thinner galaxies. There would be room for an infinite number of them, all crowded against the Hubble Radius.

Inhabitants of those galaxies would see nothing wrong, of course. They and their neighbors would be normal galaxies and space about them would be nearly empty. But at *their* Hubble Radius there would be an infinite number of paper-thinner galaxies, including our own!

It is possible, then, that within the finite volume of a nearly empty universe, there is—paradoxical though it may sound—an infinite universe after all, with an infinite number of galaxies, an infinite mass, and, to get back to the central point of this article, an infinite number of protons.

Such a picture of an infinite universe in a finite volume does not square with the "big bang" theory of the universe, which presupposes a finite quantity of mass to begin with; but it fits the "continuous creation" universe which needs an infinite universe, however finite the volume.

The weight of observation is inclining astronomers more and more to the "big bang" but I find myself emotionally attracted to the optimistic picture of "continuous creation."

So far we can only penetrate ten billion years into space, but I wait eagerly. Perhaps in my lifetime, we can make the final three billion light-years to the edge of the Observable Universe and get some indication, somehow, of the presence of an infinite number of galaxies there.

But perhaps not. The faster the galaxies recede, the less energy reaches us from them and the harder they are to detect. The paper-thin galaxies may be there—but may be indetectable.

If the results are inconclusive, I will be left with nothing but faith. And my faith is this—that the universe is boundless and without limit and that never, never, never will mankind lack for a frontier to face and conquer.*

[* Alas, in the years since this article first appeared, "continuous creation" has about vanished and no signs of accumulating galaxies toward the rim have appeared—but I retain my faith.]

Part VII

NUMBERS AND THE EARTH

15 WATER, WATER, EVERYWHERE—

THE one time in my adult life that I indulged in an ocean voyage, it wasn't voluntary.* Some nice sergeants were herding a variety of young men in soldier suits onto a vessel and I was one of the young men.

I didn't really want to leave land (being a lubber of the most fearful variety) and meant to tell the sergeants so. However, they seemed *so* careworn with their arduous duties, *so* melancholy at having to undertake the uncongenial task of telling other people what to do, that I didn't have the heart. I was afraid that if they found out one of the soldiers didn't really want to go, they might cry.

So I went aboard and we began the long six-day ocean voyage from San Francisco to Hawaii.

A luxury cruise it was not. The bunks were stacked four high and so were the soldiers. Seasickness was rampant and while I myself was not seasick even once (on my honor as a science fiction writer) that doesn't mean much when the guy in the bunk above decides to be.

My most grievous shock came the first night. I had been withstanding the swaying of the ship all day and

[* *This article first appeared in December 1965. Since then I have been on a number of ocean voyages, every one of them voluntary and every one of them enjoyable.*]

231

had waited patiently for bedtime. Bedtime came; I got into my nonluxurious bunk and suddenly realized that *they didn't turn off the ocean at night!* The boat kept swaying, pitching, yawing, heaving, rolling, and otherwise making a jackass of itself all night long! And every night!

You may well imagine, then, that what with one thing and another, I made the cruise in grim-lipped silence and was notable above all other men on board ship for my surly disposition.

Except once. On the third day out, it rained. Nothing remarkable, you think? Remember, I'm a landlubber. I had never seen it rain on the ocean; I had never *thought* of rain on the ocean. And now I saw it—a complete waste of effort. Tons of water hurling down for nothing; just landing in more water.

The thought of the futility of it all; of the inefficiency and sheer ridiculousness of a planetary design that allowed rain upon the ocean struck me so forcibly that I burst into laughter. The laughter fed upon itself and in no time at all, I was down on the deck, howling madly and flailing my arms and legs in wild glee—and getting rained on.

A sergeant (or somebody) approached and said, with warm and kindly sympathy, "What the hell's the matter with you, soldier? On your feet!"

And all I could say was, "It's raining! It's raining on the ocean!"

I kept on tittering about it all day, and that night all the bunks in the immediate neighborhood of mine were empty. The word had gone about (I imagine) that I was mad, and might turn homicidal at any moment.

But many times since, I have realized I shouldn't have laughed. I should have cried.

We here in the northeastern states are suffering from a serious drought * and when I think of all the rain on the ocean and how nicely we could use a little bit of that rain on particular portions of dry land, I could cry right now.

I'll console myself as best I may, then, by talking about water.

Actually, the Earth is not short of water and never will

[* *This was 1965, remember. Since then (knock wood) no droughts.*]

be. In fact, we are in serious and continuing danger of too much water, if the warming trend continues and the ice caps melt.*

But let's not worry about melting ice caps right now; let's just consider the Earth's water supply. To begin with, there is the ocean. I use the singular form of the noun because there is actually only one World Ocean; a continuous sheet of salt water in which the continents are set as large islands.

The total surface area of the World Ocean is 139,480,-000 square miles, while the surface area of the entire planet is 196,950,000 square miles.** As you see, then, the World Ocean covers seventy-one per cent of the Earth's surface.

The World Ocean is arbitrarily divided into smaller units partly because, in the early age of exploration, men weren't sure that there was a single ocean (this was first clearly demonstrated by the circumnavigation of the Earth by Magellan's expedition in 1519-1522) and partly because the continents do break up the World Ocean into joined segments which it is convenient to label separately.

Traditionally, one hears of the "Seven Seas" and indeed my globe and my various atlases do break up the World Ocean into seven subdivisions: 1) North Pacific, 2) South Pacific, 3) North Atlantic, 4) South Atlantic, 5) Indian, 6) Arctic, 7) Antarctic.

In addition, there are the smaller seas and bays and gulfs; portions of the ocean which are nearly surrounded by land as in the case of the Mediterranean Sea or the Gulf of Mexico or marked off from the main body of the ocean by a line of islands, as in the case of the Caribbean Sea or the South China Sea.

Let's simplify this arrangement as far as possible. In the first place, let's consider all seas, bays, and gulfs to be part of the ocean they adjoin. We can count the Mediterranean Sea, the Gulf of Mexico, and the Caribbean Sea as part of the North Atlantic, while the South China Sea is part of the North Pacific.

[* *I was a little behind here. Actually we've been experiencing a cooling trend since 1940.*]

[** *If I were writing the article today I would use "square kilometers" as my unit, but it would be tedious to make the change now. Just remember that 1 square mile equals 2.6 square kilometers and you can make the change yourself, if you wish.*]

THE OCEAN

As mentioned in the article, the ocean covers 71 per cent of the Earth's surface. But what we see is, of course, only the top of it.

On the average, the ocean is 2.3 miles (3.7 kilometers) deep, and there are places where it is over 7 miles (11 kilometers) deep. The total volume of the ocean is about 300 million cubic miles (1,200 million cubic kilometers). That means if you built a square tank 36 miles (58 kilometers) on each side and poured all the ocean water into it, you would have to build the walls as high as the Moon in order to hold it all.

Ocean water is not pure water, but is a solution of various substances, chiefly salt. It is, in fact, 3.45 per cent solids, mostly salt. This means that there are some 54,000 trillion tons of solids dissolved in the ocean, and if all of this could somehow be removed and spread out evenly over the fifty states, it would make a heap 1½ miles (2½ kilometers) high.

The solids contained in the ocean are not exclusively salt. About one seventh of the solids include substances containing every element on Earth—some present in greater quantity, some in lesser. The ocean contains as part of its normal content even such substances as uranium and gold. In every ton of ocean water there is about one ten-thousandth ounce of uranium and about one five-millionth ounce of gold. The uranium and gold are spread out so thinly that it isn't practical to try to concentrate the metals and extract them from the water. Still, the ocean is so huge that the total amount present is great. The ocean contains a total of 5 billion tons of uranium and 8 million tons of gold.

The ocean contains dissolved gases as well. Oxygen dissolves in water only slightly, but there is enough dissolved oxygen in the ocean to support its entire load of life.

Second, there is no geophysical point in separating the North Pacific from the South Pacific, or the North Atlantic from the South Atlantic. (The conventional arbitrary dividing line in each case is the equator). Let's deal with a single Pacific Ocean and a single Atlantic Ocean.

Third, if you will look at a globe, you will see that the Arctic Ocean is not a truly separate ocean. It is an off-shoot of the Atlantic Ocean to which it is connected by a thousand-mile-wide passage (the Norwegian Sea) between Greenland and Norway. Let's add the Arctic to the Atlantic, therefore.

Fourth, there is no Antarctic Ocean. The name is given to the stretch of waters neighboring Antarctica (which is the only portion of the globe where one can circumnavigate the planet along a parallel of latitude without being obstructed by land or by solid ice sheets). However, there are no nonarbitrary boundaries between this stretch of water and the larger oceans to the north. The length of arbitrary boundary can be shortened by dividing the Antarctic among those larger oceans.

That leaves us, then, with exactly three large divisions of the World Ocean—the Pacific Ocean, the Atlantic Ocean, and the Indian Ocean.

If you look at a globe, you will see that the Pacific Ocean and Atlantic Ocean stretch from north polar regions to south polar regions. The division between them in the north is clearcut, since the only connection is through the narrow Bering Strait between Alaska and Siberia. A short arbitrary line, fifty-six miles in length, can be drawn across the stretch of water to separate the oceans.

In the south the division is less clear cut. An arbitrary line must be drawn across Drake Passage from the southernmost point of South America to the northernmost point of the Antarctic Peninsula. This line is about six hundred miles long.

The Indian Ocean is the stubby one, stretching only from the tropics to the Antarctic Ocean (though it makes up for that by being wider than the Atlantic, which is the skinny one.) The Indian Ocean is less conveniently separated from the other oceans. A north-south line from the southernmost points of Africa and Australia to Antactica will separate the Indian Ocean from the Atlantic and Pacific respectively. The first of these lines is about twenty-five hundred miles long and the second eighteen hundred miles long, which makes the demarcation pretty vague, but then I told you there's really only one ocean. In addition, the Indonesian islands separate the Pacific from the Indian.

The surface areas of the three oceans, using these conventions, are expressed in Table 4 in round figures:

TABLE 4   *Area of the Oceans*

	SURFACE AREA (SQUARE MILES)	PER CENT OF WORLD OCEAN
Pacific	68,000,000	48.7
Atlantic	41,500,000	29.8
Indian	30,000,000	21.5

As you see, the Pacific Ocean is as large as the Atlantic and Indian put together. The Pacific Ocean is, by itself, twenty per cent larger than all of the Earth's land area. It's a big glob of water.

I was aware of this when I crossed the Pacific (well, half of it anyway) and I was also aware that when I was looking at all that water, I was seeing only the top of it.

The Pacific Ocean is not only the most spread out of the oceans but the deepest, with an average depth of about 2.6 miles. In comparison, the Indian Ocean has an average depth of about 2.4 miles and the Atlantic only about 2.1 miles. We can therefore work out the volume of the different oceans, as in Table 5.

As you see then the water of the World Ocean is distributed among the three oceans in just about the ratio of 2:1:1.

The total, 339,000,000 cubic miles, is a considerable amount. It makes up $\frac{1}{800}$ of the volume of the Earth—a most respectable fraction. If it were all accumulated into one place it would form a sphere about 864 miles in diameter. This is larger than any asteroid in the solar system, probably larger than all the asteroids put together.

TABLE 5   *Volume of the Oceans*

	VOLUME (CUBIC MILES)	PER CENT OF WORLD OCEAN
Pacific	177,000,000	52.2
Atlantic	87,000,000	25.7
Indian	75,000,000	22.1
Total	339,000,000	

There is therefore no shortage of water. If the oceans were divided up among the population of the Earth, each man, woman, and child would get a tenth of a cubic mile of ocean water. If you think that's not much (just a miserable tenth of a single cubic mile), consider that that equals 110,000,000,000 gallons.

Of course, the ocean consists of sea water, which has limited uses. You can travel over it and swim in it—but you can't (without treatment) drink it, water your lawn with it, wash efficiently with it, or use it in industrial processes.

For all such vital operations, you need fresh water, and there the ready-made supply is much more limited. Ocean water (including a bit of inland salt water) makes up about 98.4 per cent of all the water on Earth; and fresh water makes up 1.6 per cent or about 5,800,000 cubic miles.

That doesn't sound too bad, but it's not the whole story. Fresh water exists in three phases, solid, liquid, and gaseous. (And, incidentally, let me interrupt myself to say that water is the *only* common substance on Earth that exists in all three phases; and the only one to exist chiefly in the liquid phase. All other common substances either exist solely in the gaseous state, as do oxygen and nitrogen; or solely in the solid state, as do silica and hematite.) The distribution of the fresh water supply of the Earth among the three phases is as shown in Table 6:

TABLE 6   *The Fresh Water Supply*

	VOLUME (CUBIC MILES)
Ice	5,680,000
Liquid fresh water	120,000
Water vapor (if condensed to liquid)	3,400

Most of Earth's supply of fresh water is unavailable to us because it is tied up as ice. It is, of course, quite possible and even simple to melt ice, but the problem is one of location. Nearly ninety per cent of the world's ice is compacted into the huge ice cap that covers Antarctica and most of the rest into the smaller sheet that covers Greenland. What's left (about 200,000 cubic miles) occurs as glaciers in the higher mountains and the smaller Arctic islands plus some polar sea ice. All of this ice is quite out of the way.

That leaves us with just under 125,000 cubic miles of fresh water in liquid and gaseous form, and this represents the most valuable portion of the water resources of the planet. The fresh water supply is constantly running off into the sea through flowing rivers and seeping ground water or evaporating into the air. This loss, however, is constantly replaced by rainfall. It is estimated that the total rainfall on all the land areas of the world amounts to 30,000 cubic miles per year. This means that one-quarter of the fresh water supply is replaced each year and if there were no rain at all anywhere, Earth's dry land would become dry indeed, for in four years (if one assumes that the rate of flow, seepage, and evaporation remains constant) fresh water would be all gone.

If Earth's fresh water were evenly distributed among humanity, every man, woman, and child would own 40,000,000 gallons and every year he could use 10,000,000 gallons of his supply, collecting rain replacement in return.

But alas, the fresh water is not evenly distributed. Some areas on Earth have a far greater supply than they can use and other areas are parched. The maldistribution works in time as well as in space; for an area which is flooded one year may be drought-stricken the next.

The most spectacular reservoirs of fresh water are the lakes of the world. Of course, not all enclosed bodies of water are fresh. Only those bodies of water are fresh which have outlets to the ocean so that the efflux of water removes the salt dissolved out of the land and brought into the lake. Where a lake has no outlet to the ocean, it can lose water only through evaporation and the dissolved salts do not evaporate. More salt is constantly brought in by rivers feeding into the enclosed body and the result is a salt lake which, in some cases, is far saltier than the sea.

In fact, the largest inland body of water in the world —the Caspian Sea, located between the Soviet Union and Iran—is not fresh water. It has an area of 169,381 square miles, just about the size of California and it has 3,370 miles of shoreline.

It is sometimes stated that the Caspian Sea is not a sea but merely a lake, although a very large one. However, it seems to me that "lake" might well be restricted to enclosed bodies of *fresh* water. If "sea" is taken to mean salt water, whether in the ocean or not, then the Caspian is indeed the Caspian *Sea*.

The Caspian Sea is only 0.6 per cent salt (as compared to the 3.5 per cent salt of the oceans) but this is enough to make the waters of the Caspian undrinkable, except in the northwest corner where the fresh waters of the Volga River are discharged.

About 150 miles east of the Caspian is the Aral Sea, which is about 1.1 per cent salt. It is twice as salty as the Caspian Sea, but it is much smaller in extent, with a surface area of only about 26,000 square miles—though that is enough to make it the fourth-largest body of enclosed water in the world.

There are two other notable enclosed bodies of salt water. One is the Great Salt Lake (which I would much prefer to call the Utah Sea, since it is not "great," nor, by my definition, a lake) and the other is the Dead Sea. The Great Salt Lake is only 1,500 square miles in area and the Dead Sea is smaller still—370 square miles. The Dead Sea is not much larger, in fact, than the five boroughs of New York City.

Nevertheless, these two relatively small bodies of water are unusual for extreme salinity. The Great Salt Lake is about fifteen per cent salt and the Dead Sea is about twenty-five per cent salt, four times and seven times (respectively) as salty as the ocean.

However, looking at the surface of the water can be deceptive. How deep are these four inland seas? From data on the depth, we can work out the volume of each and the total salt * content, as in Table 7:

---

* The salt is not entirely sodium chloride by any means, but that's another matter.

TABLE 7   *The Inland Seas*

	AVERAGE DEPTH (FEET)	VOLUME (CUBIC MILES)	TOTAL SALT (TONS)
Caspian Sea	675	21,600	600,000,000,000
Aral Sea	53	260	13,000,000,000
Dead Sea	1,080	75	86,500,000,000
Great Salt Lake	20	5.7	4,000,000,000

As you see, the tiny Dead Sea isn't so tiny after all. In terms of qualtity of water it is much larger than the Great Salt Lake, and it contains 6½ times as much salt as the apparently much larger Aral Sea.

But let's turn to the true lakes—the enclosed bodies of fresh water. The largest such body in terms of surface is Lake Superior, which is about as large as the state of South Carolina. It is usually listed as the second-largest enclosed body of water on Earth (though, as I will show, it isn't really). It is, to be sure, a very poor second to the mighty Caspian, covering less than one-fifth the area of that body of water but remember, the water of Lake Superior is fresh.

Lake Superior is, however, only one of five American Great Lakes that are usually treated as separate bodies of water but which are neighboring and interconnected so that it is really quite fair to consider them all as making up one huge basin of fresh water. Statistics concerning them follow in Table 8:

TABLE 8   *The American Great Lakes*

	AREA (SQUARE MILES)	RANK IN SIZE	AVERAGE DEPTH (FEET)	VOLUME (CUBIC MILES)
Superior	31,820	2	900	5,400
Huron	23,010	5	480	2,100
Michigan	22,400	6	600	2,600
Erie	9,940	12	125	240
Ontario	7,540	14	540	770
Total	94,710			11,110

Taken as a unit, as they should be, the American Great Lakes have a little over half the surface area and

THE DEAD SEA

The Dead Sea is perhaps the most famous small body of water in the world. Although it is mentioned in the Bible (after all, Israel, both ancient and modern, borders on it) it is never called the Dead Sea. That is the name given it later by Greek geographers who were impressed by the fact that it contained no life. In the Bible it is called the Salt Sea.

The Jordan River (the most famous small river in the world) empties into the Dead Sea, descending into the Great Rift Valley, which is gradually splitting eastern Africa away from the rest of the continent and will someday form a new ocean of which the Dead Sea is now the chief portion. By the time it enters the Dead Sea, the Jordan River is 1,286 feet below sea level. The shores of the Dead Sea are the lowest regions on Earth. Despite that, the greatest depth of the Dead Sea below its water level is 1,310 feet. If the Dead Sea and the regions about it were filled with water to sea level, the maximum depth of water would be 2,600 feet, or just about half a mile.

The Dead Sea is divided into two unequal parts by a small peninsula that extends into it from the eastern shore. The northern part, making up about two thirds of the whole area, is the deep portion. The southern part, making up the remaining third, is quite shallow, with depths of from three to thirty feet.

Some people speculate that the shallow third was flooded with water as a result of an earthquake that broke the barrier protecting it from the northern portion of the lake; that the earthquake may have accompanied a volcanic eruption; that there were settlements in the southern portion when it was dry; that, in short, this accounts for the biblical account of the destruction of Sodom and Gomorrah. There is no concrete evidence for this, however.

The Granger Collection

volume of the Caspian Sea. And they contain nearly
one-tenth the total fresh water supply of the planet.

The only other group of lakes that can even faintly
compare with the American Great Lakes is a similar
series, considerably more separated, in East Africa. The
three largest are Lakes Victoria, Tanganyika, and Nyasa,
which I can lump together as the African Great Lakes.
Here are the statistics in Table 9:

TABLE 9   *The African Great Lakes*

	AREA (SQUARE MILES)	RANK IN SIZE	AVERAGE DEPTH (FEET)	VOLUME (CUBIC MILES)
Victoria	26,200	3	240	1,200
Tanganyika	12,700	8	1,900	4,500
Nyasa	11,000	10	1,800	3,800
	49,900			9,500

The African Great Lakes (two of them at least) are
remarkable for their depth, so that although they occupy
an area of only slightly more than half that of the American Great Lakes, the volume of fresh water they contain
almost rivals that present in our own larger but shallower
lakes.

But if we're going to talk about deep lakes, we've got
to mention Lake Baikal in south-central Siberia. Its area
is 13,197 square miles, making it the seventh-largest body
of enclosed water on Earth, by the usual criterion of
surface area. Its average depth, however, is 2,300, making
in the deepest lake in the world. (Its maximum depth is
4,982 feet or nearly a mile. It is so deep, I was once told,
that it is the only lake which contains the equivalent of
deep-sea fish. If so, these are the only fresh-water, deep-
sea fish in the world.)

Its depth means that Baikal contains 5,750 cubic miles
of fresh water, more than that in Lake Superior.

The only remaining lakes that would fall in the category
of "great lakes" are three in western Canada. The statistics
on the average depth of these Canadian Great Lakes are
virtually nonexistent. I have the figures on maximum
depth for two of them and nothing at all for the third.
However, I shall make what I hope is an intelligent guess

just to see what things look like, and you will find that in Table 10.

TABLE 10   *The Canadian Great Lakes*

	AREA (SQUARE MILES)	RANK IN SIZE	AVERAGE DEPTH (FEET)	VOLUME (CUBIC MILES)
Great Bear	12,200	9	240	525
Great Slave	10,719	11	240	510
Winnipeg	9,460	13	50	90

Now we are in a position to list the bodies of enclosed water in the order of their real size, their fluid contents rather than their surface area. To be sure, surface area of any lake can be determined with reasonable accuracy, whereas the fluid contents can only be roughly estimated, so it makes sense to list them in order of decreasing surface area. However, I will do as I choose. The fourteen largest bodies of enclosed water (in terms of surface area) rank in terms of fluid content as shown in Table 11.

TABLE 11   *The Large Lakes of the Earth*

	VOLUME (CUBIC MILES)
* Caspian	21,600
Baikal	5,750
Superior	5,400
Tanganyika	4,500
Nyasa	3,800
Michigan	2,600
Huron	2,100
Victoria	1,200
Ontario	770
Great Bear	525
Great Slave	510
* Aral	260
Erie	240
Winnipeg	90

This list is not only a rough one, with several of the

---

* *do not contain fresh water*

figures so rough as to be worthless, but in addition there are lakes with smaller areas than any on the list which are deep enough to deserve a listing somewhere ahead of Winnipeg. These include Lake Ladoga and Lake Onega in the northwestern stretch of European Russia, and Lake Titicaca in the Andes between Bolivia and Peru.

But what's the use? All this talk about water isn't helping the parching Northeast at all. Indeed, the water level in the American Great Lakes has been falling disturbingly in recent years, I understand, and even the Caspian Sea is shrinking.

Maybe old Mother Earth is getting tired of us. . . . In my more morose moments, I wonder if I could bring myself to blame her if she were.

16 UP AND DOWN THE EARTH

BOSTON is getting its face lifted, and we now have "The New Boston." *

The outstanding feature of the New Boston is the Prudential Center, which is an area of the Back Bay that has been renovated into New York–like luxury. It possesses a new hotel, the Sheraton-Boston, and, most spectacular of all, a beautiful skyscraper, the fifty-two-story Prudential Tower, which is 750 feet tall.

In the summer of 1965, I invaded the center for the first time. I was asked to join a panel discussion dealing with the future of industrial management. The panel was held in the Sheraton-Boston under conditions of great splendor, and after the dinner that followed, the manager of the hotel announced, in the course of a short talk, that the Prudential Tower was the tallest office building in continental North America.

We registered amazement and he at once explained that yes, there were indeed taller office buildings not far from Boston, but they were not on continental North America. They were on an island off the shores of the continent; an island named Manhattan.

[* This article first appeared in February 1966, at which time I lived in the Boston area. In 1970, however, I moved to New York City and it is there I have been ever since.]

And he was right. Outside the island of Manhattan, there is, at the moment of writing, no office building taller than the Prudential Tower anywhere in North America. (Perhaps anywhere in the world.) *

It made me think at once that you can play a large number of games, if you are the record-gathering type (as I am), by altering qualifications slightly. Long before the manager's speech was over, I was thinking of mountains.

Everyone knows the name of the highest mountain of the world. It is Mount Everest, located in the Himalayan Mountain Range, exactly on the border between Nepal and Tibet.

It is named for a British military engineer, George Everest, who spent much of his adult life surveying Java and India and who, from 1830 to 1843, was surveyor general of India. In 1852, when a mountain was discovered in the north, one which was at once suspected of being height champion, it was named for him. At that, his name is easier to pronounce than the native Tibetan name for the mountain—Chomolungma.

The height of Mount Everest is usually given in the reference books as 29,002 feet above sea level, a value first obtained in 1860, though I believe that the most recent trigonometric measurements make it 29,141 feet. In either case, the tippy, tippy top of Mount Everest is the only piece of solid land on the face of the globe that is more than 29,000 feet above sea level, so that the mountain qualifies nicely as something quite unique. Using another unit of measure, Mount Everest is just a trifle more than five and a half miles high and all other land is less than five and a half miles above sea level.

Except by members of the "Anglo-Saxon nations," however, mountain heights are generally measured in meters rather than in feet or miles.** There are 3.28 feet in a meter and Mount Everest stands 8,886 meters above sea level.

At once this gives rise to the question: how many other mountains are there that belong to the rarefied

[* Since this article appeared, two office buildings higher than the Prudential Tower have been constructed in Chicago.]
[** Nowadays, even the Anglo-Saxon nations are falling into line. Right now, the United States is the only holdout of consequence.]

aristocracy of those that tower more than 8,000 meters
above sea level. The answer is; Not many. Just thirteen! *
And here they are in Table 12.

Of these thirteen aristocrats all but four are in the
Himalaya Mountain Range, spread out over a stretch of
a little over three hundred miles. The tallest exception is
Mount Godwin Austen, which is named for Henry Haver-
sham Godwin-Austen, another Britisher who was engaged
in the nineteenth-century trigonometric surveys of India.
It is only recently that the mountain came to be officially
known by his name. Previously, it was known simply as
K-2. Its native name is Dapsang.

Mount Godwin Austen is located about eight hundred
miles northwest of Mount Everest and the other Himalayan towers. It is the highest peak of the Karakorum
Mountain Range, running between Kashmir and Sinkiang.

TABLE 12   *The 8,000-Meter Mountains*

| | | HEIGHT | |
MOUNTAINS	FEET	MILES	METERS
Everest	29,141	5.52	8,886
Godwin Austen	28,250	5.36	8,613
Kanchenjunga	28,108	5.33	8,570
Lhotse	27,923	5.29	8,542
Makalu	27,824	5.28	8,510
Dhaulagiri	26,810	5.10	8,175
Manaslu	26,760	5.06	8,159
Cho Oyu	26,750	5.06	8,155
Nanga Parbat	26,660	5.05	8,125
Annapurna	26,504	5.03	8,080
Gasherbrum	26,470	5.02	8,075
Broad	26,400	5.00	8,052
Gosainthan	26,291	4.98	8,016

All thirteen of the eight-thousanders are located in Asia
and all are located in the borderlands that separate India
and China.

This is true, indeed, not only for the thirteen highest

[* *I'm not as confident about that statement now as I was at the time
the article was written. The* Guinness Book of World Records *speaks of
Gasherbrum as the fifteenth tallest mountain and if that is so (and I trust
Guinness) then there are at least four 8,000-meter mountains I have not
listed in the table and which I cannot find in my library.*]

but for the sixty highest (!) mountains in the world, at least, so that the area is *the* place for mountaineers.*

And of all mountains, Everest is obviously *the* mountain to climb. The first serious attempt to climb it was made in 1922 and after a full generation of effort, eleven lives had been lost on its slopes and no successes were scored. Then, on May 29, 1953, the New Zealander Edmund Percival Hillary and the Sherpa Tenzing Norgay made it. Since then, others have too.

You would think that with even Everest conquered, there would remain no more mountains unclimbed, but that is not so. Everest received a lot more attention than some of the other peaks. As of now (unless someone has sneaked up the slopes while I wasn't looking) the highest mountain still unconquered is Gosainthan, which is only the thirteenth highest.**

The highest mountain range outside Asia is the Andes Mountain Range, running down the western edge of South America. The highest peak in the Andes is Mount Aconcagua, which stands 22,834 feet high. Despite the fact that Mount Aconcagua is the highest mountain peak in the world outside Asia, there are scores of higher peaks in Asia.

TABLE 13   *The Highest Mountains by Regions*

| | | | HEIGHT | |
REGION	MOUNTAIN	FEET	MILES	METERS
Asia	Everest	29,141	5.52	8,886
South America	Aconcagua	22,834	4.34	6,962
North America	McKinley	20,320	3.85	6,195
Africa	Kilimanjaro	19,319	3.67	5,890
Europe	Elbrus	18,481	3.50	5,634
Antarctica	Vinson Massif	16,860	3.19	5,080
48 States	Whitney	14,496	2.75	4,419
Australia	Kosciusko	7,328	1.39	2,204
New England	Washington	6,288	1.19	1,918

[* *The Himalayas, I have recently been told, contain 96 of the 108 highest peaks in the world.*]

[** *The* Guinness Book of World Records *says it is Gasherbrum, the fifteenth highest.*]

For the records, here, in Table 13, are the highest peaks in each of the continents. To soothe my national and regional pride, I will add the highest mountain in the forty-eight contiguous states, and in New England, too. (After all, I'm writing the chapter and can do as I please.)

To locate these mountains—

Mount Aconcagua is in Argentina, very close to the border of Chile, only a hundred miles east of Valparaiso.

Mount McKinley is in south-central Alaska, about one hundred fifty miles southwest of Fairbanks. The fact that it was the highest land in North America was discovered in 1896 and it was named after William McKinley, who had just been elected President of the United States. The Russians (who had owned Alaska before 1867) had called it "Bolshaya" ("large").

Mount Kilimanjaro is in northeastern Tanganyika, near the border of Kenya, and is about two hundred miles from the Indian Ocean. Mount Elbrus is in the Caucasus Mountain Range, about sixty miles northeast of the Black Sea.

Concerning the Vinson Massif, alas, I know virtually nothing. Even its height is only a rough estimate.

Mount Whitney is in California, on the eastern border of Sequoia National Park. It is only eighty miles west of Death Valley in which is to be found the lowest point of land in the forty-eight states (a pool called Badwater—and I'll bet it is—which is two hundred eighty feet below sea level). Mount Whitney is named for the American geologist Josiah Dwight Whitney, who measured its height in 1864.

Mount Kosciusko is in the southeastern corner of Australia, on the boundary between the states of Victoria and New South Wales? It is the highest point of the range called the Australian Alps. I suspect it was discovered at the end of the eighteenth century, when the Polish patriot Thaddeus Kosciusko was leading the last, forlorn fight for Polish independence, but I can't be sure.

Mount Washington is located in the Presidential Mountain Range in northern New Hampshire, and we all know who it is named after.

By listing the high mountains by continents, I don't mean to imply that all high mountains are on continents. In fact, Australia, usually considered a continent (though a small one) possesses no particularly high mountains, while New Guinea to its north (definitely an island, though a large one) is much more mountainous and possesses dozens of peaks higher than any in continental Australia, and some that are quite respectable by any standards. Three Pacific islands are notably mountainous and these are listed in Table 14.

TABLE 14   *Notable Island Mountains*

ISLAND	MOUNTAIN	FEET	HEIGHT MILES	METERS
New Guinea	Carstensz	16,404	3.12	5,000
Hawaii	{ Mauna Kea	13,784	2.61	4,200
	{ Mauna Loa	13,680	2.59	4,171
Sumatra	Kerintji	12,484	2.36	3,807
New Zealand	Cook	12,349	2.34	3,662

Mount Carstensz is the highest mountain in the world that is not on a continent. Whom it is named for I do not know, but it is in the western portion of New Guinea and is part of the Nassau Mountain Range, which is named for the Dutch royal family. I suspect that by now Indonesia has renamed both the range and the mountain or, more likely, has restored the original names, but I don't know what these might be.*

Mount Cook is just a little west of center in New Zealand's southern island. It is named for the famous explorer Captain Cook, of course, and its Maori name is Aorangi.

All the heights I have given for the mountains, so far, are "above sea level."

However, remembering the manager of the Sheraton-Boston Hotel, let's improve the fun by qualifying matters.

After all, the height of a mountain depends a good deal upon the height of its base. The Himalayan mountain peaks are by far the most majestic in the world; there is no disputing that. Nevertheless, it is also true that they sit upon the Tibetan plateau, which is the highest in the world. The Tibetan "lowlands" are nowhere lower than some 12,000 feet above sea level.

[* *I have found out since. Mount Carstensz is now officially Mount Djaja of the Sudirman Range.*]

If we subtract 12,000 feet from Mount Everest's height, we can say that its peak is only 17,000 feet above the land mass upon which it rests.

This is not exactly contemptible, but by this new standard (base to top, instead of sea level to top) are there any mountains that are higher than Mount Everest? Yes, indeed, there is one, and the new champion is not in the Himalayas, or in Asia, or on any continent.

This stands to reason after all. Suppose you had a mountain on a relatively small island. That island may *be* the mountain, and the mountain wouldn't look impressive because it was standing with its base in the ocean depth and with the ocean lapping who knows how many feet up its slopes.

This is actually the case for a particular island. That island is Hawaii—the largest single unit of the Hawaiian Islands. The island of Hawaii, with an area of 4,021 square miles (about twice the size of Delaware) is actually a huge mountain rising out of the Pacific. It comes to four peaks, of which the two highest are Mauna Kea and Mauna Loa (*See* Table 13).

The mountain that makes up Hawaii is a volcano actually, but most of it is extinct. Mauna Loa alone remains active. It, all by itself, is the largest single mountain in the world in terms of cubic content of rock, so you can imagine how large the whole mountain above and below sea level must be.

The central crater pit of Mauna Loa is sometimes active but has not actually erupted in historic times. Instead, the lava flow comes from openings on the sides. The largest of these is Kilauea, which is on the eastern side of Mauna Loa, some 4,088 feet (0.77 mile, or 1,246 meters) above sea level. Kilauea is the largest active crater in the world and is more than two miles in diameter.

As though these distinctions are not enough, this tremendous four-peaked mount we call Hawaii becomes totally astounding if viewed as a whole. If one plumbs the ocean depths, one find that Hawaii stands on a land base that is over 18,000 feet below sea level.

If the oceans were removed from Earth's surface (only temporarily, please), then no single mountain on Earth could possibly compare with the breathtaking towering majesty of Hawaii. It would be by far the tallest mountain on Earth, counting from base to peak. Its height on that basis would be 32,036 feet (6.08 miles or 9,767 meters). It is the only mountain on earth that extends more than six miles from base to tip.

The vanishing of the ocean would reveal a similar, though smaller, peak in the Atlantic Ocean; one that is part of the Mid-Atlantic Mountain Range. For the most part, we are unaware of the mountain range because it is drowned by the ocean, but it is larger and longer and more spectacular than any of the mountain ranges on dry land, even than the Himalayas. It is 7,000 miles long and 500 miles wide and that's not bad.

Some of the highest peaks of the range do manage to poke their heads above the surface of the Atlantic. The Azores, a group of nine islands and several inlets (belonging to Portugal), are formed in this manner. They are about 800 miles west of Portugal and have a total land area of 888 square miles, rather less than that of Rhode Island.

On Pico Island in the Azores stands the highest point of land on the island group. This is Pico Alto ("High Mountain"), which reaches 7,460 feet (1.42 miles or 2,274 meters) above sea level. However, if you slide down the slopes of the mountain and proceed all the way down to the sea bottom, you find that only one-quarter of the mountain shows above water.

The total height of Pico Alto from underwater base to peak is about 27,500 feet (5.22 miles or 8,384 meters), which makes it a peak of Himalayan dimensions.

While we have the oceans temporarily gone from the Earth, we might as well see how deep the ocean goes.

About 1.2 per cent of the sea bottom lies more than 6,000 meters below sea level, and where this happens we have the various "Trenches." There are a number of these, most of them in the Pacific Ocean. All are near island chains and presumably the same process that burrows out the deeps also heaves up the island chain.

The greatest depth so far recorded in some of these deeps (according to the material available to me) is given in Table 15.

The figures for the depth of the deeps are by no means as reliable as those for the heights of mountains, of course, and I can't tell when some oceanographic ship will plumb a deeper depth in one or more of these deeps. The greatest recorded depth in the Mindanao Trench—and in the world—was plumbed only as recently as March, 1959, by the Russian oceanographic vessel the *Vityaz.*

The greatest depth in the Mariana Trench was actually reached by Jacques Piccard and Don Walsh in person on January 23, 1960, in the bathyscaphe *Trieste.* This has been named the "Challenger Deep" in honor of the oceanographic vessel the H.M.S. *Challenger,* which conducted a scientific cruise from 1872 to 1876 all over the oceans and established modern oceanography.

In any case, the oceans are deeper than any mountain is high, which is the point I want to make, and in several places.

Consider the greatest depth of the Mindanao Trench. If Mount Everest could be placed in it and made to nestle all the way in, the mountain would sink below the waves and waters would roll for 7,000 feet (1⅓ miles) over its peak. If the island of Hawaii were moved from its present location, 4,500 miles westward, and sunk into the Mindanao Trench, it too would disappear entirely and 4,162 feet of water (⅘ of a mile) would flow above its tip.

TABLE 15 *Some Ocean Trenches*

TRENCH	GENERAL LOCATION	DEPTH FEET	MILES	METERS
Bartlett	S. of Cuba	22,788	4.31	6,948
Java	S. of Java	24,442	4.64	7,252
Puerto Rico	N. of Puerto Rico	30,184	5.71	9,392
Japan	S. of Japan	32,153	6.09	9,800
Kurile	E. of Kamchatka	34,580	6.56	10,543
Tonga	E. of New Zealand	35,597	6.75	10,853
Mariana	E. of Guam	35,800	6.79	10,915
Mindanao	E. of Philippines	36,198	6.86	11,036

If sea level is the standard, then the lowest bit of the solid land surface on Earth, just off the Philippines, is about 3,200 miles east of the highest bit at the top of Mount Everest. The total difference in height is 65,339 feet (12.3 miles or 19,921 meters).

This sounds like a lot but the diameter of the Earth is about 7,900 miles so that this difference in low-high makes up only 0.15 percent of the Earth's total thickness.

KILAUEA

Mauna Loa is the largest mountain mass in the world and together with Mauna Kea virtually makes up the island of Hawaii. Mauna Loa means "long mountain," which is a good name since from end to end it is seventy-five miles wide. Mauna Kea means "white mountain" because it is usually snowcapped. The snowcap indicates that Mauna Kea is a dormant volcano, but Mauna Loa is active, and near it is Kilauea (here illustrated), which is the largest crater in the world, with an area of four square miles.

Kilauea is not known for spectacular eruptions. Rather, it is always simmering, and within the crater is a boiling lake of molten rock that occasionally rises and overflows its sides. Occasionally such a lava flow is copious and long-sustained and in 1935 even threatened the city of Hilo, largest on the island.

The native Hawaiians considered the most active vent of Kilauea to be the home of Pele, the fire goddess—which makes sense if we assume the existence of divine beings.

Here, however, rests a peculiar coincidence. The Hawaiian fire goddess is Pele, and on the island of Martinique is a mountain called Pelée. The two names have nothing in common despite appearances, since "Montagne Pelée" is merely "Bald Mountain" in French (or "peeled" mountain, if you want to preserve the sound), because the top was denuded.

The name, however, was fateful, for the mountain is a volcano and that is why the top is denuded. It was not taken as a very serious volcano, for two minor eruptions, one in 1792 and one in 1851, impressed nobody. But then, on May 8, 1902, the mountain suddenly exploded. An avalanche of lava went rolling down the side right down onto St. Pierre, then the capital of Martinique. One moment it was a city of 30,000 people; the next a collection of 30,000 corpses. Only two people survived.

If the Earth were shrunk to the size of my library globe (16 inches in diameter), the peak of Mount Everest would project only 0.01 inch above the surface and the Mindanao Trench would sink only 0.014 inch below the surface.

You can see then that despite all the extreme ups and downs I have been talking about, the surface of the Earth, viewed in proportion to the size of the Earth, is very smooth. It would be smooth, even if the oceans were gone and the unevenness of the ocean bottom were exposed. With the oceans filling up most of the Earth's hollows (and concealing the worst of the unevennesses), what remains is nothing.

But let's think about sea level again. If the Earth consisted of a universal ocean, it would take on the shape of an ellipsoid of revolution, thanks to the fact that the planet is rotating. It wouldn't be a perfect ellipsoid because, for various reasons, there are deviations of a few feet here and there. Such deviations are, however, of only the most academic interest and for our purposes we can be satisfied with the ellipsoid.

This means that if Earth were bisected by a plane cutting through the center, and through both poles, the cross-sectional outline would be an ellipse. The minor axis (or shortest possible Earth-radius) would be from the center to either pole, and that would be 6,356,912 meters. The longest radius, or major axis, is from the center to any point on the equator. This is 6,378,388 meters (on the average, if we wish to allow for the fact that the equator is itself very slightly elliptical).

The equatorial sea level surface, then, is 21,476 meters (70,000 feet or 13.3 miles) farther from the center than the polar sea level surface is. This is the well-known "equatorial bulge."

However, the bulge does not exist at the equator alone. The distance from center to sea level surface increases smoothly as one goes from the poles to the equator. Unfortunately, I have never seen any data on the extra length of the radius (over and above its minimum length at the poles) for different latitudes.

I have therefore had to calculate it for myself, making use of the manner in which the gravitational field varies from latitude to latitude. (I *could* find figures on the gravitational field.) The results, which I hope are approximately right anyway, are included in Table 16.

TABLE 16 *The Earth's Bulge*

| | EXTRA LENGTH OF EARTH'S RADIUS | | |
LATITUDE	FEET	MILES	METERS
0° (equator)	70,000	13.3	21,400
5°	69,500	13.2	21,200
10°	68,000	12.9	20,800
15°	65,500	12.4	20,000
20°	62,300	11.8	19,000
25°	58,000	11.0	17,700
30°	52,800	10.0	16,100
35°	47,500	9.0	14,500
40°	41,100	7.8	12,550
45°	35,100	6.65	10,700
50°	29,000	5.50	8,850
55°	23,200	4.40	7,050
60°	17,700	3.35	5,400
65°	12,500	2.37	3,800
70°	8,250	1.56	2,500
75°	4,800	0.91	1,460
80°	2,160	0.41	660
85°	530	0.10	160
90° (poles)	0	0.00	0

Suppose, now, we measure heights of mountains not from just any old sea level, but from the polar sea level. This would serve to compare distances *from the center of the Earth,* and certainly that is another legitimate way of comparing mountain heights.

If we did this, we would instantly get a completely new perspective on matters.

For instance, the Mindanao Trench dips down to 11,036 meters below sea level; but that means below the sea level at its own latitude, which is 10.0° N. That sea level is 20,800 meters above the polar sea level so that the greatest depth of the Mindanao Trench is still some 9,800 meters (6.1 miles) *above* the polar sea level.

In other words, when Peary stood on the sea ice at the North Pole, he was six miles closer to the center of the Earth than if he had been in a bathyscaphe probing the bottom of the Mindanao Trench.

Of course, the Arctic Ocean has a depth of its own. Depths of 4,500 meters (2.8 miles) have, I believe, been recorded in the Arctic. This means that the bottom of the Arctic Ocean is nearly nine miles closer to the center of the Earth than the bottom of the Mindanao Trench, and from this point of view, we have a new candidate for the mark of "deepest deep." (The south polar regions are filled up by the continent of Antarctica, so it is out of the running in this respect.)

And the mountains?

Mount Everest is at a latitude of about 30.0°. Sea level there is 16,100 meters higher than polar sea level. Add that to the 8,886 meters that Mount Everest is above its own sea level mark and you find that the mountain is just about 25,000 meters (15.5 miles) above polar sea level. But it is only 2.2 miles above equatorial sea level.

In other words, when a ship is crossing the equator, its passengers are only 2.2 miles closer to the center of the Earth than Hillary was when he stood on Mount Everest's peak.

Are there mountains that can do better than Mount Everest by this new standard? The other towers of Asia are in approximately Mount Everest's latitude. So are Mount Aconcagua and some of the other high peaks of the Andes (though on the other side of the equator).

Mount McKinley is a little over 60.0° N so that its sea level is only some 5,000 meters above polar sea level. Its total height above polar sea level is only 11,200 meters (7.0 miles), which is less than half the height of Mount Everest.

No, what we need are some good high mountains near the equator, where they can take full advantage of the maximum bulge of the Earth's midriff. A good candidate is the tallest mountain in Africa, Mount Kilimanjaro. It is about 3.0° S and is 5,890 meters high. To this one can add the 21,300-meter-high bulge it stands on, so that it is some 27,200 meters above polar sea level (16.9 miles), or nearly a mile and a half higher than Mount Everest, counting from the center of the Earth.

And that is not the best, either. My candidate for highest peak by these standards is Mount Chimborazo in Ecuador. It is part of the Andes Mountain Range, in which there are at least thirty peaks higher than Mount

Chimborazo. Mount Chimborazo, is, however, at 2.0° S. Its height above its own sea level is 6,300 meters. If we add the equatorial bulge, we have a total height of 27,600 meters above polar sea level (17.2 miles).*

If we go by the distance from the center of the Earth, then, we can pass from the bottom of the Arctic Ocean to the top of Mount Chimborazo and increase that distance by 32,100 meters, or just about 20.0 miles—a nice even number.

By changing the point of view then, we have three different candidates for tallest mountain on Earth: Mount Everest, Mauna Kea, and Mount Chimborazo. We also have two different candidates for the deepest deep: the bottom of the Arctic Ocean and the bottom of the Mindanao Trench.

But let's face it. What counts in penetrating extreme depths or extreme heights is not mere distance, but difficulty of attainment. The greatest single measure of difficulty in plumbing depths is the increase of water pressure; and the greatest single measure of difficulty in climbing heights is the decrease of air pressure.

By that token, water pressure is highest at the bottom of the Mindanao Trench, and air pressure is lowest at the top of Mount Everest, and therefore those are the extremes in practice.

———————

[* *Since this article first appeared Chimborazo has been announced as the highest mountain in the world by others and the news has been printed with considerable excitement by* Scientific American *and by* Newsweek. *Neither took note of this article's precedence.*]

17 THE ISLES OF EARTH

ONE OF THE NICEST things about the science essays I write is the mail it brings me—almost invariably good-humored and interesting.

Consider, for instance, the previous chapter "Up and Down the Earth," in which I maintain that Boston's Prudential is the tallest office building on continental North America (as opposed to the higher ones on the *island* of Manhattan). The moment that essay first appeared I received a card from a resident of Greater Boston, advising me to follow the Charles and Neponset rivers back to their source and see if Boston could not be considered an island.

I followed his advice and, in a way, he was right. The Charles River flows north of Boston and the Neponset River flows south of it. In southwestern Boston they approach within two and one-half miles of each other. Across that gap there meanders a stream from one to the other so that most of Boston and parts of some western suburbs (including the one I live in)* are surrounded on all sides by surface water. The Prudential Tower, and my house, too, might therefore be considered, by a purist, to be located on an island.

[* *Not anymore. As I said before, I've returned to New York.*]

Well!

But before I grow panicky, let me stop and consider. What is an island, anyway?

The word "island" comes from the Anglo-Saxon "eglond," and this may mean, literally, "water-land"; that is "land surrounded by water."

This Anglo-Saxon word, undergoing natural changes with time, ought to have come down to us as "eyland" or "iland." An "s" was mistakenly inserted, however, though the influence of the word "isle," which is synonymous with "island" yet, oddly enough, is not etymologically related to it.

For "isle" we have to go back to classical times.

The ancient Greeks in their period of greatness were a seafaring people who inhabited many islands in the Mediterranean Sea as well as sections of the mainland. They, and the Romans who followed, were well aware of the apparently fundamental difference between the two types of land. An island was to them a relatively small bit of land surrounded by the sea. The mainland (of which Greece and Italy were part) was, on the other hand, continuous land with no known boundary.

To be sure, the Greek geographers assumed that the land surface was finite and that the mainland was surrounded on all sides by a rim of ocean but, except for the west, that was pure theory. In the west, beyond the Strait of Gibraltar, the Mediterranean Sea did indeed open up into the broad ocean. No Greek or Roman, however, succeeded in traveling overland to Lapland, South Africa, or China, as to stand on the edge of land and, with his own eyes, gaze at the sea.

In Latin, then, the mainland was *terra continens;* that is, "land that holds together." The notion was that when you traveled on the mainland, there was always another piece of land holding on to the part you were traversing. There was no end. The phrase has come down to us as the word "continent."

On the other hand, a small bit of land, which did *not* hold together with the mainland, but which was separate and surrounded by the sea was *terra in salo* or "land in the sea." This shortened to *insula* in Latin; and, by successive steps, to *isola* in Italian, "isle" in English, and *île* in French.

The *strict* meaning of the word "isle," then (and by extension the word "island"), is that of land surrounded by salt water. Of course, this is undoubtedly *too* strict. It would render Manhattan's status rather dubious since it is bounded on the west by the Hudson River. Then, too, there are certainly bodies of land, usually called islands, nestled within lakes or rivers, which are certainly surrounded by fresh water. However, even such islands must be surrounded by a thickness of water that is fairly large compared to the island's diameter. No one would dream of calling a large tract of land an island just because a creek marked it off. So Boston is *not* an island, practically speaking, and Manhattan is.

However, for the purposes of the remainder of this article I am going to stick to the strict definition of the term and discuss only those islands that are surrounded by salt water—

If we do this, however, then, again strictly speaking, the land surface of the Earth consists of nothing but islands. There are no continents in the literal meaning of the word. The mainland is never endless. The Venetian traveler Marco Polo reached the eastern edge of the anciently known mainland in 1275; the Portuguese navigator Bartholomew Diaz reached the southern edge in 1488; and Russian explorers marked off the northern edge in the seventeenth and early eighteenth centuries.

The mainland I refer to here is usually considered as making up the three continents of Asia, Europe, and Africa. But why *three* continents, where there is only a single continuous sheet of land, if one ignores rivers and the man-made Suez Canal?

The multiplicity of continents dates back to Greek days. The Greeks of Homeric times were concentrated on the mainland of Greece and faced a hostile second mainland to the east of the Aegean. The earliest Greeks had no reason to suspect that there was any land connection between the two mainlands and they gave them two different names; their own was Europe, the other Asia.

These terms are of uncertain origin but the theory I like best suggests they stem from the Semitic words *assu* and *erev*, meaning "east" and "west" respectively. (The Greeks may have picked up these words from the Phoenicians, by way of Crete, just as they picked up the Phoenician alphabet.) The Trojan War of 1200 B.C. begins the confrontation of, literally, the West and the East; a confrontation that is still with us.

Of course, Greek explorers must have learned, early in the game, that there was indeed a land connection between the two mainlands. The myth of Jason and the Argonauts, and their pursuit of the Golden Fleece, probably reflects trading expeditions antedating the Trojan War. The Argonauts reached Colchis (usually placed at the eastern extremity of the Black Sea) and there the two mainlands merged.

Indeed, as we now know, there is some fifteen hundred miles of land north of the Black Sea, and a traveler can pass from one side of the Aegean Sea to the other—from Europe to Asia and back—by way of this fifteen-hundred-mile connection. Consequently, Europe and Asia are separate continents only by geographic convention and there is no real boundary between them at all. The combined land mass is frequently spoken of. as "Eurasia."

The Ural Mountains are arbitrarily set as the boundary between Europe and Asia in the geography books. Partly, this is because the Urals represent a mild break in a huge plain stretching for over six thousand miles from Germany to the Pacific Ocean, and partly because there is political sense in considering Russia (which, until about 1580, was confined to the region west of the Urals) part of Europe. Nevertheless, the Asian portion of Eurasia is so much larger than the European portion that Europe is often looked upon as a mere peninsula of Eurasia.

Africa is much more nearly a separate continent than Europe is. Its only land connection to Eurasia is the Suez Isthmus, which nowadays is about a hundred miles wide, and in ancient times was narrower.

Still the connection was there and it was a well-traveled one, with civilized men (and armies too) crisscrossing it now and again—whereas they rarely crossed the land north of the Black Sea. The Greeks were aware of the link between the nations they called Syria and Egypt, and they therefore considered Egypt and the land west of it to be a portion of Asia.

The matter was different to the Romans. They were farther from the Suez Isthmus and throughout their early history that connection was merely of academic interest to them. Their connection with Africa was entirely by way of the sea. Furthermore, as the Greeks had once faced

Troy on opposing mainlands with the sea between, so—a thousand years later—the Romans faced the Carthaginians on opposing mainlands with the sea between. The struggle with Hannibal was every bit as momentous to the Romans as the struggle with Hector had been to the Greeks.

The Carthaginians called the region about their city by a word which, in Latin, became Africa. The word spread, in Roman consciousness, from the immediate neighborhood of Carthage (what is now northern Tunisia) to the entire mainland the Romans felt themselves to be facing. The geographers of Roman times, therefore—notably the Greek-Egyptian Ptolemy—granted Africa the dignity of being a third continent.

But let's face facts and ignore the accidents of history. If one ignores the Suez Canal, one can travel from the Cape of Good Hope to the Bering Strait, or to Portugal or Lapland, without crossing salt water, so that the whole body of land forms a single continent. This single continent has no generally accepted name and to call it "Eurafrasia," as I have sometimes felt the urge to do, is ridiculous.

We can think of it this way, though. This tract of land is enormous but it is finite and it is bounded on all sides by ocean. Therefore it is an island; a vast one, to be sure, but an island. If we take that into account then there is a name for it; one that is sometimes used by geopoliticians. It is "the World Island."

The name seems to imply that the triple continent of Europe-Asia-Africa makes up the whole world and, you know, it nearly does. Consider Table 17. (And let me point out that in this and the succeeding tables in this article, the figures for area are good but those for population are often quite shaky. I have tried to choke mid-1960s' population figures * out of my library, but I haven't always been able to succeed. Furthermore, even when such figures are given they are all too frequently marked "estimate" and may be quite far off the truth. . . . But let's do our best.)

TABLE 17   *The World Island* *

	AREA (SQUARE MILES)	POPULATION
Asia	16,500,000	1,950,000,000
Africa	11,500,000	336,000,000
Europe	3,800,000	653,000,000
The World Island	31,800,000	2,939,000,000

The World Island contains a little more than half the total land area of the globe. Even more significantly, it contains three-quarters of the Earth's population. It has a fair claim to the name.

The only tract of land that even faintly compares to the World Island in area and population is the American mainland, first discovered by primitive Asians many thousands of years ago, again by the Icelandic navigator Leif Ericsson in 1000 A.D., and finally by the Italian navigator Giovanni Caboto (John Cabot to the English nation, which employed his services) in 1497. . . . I don't mention Columbus because he discovered only islands prior to 1497. He did not touch the American mainland until 1498.

Columbus thought that the new mainland was part of Asia, and so indeed it might have been. Its complete physical independence of Asia was not demonstrated till 1728, when the Danish navigator Vitus Bering (employed by the Russians) explored what is now known as the Bering Sea and sailed through what is now called the Bering Strait, to show that Siberia and Alaska were not connected.

There is, therefore, a second immense island on Earth and this one is, traditionally, divided into two continents: North America and South America. These, however, if one ignores the man-made Panama Canal, are connected, and a man can travel from Alaska to Patagonia without crossing salt water.

There is no convenient name for the combined continents. It can be called "the Americas" but that makes

[* *This article first appeared in June 1966. In the years since, populations have, of course, increased. I have changed all the tables in this article, therefore, to reflect that increase.*]

use of a plural term for what is a single tract of land and I reject it for that reason.

I would like to suggest a name of my own—"the New World Island." This capitalizes on the common (if old-fashioned) phrase "the New World" for the Americas. It also indicates the same sort of relationship between the World Island and the New World Island that there is between England and New England, or between York and New York.

The vital statistics on the New World Island are presented in Table 18. As you see, the New World Island has about half the area of the World Island, but only a little over one-sixth the population.

TABLE 18   *The New World Island*

	AREA (SQUARE MILES)	POPULATION
North America	9,385,000	321,000,000
South America	7,035,000	190,000,000
The New World Island	16,420,000	511,000,000

There are two other tracts of land large enough to be considered continents, and one tract which is borderline and is usually considered too small to be a continent. These are, in order of decreasing area: Antarctica (counting its ice cap), Australia, and Greenland.

Since Greenland is almost uninhabited, I would like (as a pure formality) to lump it in with the group of what we may call "continental islands" just to get it out of the way. We can then turn to the bodies of land smaller than Greenland and concentrate on those as a group.

Table 19 lists the data on the continental-islands.

TABLE 19   *The Continental-Islands*

	AREA (SQUARE MILES)	POPULATION
The World Island	31,800,000	2,939,000,000
The New World Island	16,420,000	511,000,000
Antarctica	5,100,000	——
Australia	2,970,000	12,550,000
Greenland	840,000	47,000

The bodies of land that remain—all smaller than Greenland—are what we usually refer to when we speak of "islands." From here on in, then, when I speak of "islands" in this essay, I mean bodies of land smaller than Greenland and entirely surrounded by the sea.

There are many thousands of such islands and they represent a portion of the land surface of the globe that is by no means negligible. Altogether (as nearly as I can estimate it) the islands have a total area of about 2,500,000 square miles—so that in combination they are continental in size, having almost the area of Australia. The total population is about 400,000,000, which is even more clearly continental in size, being well above the total population of North America.

Let's put it this way, one human being out of every ten lives on an island smaller than Greenland.

There are some useful statistics we can bring up in connection with the islands. First and most obvious is the matter of area. The five largest islands in terms of area are listed in Table 20.

TABLE 20   *The Largest Islands* *

	AREA (SQUARE MILES)
New Guinea	312,329
Borneo	290,285
Madagascar	230,035
Baffin	201,600
Sumatra	163,145

The largest island, New Guinea, spreads out over an extreme length of 1,600 miles. If superimposed on the United States, it would stretch from New York to Denver. In area, it is fifteen per cent larger than Texas. It has the largest and tallest mountain range outside those on the World Island and the New World Island, and some of the most primitive people in the world.

Two other islands of the first five are members of the same group as New Guinea. It, Borneo, and Sumatra are

[* *These days it is becoming more customary to use the geographic names used by the inhabitants. Borneo is really Kalimantan, for instance. I will, however, use the more familiar name in every case.*]

all part of what used to be called the "East Indies," an archipelago stretching across four thousand miles of ocean between Asia and Australia, and making up by far the largest island grouping in the world. The archipelago has an area of nearly one million square miles, and thus contains about forty per cent of all the island area in the world. The archipelago bears a population of perhaps 121,000,000 or about thirty per cent that of all the island population in the world.

In a way, Madagascar is like an East Indian island displaced four thousand miles westward to the other end of the Indian Ocean. It has roughly the shape of Sumatra and in size is midway between Sumatra and Borneo. Even its native population is more closely akin to those of Southeast Asia than to those of nearby Africa.

Only Baffin Island of the five giants falls outside this pattern. It is a member of the archipelago lying in the north of Canada. It is located between the mouth of Hudson Bay and the coast of Greenland.

Oddly enough, not one of the five largest islands is a giant in respect to population. There are three islands, indeed (not one of which is among the five largest), which, among them, contain well over half of all the island people in the world. The most populous is probably not known by name to very many Americans. It is Honshu and, before you register a blank, let me explain that it is the largest of the Japanese islands, the one on which Tokyo is located.

The three islands are given in Table 21.

TABLE 21   *The Most Populous Islands*

	AREA SQUARE MILES	RANK	POPULATION
Honshu	91,278	6	83,000,000
Java	48,504	12	78,000,000
Great Britain	88,133	7	56,000,000

Java is easily the most densely populated of the large islands. (I say "large islands" in order to exclude islands such as Manhattan.) It has a density of 1,600 people per square mile which makes it just nine times as densely populated as Europe. It is 1¾ times as densely populated as the Netherlands, Europe's most thickly peopled nation. This is all the more remarkable since the Netherlands is highly industrialized and Java is largely agricultural. After all, one usually expects an industrialized area to support a larger population than an agricultural one would. (And, to be sure, the Netherlands' standard of living is much higher than Java's.)

Lagging far behind the big three are four other islands, each with more than ten million population. These are given in Table 22. (Kyushu, by the way, is another of the Japanese islands.)

Notice that the seven most populous islands are all in the Eastern Hemisphere, all lying off the World Island or between the World Island and Australia. The most populous island of the Western Hemisphere is again one which most Americans probably can't name. It is Hispaniola, the island on which Haiti and the Dominican Republic are located. It's population is 9,000,000.

TABLE 22   *The Moderately Populous Islands* *

	AREA (SQUARE MILES)	RANK	POPULATION
Sumatra	163,145	5	20,000,000
Formosa	13,855	34	15,000,000
Ceylon	25,332	24	15,000,000
Kyushu	14,791	31	12,000,000

One generally thinks of great powers as located on the continents. All but one in history among the continental great powers were located on the World Island. (The one exception is the United States.)

The great exception to the rule of continentalism among the great powers is, of course, Great Britain.** In more recent times, Japan proved another. In fact, Great Britain and Japan are the only island nations that have been completely independent throughout medieval and modern history.

[* *Formosa is more properly known as Taiwan; Ceylon as Sri Lanka.*]
** *I'm not going to distinguish between England, Great Britain, the United Kingdom, and the British Isles. I can if I want to, though, never you fear!*

Nowadays, however (unless I have miscounted and I am sure that if I have I will be quickly enlightened by a number of Gentle Readers), there are no less than thirty-one island nations; thirty-one independent nations, that is, whose territory is to be found on an island or group of islands, and who lack any significant base on either the World Island or the New World Island.

One of these nations, Australia, is actually a continent-nation by ordinary convention, but I'll include it here to be complete. The thirty-one island nations (including Australia) are listed in Table 23, in order of population.*

Some little explanatory points should accompany this table. First the discrepancy between Great Britain's area as an island and as a nation is caused by the fact that as a nation it includes certain regions outside its home island, notably Northern Ireland. Indonesia includes most but not all the archipelago I previously referred to as the East Indies.

Virtually all the island people are now part of independent island nations. The largest island area that is still colonial is Papua New Guinea, the eastern half of the island of New Guinea. It has an area of 182,700 square miles, a population of 2,300,000, and is administered by Australia. I frankly don't know how to classify Puerto Rico. It is self-governing to a considerable extent but if it is counted as an American colony, I think it may qualify as the most populous (pop. 2,700,000) nonindependent island remaining.

As you see from Table 23, the most populous island nation is neither Japan nor Great Britain, but Indonesia. It is, in fact, the fifth-most-populous nation in the world. Only China, India, the Soviet Union, and the United States (all giants in area) are more populous than Indonesia.

The only island nations that occupy less than a single island are Haiti and the Dominican Republic (which share Hispaniola) and Ireland, where the six northeastern counties are still part of Great Britain. The only island nation which has part of its islands belonging to nations

---

[* When this article first appeared nine years ago, there were only twenty-one island nations. Since then, ten more islands or island groups have become independent, and I have prepared a revised table, with updated population figures, to reflect that fact.]

TABLE 23 *The Island Nations*

	AREA (SQUARE MILES)	POPULATION
Indonesia	735,268	121,000,000
Japan	142,726	105,000,000
Great Britain	94,220	56,000,000
Philippines	115,707	37,000,000
Formosa	13,885	15,000,000
Australia	2,971,021	12,500,000
Ceylon	25,332	12,500,000
Cuba	44,218	8,500,000
Madagascar	230,035	7,500,000
Haiti	10,714	5,000,000
Dominican Republic	18,816	4,000,000
Ireland	27,135	3,000,000
New Zealand	103,376	2,900,000
Singapore	224	2,200,000
Jamaica	4,232	2,000,000
Trinidad	1,980	950,000
Mauritius	720	900,000
Cyprus	3,572	630,000
Fiji	7,055	575,000
Malta	122	330,000
Comoro	864	300,000
Barbados	166	275,000
Bahrain	256	230,000
Bahamas	5,382	215,000
Iceland	39,768	210,000
Western Samoa	1,097	150,000
Maldive Islands	115	115,000
Grenada	133	110,000
Tonga	269	100,000
São Tomé	372	69,000
Nauru	8	8,000

based on some continent is Indonesia. Part of the island of Borneo (most of which is Indonesian) makes up a portion of the new nation of Malaysia, based on nearby Asia. The eastern half of New Guinea (the western half of which is Indonesian) belongs to Australia.

There are eighteen cities within these island nations which contain one million or more people. These are

listed, in order of decreasing population, in Table 24—
and I warn you that some of the figures are not particularly trustworthy.

TABLE 24   *The Island Cities*

CITY	NATION	POPULATION
Tokyo	Japan	11,400,000
London	Great Britain	8,200,000
Djakarta	Indonesia	4,500,000
Osaka	Japan	3,000,000
Sydney	Australia	2,800,000
Melbourne	Australia	2,400,000
Yokohama	Japan	2,300,000
Nagoya	Japan	2,000,000
Taipei	Formosa	1,750,000
Havana	Cuba	1,700,000
Kyoto	Japan	1,400,000
Kobe	Japan	1,300,000
Manila	Philippines	1,300,000
Surabaja	Indonesia	1,300,000
Bandung	Indonesia	1,100,000
Kitakyushu	Japan	1,050,000
Sapporo	Japan	1,000,000
Birmingham	Great Britain	1,000,000

Of these, Tokyo is certainly remarkable since it may
be the largest city in the world. I say "may be" because
there is a second candidate for the post—Shanghai. Population statistics for the Chinese People's Republic (Com-
munist China) are shaky indeed but there is a possibility
that the population of Shanghai—a continental city—may
be as high as 11,000,000, though figures as low as 7,000,-
000 are also given.

New York City, the largest city on the New World
Island, is no better than a good fourth, behind Tokyo,
Shanghai, and Greater London. New York is located
mostly on islands, of course. Only one of its boroughs,
the Bronx, is indisputably on the mainland. Still it is not
on an island nation in the same sense that Tokyo or
London is.

If we exclude New York as a doubtful case, then the
largest island city in the Western Hemisphere, and the

only one in that half of the world to have a population of over a million, is Havana.

That leaves only one item. In restricting the discussion of islands to those which are surrounded by salt water, have we been forced to neglect any important fresh water islands?

In terms of size (rather than population) there is only one that is worth mentioning. It is a river island that very few in the world (outside Brazil) can be aware of. It is the island of Marajó, which nestles like a huge basketball in the recess formed by the mouth of the Amazon River.

It is one hundred miles across and has an area of fifteen thousand square miles. It is larger than Formosa and if it were counted among the true islands of the sea it would be among the top thirty islands of the world, which is certainly not bad for a river island. However, it is a low-lying piece of land, swampy, often flooded, and right on the equator. Hardly anyone lives there.

Its mere existence, though, shows what a monster of a river the Amazon is.

INDEX

INDEX

INFORMATION IS POWER

With these almanacs, compendiums,
encyclopedias, and dictionaries at your fingertips,
you'll always be in the know.
Pocket Books has a complete list of essential
reference volumes.